CATHEDRAL CITIES
OF SPAIN

Cathedral Cities Of Spain

W W. Collins

Nabu Public Domain Reprints:

You are holding a reproduction of an original work published before 1923 that is in the public domain in the United States of America, and possibly other countries. You may freely copy and distribute this work as no entity (individual or corporate) has a copyright on the body of the work. This book may contain prior copyright references, and library stamps (as most of these works were scanned from library copies). These have been scanned and retained as part of the historical artifact.

This book may have occasional imperfections such as missing or blurred pages, poor pictures, errant marks, etc. that were either part of the original artifact, or were introduced by the scanning process. We believe this work is culturally important, and despite the imperfections, have elected to bring it back into print as part of our continuing commitment to the preservation of printed works worldwide. We appreciate your understanding of the imperfections in the preservation process, and hope you enjoy this valuable book.

BURGOS.　THE CATHEDRAL

CATHEDRAL CITIES
OF SPAIN

WRITTEN AND ILLUSTRATED
BY
W. W. COLLINS, R.I.

LONDON: WILLIAM HEINEMANN
NEW YORK: DODD, MEAD AND COMPANY
1909

PREFACE

SPAIN, the country of contrasts, of races differing from one another in habits, customs, and language, has one great thing that welds it into a homogeneous nation, and this is its Religion. Wherever one's footsteps wander, be it in the progressive provinces of the north, the mediævalism of the Great Plain, or in that still eastern portion of the south, Andalusia, this one thing is ever omnipresent and stamps itself on the memory as the great living force throughout the Peninsula.

In her Cathedrals and Churches, her ruined Monasteries and Convents, there is more than abundant evidence of the vitality of her Faith; and we can see how, after the expulsion of the Moor, the wealth of the nation poured into the coffers of the Church and there centralised the life of the nation.

In the mountain fastnesses of Asturias the Churches of Santa Maria de Naranco and San

PREFACE

Miguel de Lino, dating from the ninth century and contemporary with San Pablo and Santa Cristina, in Barcelona, are the earliest Christian buildings in Spain. As the Moor was pushed further south, a new style followed his retreating steps; and the Romanesque, introduced from over the Pyrenees, became the adopted form of architecture in the more or less settled parts of the country. Creeping south through Leon, where San Isidoro is well worth mention, we find the finest examples of the period in the eleventh and twelfth centuries, at Segovia, Avila, and the grand Catedral Vieja of Salamanca.

Spain sought help from France to expel the Moor, and it is but natural that the more advanced nation should leave her mark somewhere and in some way in the country she pacifically invaded. Before the spread of this influence became general, we find at least one great monument of native genius rise up at Tarragona. The Transition Cathedral there can lay claim to be entirely Spanish. It is the epitome and outcome of a yearning for the display of Spain's own talent, and is one of the most interesting and beautiful in the whole country.

Toledo, Leon, and Burgos are the three

PREFACE

... known as the "French" Cathedrals or ... are Gothic and the first named is the ... of all. Spanish Gothic is best exemplified ... Cathedral of Barcelona. For late-Gothic, ... go to the huge structures of Salamanca, ... and the Cathedral at Seville which ... overwhelms in the grandeur of its scale.

... the close of the fifteenth century Italian ... influence began to be felt, and ... of the Plateresque style became ... San Marcos at Leon, the University ... Salamanca, and the Casa de Ayuntamiento at ... are among the best examples of this. The ... of Churriguera, who evolved the Churri-... style, is to be met with in almost every ... in the country. He it is who was ... for those great gilded altars with their ... twisted pillars so familiar to travellers in ... and which, though no doubt a tribute to ... of God, one feels are more a vulgar ... of wealth than a tasteful or artistic addition ... architecture. The finest of the Renaissance ... is that of Granada, and the most ... piece of Churrigueresque is the Cartuja ... city.

PREFACE

Taking the Cathedrals as a whole the two most unfamiliar and notable features are the Coros or Choirs, and the Retablos. These latter—gorgeous backings to the High Altar, generally ill-lit, with a superabundance of carving sometimes coloured and gilded, sometimes of plain stone—are of Low-country or Flemish origin. The former, with one exception at Oviedo, are placed in the nave west of the crossing, and enclose, as a rule, two or more bays in this direction. Every Cathedral is a museum of art, and these two features are the most worth study.

NOTE.—*Since the revolution in Catalonia of July–August 1909, the King has decreed that no one can secure exemption from military service by the payment of a sum of money.*

CONTENTS

	PAGE
CADIZ	1
SEVILLE	7
CORDOVA	23
GRANADA	31
MALAGA	57
VALENCIA	65
TORTOSA	77
TARRAGONA	83
BARCELONA	91
GERONA	101
TOLEDO	107
SALAMANCA	121
AVILA	137
SEGOVIA	145
SARAGOSSA	159
SANTIAGO	174
TUY	183
ORENSE	187
ASTORGA	193
ZAMORA	199
LEON	205
OVIEDO	217
VALLADOLID	225
BURGOS	233
INDEX	249

ILLUSTRATIONS

		To face page
Burgos.	The Cathedral	*Frontispiece*
Cadiz.	The Cathedral	2
Cadiz.	The Market Place	4
Seville.	In the Cathedral	8
Seville.	The Giralda Tower	12
Seville.	In the Alcázar, the Patio de las Doncellas	14
Seville.	View over the Town	18
Cordova.	Interior of the Mesquita	24
Cordova.	The Campanario Tower	26
Cordova.	The Bridge	28
Cordova.	Fountain in the Court of Oranges	30
Granada.	Carrera de Darro	32
Granada.	Exterior of the Cathedral	38
Granada.	The Alhambra	46
Granada.	The Alhambra, Court of Lions	50
Granada.	Generalife	54
Malaga.	View from the Harbour	58
Malaga.	The Market	62
Valencia.	San Pablo	66
Valencia.	Door of the Cathedral	68
Valencia.	Religious Procession	72
Tortosa		80
Tarragona		84
Tarragona.	The Archbishop's Tower	86
Tarragona.	The Cloisters	88
Barcelona.	The Cathedral	92
Barcelona.	The Rambla	96
Gerona.	The Cattle Market	102

ILLUSTRATIONS

To face page

Gerona. The Cathedral	104
Toledo. The Cathedral	108
Toledo. The South Transept	110
Toledo. The Zócodover	114
Toledo. The Alcántara Bridge	116
Salamanca	122
Salamanca. The Old Cathedral	124
Salamanca. An Old Street	128
Avila	138
Avila. Puerta de San Vicente	142
Segovia at Sunset	146
Segovia. The Aqueduct	148
Segovia. Plaza Mayor	152
Saragossa. La Seo	160
Saragossa. In the Old Cathedral	164
Saragossa. Easter Procession	166
Santiago. The Cathedral	172
Santiago. South Door of the Cathedral	174
Santiago. Interior of the Cathedral	178
Tuy	184
Orense. In the Cathedral	188
Astorga	194
Zamora. The Cathedral	202
Leon. The Cathedral	208
Leon. The West Porch of the Cathedral	210
Leon. San Marcos	214
Oviedo. In the Cathedral	218
Oviedo. The Cloisters	222
Valladolid. Santa Maria la Antigua	226
Valladolid. San Pablo	228
Burgos. The Capilla Mayor	236
Burgos. Arch of Santa Maria	242

CADIZ

AT one time the greatest port in the world—
"Where are thy glories now, oh, Cadiz?"
She is still a White City lying em-
bosomed on a sea of emerald and topaz. Her
streets are still full of the colour of the East, but
that Seville has robbed her of her trade, and in
the bustle of modern life she is too far from the
busy centre, too much on the outskirts of everything, to be anything more than a port of call for
American tourists and a point from whence the
emigrant leaves his native country.

This isolation is one of her great charms, and
the recollections I have carried away of her quiet
clean streets, her white or pink washed houses
with their flat roofs and *miradores*, her brilliant sun
and blue sea, can never be effaced by Time's subtle
touch.

Landing from a coasting-boat from Gibraltar, I
began my travels through Spain at Cadiz; and it
was with intense regret, so pleasant was the change
from the grey skies and cold winds of England, that
I took my final stroll along the broad Alameda

CADIZ

most enchanting of Spain's seaports, began my acquaintance with her many glorious cities.

In ancient times Cadiz was the chief mart for the tin of the Cassiterides and the amber of the Baltic. Founded by the Tyrians as far back as 1100 B.C., it was the Gadir (fortress) of the Phœnicians. Later on Hamilcar and Hannibal equipped their armies and built their fleets here. The Romans named the city Gades, and it became second only to Padua and Rome. After the discovery of America, Cadiz became once more a busy port, the great silver fleets discharged their precious cargoes in its harbour and from the estuary sailed many a man whose descendants have created the great Spain over the water.

The loss of the Spanish colonies ruined Cadiz and it has never regained the place in the world it once held. Huge quays are about to be constructed and the present King has just laid the first stone of these, in the hopes that trade may once more be brought to a city that sleeps.

There are two Cathedrals in Cadiz. The Catedral Nueva is a modern structure commenced in 1722 and finished in 1838 by the bishop whose statue faces the rather imposing west façade. Built of limestone and Jérez sandstone, it is white—dazzling white, and rich ochre brown. There is very little of interest in the interior. The *silleria del coro* (choir stalls) were given by Queen Isabel, and came originally from a suppressed Carthusian Convent near Seville. The exterior can claim a certain grandeur, especially when seen from the sea. The drum of the *cimborio* with the great yellow dome above, and the towers of the west façade give it from a distance somewhat the appearance of a mosque.

The Catedral Vieja, built in the thirteenth century, was originally Gothic, but being almost entirely destroyed during Lord Essex's siege in 1596, was rebuilt in its present unpretentious Renaissance form.

Cadiz possesses an Académia de Bellas Artes where Zurbaran, Murillo and Alfonso Cano are represented by second-rate paintings. To the suppressed convent of San Francisco is attached the melancholy interest of Murillo's fatal fall from the scaffolding while at work on the *Marriage of St. Catherine*. The picture was finished by his apt pupil Meneses Osorio. Another work by the master, a *San Francisco*, quite in his best style also hangs here.

The churches of Cadiz contain nothing to attract one, indeed if it were not for the fine setting of the city surrounded by water, and the semi-eastern atmosphere that pervades the place, there is but little to hold the ordinary tourist. The Mercado,

CADIZ. THE MARKET PLACE

CADIZ

or market-place, is a busy scene and full of colour; the Fish Market, too, abounds in varieties of finny inhabitants of the deep and compares favourably in this respect with that of Bergen in far away Norway. The sole attraction in this City of the Past—in fact, I might say in the Past of Spain as far as it concerns Cadiz—lies on the stretch of water into which the rivers Guadalete and San Pedro empty themselves. From the very earliest days down to the time when Columbus sailed on his voyage which altered the face of the then known globe, and so on to our own day, it is in the Bahia de Cadiz that her history has been written.

SEVILLE

SEVILLE, the "Sephela" of the Phœnicians, "Hispalis" of the Romans, and "Ishbilyah" of the Moors, is by far the largest and most interesting city of Southern Spain. In Visigothic times Seville was the capital of the Silingi until Leovigild moved his court to Toledo. It was captured by Julius Cæsar in 45 B.C., but during the Roman occupation was overshadowed by Italica, the birthplace of the Emperors Trajan, Adrian, and Theodosius, and the greatest of Rome's cities in Hispania. This once magnificent place is now a desolate ruin, plundered of its glories and the haunt of gipsies.

Under the Moors, who ruled it for five hundred and thirty-six years, Seville was second only to Cordova, to which city it became subject when Abdurrhaman established the Western Kalifate there in the year 756.

San Ferdinand, King of Leon and Castile, pushed his conquests far south and Seville succumbed to the force of his arms in 1248.

Seville is the most fascinating city in Spain. It

SEVILLE

simple iron-gilt *reja*. The *silleria*, by Sanchez, Dancart, and Guillier are very fine and took seventy years to execute. Between the *coro* and Capilla Mayor, in Holy Week the great bronze candlestick, twenty-five feet high, a fine specimen of sixteenth-century work, is placed alight. When the *Miserr* is chanted during service, twelve of its thirteen candles are put out, one by one, indicating the desertion of Christ by his apostles. The thirteenth left burning symbolises the Virgin, faithful to the end. From this single light all the other candles in the Cathedral are lit.

The *reja* of the Capilla Mayor is a grand example of an iron-gilt screen, and with those to the north and south, is due to the talent of the Dominican, Francisco de Salamanca.

The fine Gothic *retablo* of the High Altar surpasses all others in Spain in size and elaboration of detail. It was designed by Dancart and many artists were employed in its execution. When the sun finds his way through the magnificent coloured glass of the windows between noon and three o'clock, and glints across it, few "interior" subjects surpass the beautiful effect on this fine piece of work.

In front of the High Altar at the feast of Corpus Christi and on three other occasions, the *Seises's* dance takes place. This strange ceremony is performed by chorister boys who dance a sort of minuet with castanets. Their costume is of the time of Philip III., *i.e.*, 1630, and they wear plumed hats. Of the numerous chapels the most interesting is the Capilla Real. It possesses a staff of clergy all to itself. Begun in 1514 by Martin de Gainza, it was finished fifty years later. Over the High Altar is the almost life-size figure of the Virgin de los Reyes, given by St. Louis of France to San Ferdinand. Its hair is of spun gold and its numerous vestments are marvellous examples of early embroidery. The throne on which the Virgin is seated is a thirteenth-century piece of silver work, with the arms of Castile and Leon, San Ferdinand's two kingdoms. Before it lies the King himself in a silver shrine. Three times a year, in May, August and November, a great military Mass takes place before this royal shrine, when the garrison of Seville marches through the chapel and colours are lowered in front of the altar. In the vault beneath are the coffins of Pedro the Cruel and Maria Padilla his mistress, the only living being who was humanly treated by this scourge of Spain. Their three sons rest close to them.

On the north and south sides of this remarkable chapel, within arched recesses, are the sarcophagi of Beatrice of Swabia and Alfonso the Learned. They

SEVILLE

are covered with cloth of gold emblazoned with coats-of-arms. A crown and sceptre rest on the cushion which lies on each tomb. In the dim light, high above and beyond mortal reach rest these two—it is very impressive.

Each of the remaining twenty-nine chapels contains something of interest. In the Capilla de Santiago is a beautiful painted window of the conversion of St. Paul. The *retablo* in the Capilla de San Pedro contains pictures by Zurbaran. In the north transept in a small chapel is a good Virgin and Child by Alonso Cano; in the south is the Altar de la Gamba, over which hangs the celebrated *La Generacion* of Louis de Vargas, known as *La Gamba* from the well-drawn leg of Adam. On the other side of this transept is the Altar de la Santa Cruz and between these two altars is the monument to Christopher Columbus. Erected in Havana it was brought to Spain after the late war and put up here.

Murillo's work outshines all other's in the cathedral. The grand *San Antonio de Padua*, in the second chapel west of the north aisle, is difficult to see. The window which lights it is covered by a curtain, which, however, the silver key will pull aside. Over the Altar of Nuestra Señora del Consuelo is a beautiful Guardian Angel by the same brush. Close by is another, *Santa*

CATHEDRAL CITIES OF SPAIN

Dorotea, a very choice little picture. In the Sacristy are two more, *S.S. Isidore and Leander*. In the Sala Capitular a *Conception* and a *Mater Dolorosa* in the small sacristy attached to the Capilla Real complete the list.

Besides these fine pictures there are others which one can include in the same category by Cano, Zurbaran, Morales, Vargas, Pedro Campaña and the Flemish painter Sturm, a veritable gallery! And when I went into the Treasury and saw the priceless relics which belong to Seville's Cathedral, priceless in value and interest, and priceless from my own art point of view, "Surely," thought I, "not only is it a picture gallery, it is a museum as well."

The original mosque of Abu Yusuf Yakub was used as a Cathedral until 1401, when it was pulled down, the present building, which took its place, being finished in 1506. The dome of this collapsed five years later and was re-erected by Juan Gil de Hontañon. Earthquake shocks and "jerry-building" were responsible for a second collapse in the August of 1888. The restoration has since been completed in a most satisfactory manner—let us hope it will last.

The exterior of the Cathedral is a very irregular mass of towers, domes, pinnacles and flying buttresses, which give no clue to the almost overpowering solemnity within the walls. Three

SEVILLE. THE GIRALDA TOWER

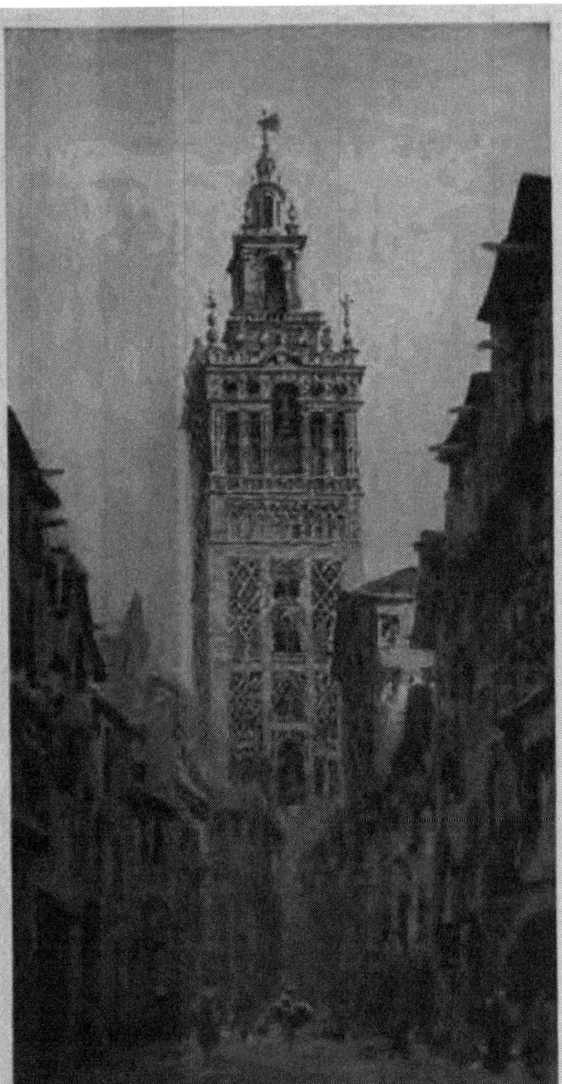

SEVILLE

doorways occupy the west façade, which is of modern construction, and there are three also on the north side of the Cathedral, one of which opens into the *Sagrario*, another into the Patio de los Naranjos and the third into the arcade of the same patio. This last retains the horse-shoe arch of the old mosque. In the porch hangs the stuffed crocodile which was sent by the Sultan of Egypt to Alfonso el Sabio with a request for the hand of his daughter. On the south is one huge door seldom opened. On the east there are two more, that of La Puerta de los Palos being under the shadow of the great Giralda Tower.

This magnificent relic of the Moslem's rule rears its height far above everything else in Seville. Erected at the close of the twelfth century by order of Abu Yusuf Yakub, it belongs to the second and best period of Moorish architecture.

On its summit at the four corners rested four brazen balls of enormous size overthrown by one of the numerous earthquakes which have shaken Seville in days gone by. The belfry above the Moorish portion of the tower, which ends where the solid walls stop, was put up in 1568, and has a second rectangular stage of smaller dimensions above. Both these are in keeping with the Moorish work below and in no way detract from its beauty. On top of the small cupola which caps the whole is the world-famed figure of Faith. Cast in bronze, with the banner of Constantine spread out to the winds of heaven, this, the *Giraldilla*, or weather-cock, moves to the slightest breeze. It is thirteen feet high, and weighs one and a quarter tons. Over three hundred feet above the ground, the wonder is—how did it get there? and how has it preserved its equipoise these last three hundred years?

It is difficult to find a point from which one can see the Giralda Tower, in fact the only street from which it is visible from base to summit is the one in which I made my sketch. Even this view does not really convey its marvellous elegance and beauty.

Next to the Cathedral the Alcázar is the most famous building in Seville. It is now a royal residence in the early part of the year, and when the King and Queen are there, no stranger under any pretext whatever is admitted.

Its courtyards and gardens are its glory. The scent of orange blossom perfumes the air, the fountains splash and play, all is still within these fascinating courts save the tinkle of the water and cooing of doves. Of its orange trees, one was pointed out to me which Pedro the Cruel planted! and many others are known to be over two hundred years old.

SEVILLE. IN THE ALCÁZAR, THE PATIO DE LAS
DONCELLAS

SEVILLE

Of all its courts, the Patio de las Doncellas is the most perfect. Fifty-two marble columns support the closed gallery and rooms above, and the walls of the arcade are rich with glazed tiles.

Of all its chambers, the Hall of Ambassadors is the finest and is certainly the architectural gem of the Alcázar. Its dome is a marvel of Media Naranja form, and the frieze of window-shaped niches but adds to its beauty.

Very little remains of the first Alcázar, which, by the way, is a derivation of Al-Kasr or house of Cæsar, and the present building as it now stands was due to Pedro the Cruel, Henry II., Charles V. and Philip V. The first named employed Moorish workmen from Granada, who emulated, under his directions, the newly finished Palace of the Alhambra. Many a treacherous deed has taken place within these walls, and none more loathsome than those credited to Pedro the Cruel. However, one thing can be put to his credit and that is this fairy Palace, this flower from the East, by the possession of which Seville is the gainer.

To the east of the Alcázar is the old Jewish quarter, the most puzzling in plan, if plan it has, and the oldest part of Seville.

The balconies of the houses opposite one another almost touch; there certainly, in some cases, would be no difficulty in getting across the street by using them as steps, and if a laden donkey essayed the passage below I doubt if he could get through. Poking about in these narrow alley-ways one day, I fell into conversation with a *guardia municipal* who entertained me greatly with his own version of Seville's history, which ended, as he melodramatically pointed down the lane in which we were standing—" And here, señor, one man with a sword could keep an army at bay, and "—this in confidence, whispered—" I should not like to be the first man of the army " !

In almost every quarter of the city fine old houses are to be found amidst most squalid and dirty surroundings. You may wander down some mean *calle*, where children in dozens are playing on the uneven pavement, their mothers sit about in the doorways shouting to one another across the street. Suddenly a wall, windowless save for a row of small openings under the roof, is met. A huge portal, above which is a sculptured coat-of-arms, with some old knight's helmet betokening a noble owner, is let into this, look inside, as you pass by—behind the iron grille is a deliciously cool *patio*, full of palms and shrubs. A Moorish arcade runs round supporting the glazed galleries of the first floor. A man in livery sits in a rocking chair dosing with the eternal cigarette between his lips. Beyond the first *patio* you can see another, a bigger which the sun is lighting up. The life in this house is as different to the life of its next door neighbours, as Park Lane is to Shoreditch. One of these great houses—owned by the Duke of Medinaceli—the Casa del Pilatos, has a large Moorish court, very similar to those of the Alcázar. They will tell you in Seville, that Pilate was a Spaniard, a lawyer, and failing to win the case for Christ, left the Holy Land, where he had a good practice, and returned to Spain to assist Ferdinand to drive out the Moors. "Yes, señor, he settled here and built this fine house about five hundred years ago."

As a rule, in the better-class houses a porch opens into the street. On the inner side of this there is always a strong iron gate with a grille beyond to prevent any entry. These gates served a purpose in the days of the Inquisition, when none knew if the Holy Office might not suddenly descend upon and raid the house. Seville suffered terribly from the horrors of those dark times; even now,—when a ring at the bell calls forth: "Who is there?" from the servant in the balcony above, before she pulls the handle which connects with the catch that releases the lock of the gate—the answer often is: "People of Peace." Some houses have interior walls six feet thick and more, which being hollow contain hiding-places with access from the roof by a rope.

CATHEDRAL CITIES OF SPAIN

In the heat of summer—and Seville is called the "frying-pan of Europe"—when the temperature in the shade of the streets rises to over 115° Fahr. family life is spent below in the cool *patio*. A real house moving takes place as the heat comes on. The upper rooms, which are always inhabited in the winter, the kitchen, servants' rooms and all are deserted, every one migrates with the furniture to the lower floors. The upper windows are closed, shutters put up and a great awning drawn across the top of the courtyard. Despite the great heat, summer is a perfectly healthy period. No one dreams of going out in the daytime, and all Seville begins life towards five o'clock in the afternoon; 2 A.M. to 4 A.M. being the time to retire for the night! Seville can be very gay, and *Sevillanos* worship the *Torrero* or bull-fighter (*Toreador* is a word unknown to the Spaniard). If a favourite *Torrero*, who has done well in the ring during the afternoon, enters the dining-room of a hotel or goes into a café it is not unusual for every one at table to rise and salute him.

There is another life in Seville, the life of the roofs. In early spring before the great heat comes, and in autumn before the cold winds arrive, the life of the roofs fascinated me. Up on the roofs in the dry atmosphere, Seville's washing hangs out to air, and up on the roofs, in the warm sun, with the

SEVILLE. VIEW OVER THE TOWN

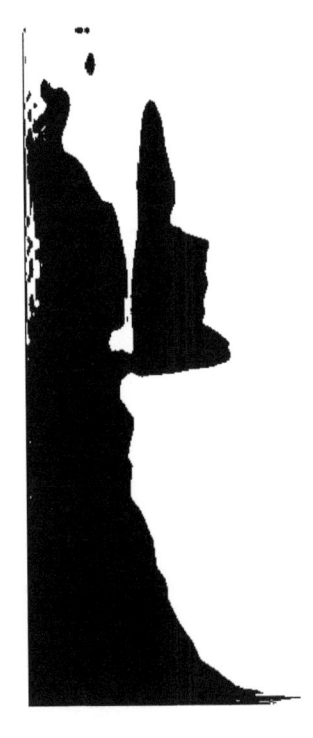

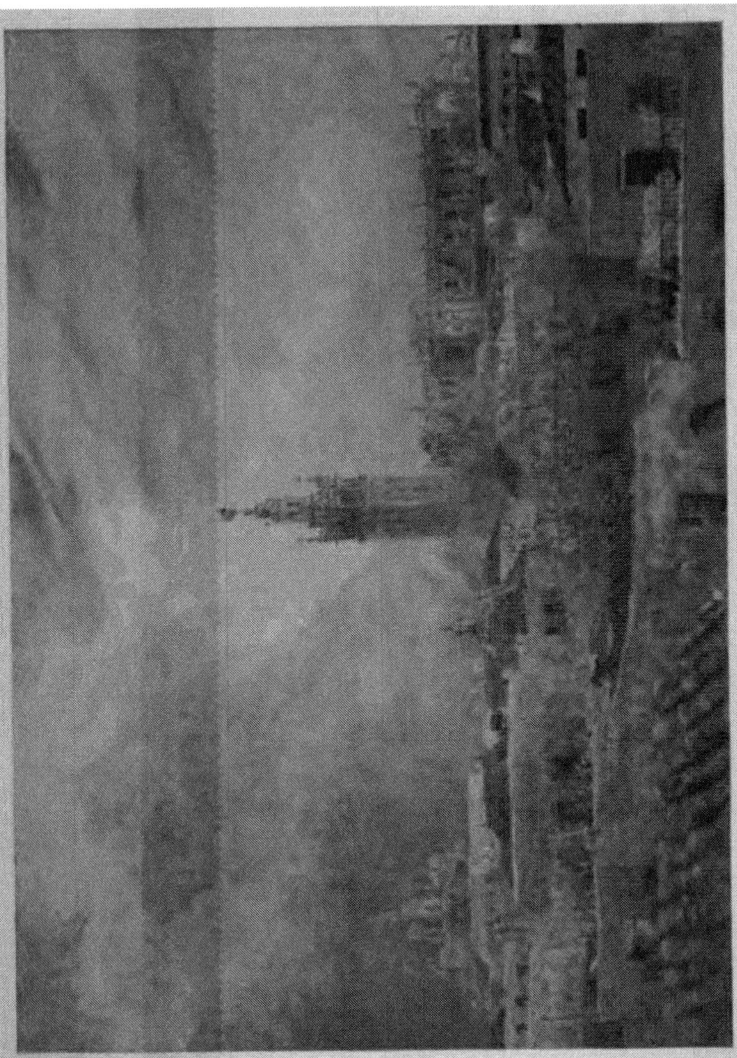

SEVILLE

hum of the streets far below, you will hear the quaint song—so Arabian in character—of the *lavandera*, as she pegs out the damp linen in rows. In the evening the click-a-click-click of the castanets and the sound of the guitar, broken by merry laughter, tells one that perhaps the *Sevillano* has fathomed the mystery of knowing how best to live. And as sundown approaches what lovely colour effects creep o'er this city in the air! The light below fades from housetop and *miradore*, pinnacle and dome, until the last rays of the departing majesty touch the vane of the Giralda, that superb symbol of Faith,—and all is steely grey.

Over the Guadalquiver lies Triana, and as I crossed the bridge for the first time the remains of an old tower were pointed out to me on the river bank. The subterranean passage through which the victims of the Inquisition found their exit to another world in the dark waters below is exposed to view, the walls having fallen away. It was therefore with something akin to relief I reached the gipsy quarter in this quaint, dirty suburb and feasted my eyes on the colours worn by its dark-skinned people. The potteries of Triana are world-renowned, and still bear traces in their output of Moorish tradition and design.

Seville's quays are the busiest part of the city, and the constant dredging of the river permits of vessels of four thousand tons making this a port of call.

Next to the Prado in Madrid, the Museum of Seville is more full of interest than any other. It is here that Murillo is seen at his best. The building was at one time the Convento de la Mercede founded by San Ferdinand. The exhibits in the archæological portion nearly all come from that ruin, the wonderful city of Italica. Among the best of Murillo's work are *St. Thomas de Villa Nueva Distributing Alms*, *Saint Felix of Cantalicio* and a *Saint Anthony of Padua*. A large collection of Zurbaran's works also hangs in the gallery, but his big composition of the *Apotheosis of Saint Anthony*, is not so good as his single-figure subjects, and none of these approach in quality the fine *Monk* in the possession of the Bankes family at Kingston Lacy in Dorset.

Seville is the home of bull-fights. The first ever recorded took place in 1405, in the Plaza del Triunfo, in honour of the birth of a son to Henry II. of Castile. The world of Fashion takes the air every evening in the beautiful Paseo de las Delicias. The humbler members of society throng the walks watching their wealthier sisters drive down its fine avenues—this daily drive being the only exercise the ladies of Seville permit themselves to take.

SEVILLE

It is a pretty sight to watch the carriages coming home as twilight begins, and the last rays of the sun light up the Torre del Oro. Built by the Almohades this Moorish octagon stood at the river extremity of Moslem Seville. The golden yellow of the stone no doubt gave it the name of "Borju-d-dahab," "the tower of gold," which has stuck to it under Christian rule. But " how are the mighty fallen," and one of the glories of the Moor debased. It is now an office used by clerks of the Port, and, instead of the dignified tread of the sentinel, resounds to the scribble of pens.

CORDOVA

It is hard to realise that the Cordova of to-day was, under the rule of the Moor, a city famous all the world over and second only to the great Damascus. Long before the Moor's beneficent advent, in the far-off days of Carthage, Cordova was known as "the gem of the south." Its position on the mighty Guadalquiver, backed by mountains on the north, always seems to have attracted the best of those who conquered. In the time of the Romans, Marcellus peopled it with poor Patricians from Rome, and Cordova became Colonia Patricia, the capital of Hispania Ulterior. But it was left to the Infidel to make it what is now so difficult to realise—the first city in Western Europe.

The zenith of its fame was reached during the tenth century, when the mighty Abderrhaman III., ruler of the Omayyades reigned, and did not begin to decrease until the death of Almanzor at the beginning of the next century. If we are to believe the historian Almakkari, Cordova contained at one time a million inhabitants, for whose worship were provided three hundred Mosques, and for whose ablutions nine hundred baths were no more than was necessary. (The arch-destroyer of all things Infidel, Philip II., demolished these.) It was the centre of art and literature, students from all parts flocked hither, its wealth increased and its fame spread, riches and their concomitant luxury made it the most famous place in Western Europe. Nothing could exceed the grace and elegance of its life, the courtly manners of its people, nor the magnificence of its buildings.

From the years 711 to 1295, when Ferdinand drove him out, the cultivated Moslem reigned in this his second Mecca. And now?—under Christian rule it has dwindled down to what one finds it to-day—a quiet, partly ruinous town. Of all its great buildings nothing remains to remind one of the past but the ruins of the Alcázar—now a prison, a portion of its walls, and the much mutilated Mesquita—the Cathedral.

I could not at first entry grasp the size of this the second largest church of any in existence Coming suddenly into the cool shade of its many pillared avenues, I felt as if transplanted into the silent depths of a great forest. In every direction I looked the trunks of huge trees apparently rose upwards in ordered array. The light here and there filtered through gaps on to the red-tiled

CORDOVA. INTERIOR OF THE MESQUITA

CORDOVA

foot, which only made the deception greater by its resemblance to the needles of a pine-wood or the dead leaves of autumn. Then the organ boomed out a note and the deep bass of a priest in the *coro* shattered the illusion.

The first Mosque built on the site of Leovigild's Visigothic Cathedral, occupied one-fifth of the present Mezquita. It was "Ceca" or House of Purification, and a pilgrimage to it was equivalent to a visit to Mecca. It contained ten rows of columns, and is that portion which occupies the north-west corner ending at the south-east extremity where the present *coro* begins. This space soon became insufficient for the population, and the Mosque was extended as far as the present Capilla de Nuestra Senora de Villaviciosa.

Subsequent additions were made by different rulers. The Caliph Al-Hakim II., who followed Abderrhaman III., expanded its size by building southwards as far as the inclination of the sloping ground would allow. To him is due the third Mihráb, or Holy of Holies, the pavement of which is worn by the knees of the devout who went thus round the Mihráb seven times. This Mihráb is the most beautiful chamber I came across in all Spain. The Byzantine Mosaics which adorn it are among the most superb that exist, the domed ceiling of the recess is hewn out of a solid block of marble, and its walls, which Leo the Emperor of Constantinople sent a Greek artist and skilled workmen to put up, are chiselled in marble arabesques and moulded in stucco. The entrance archway to this gem of the East, an intricate and well-proportioned feature, rests on two green and two dark coloured columns. Close by is the private door of the Sultan which led from the Alcázar to the Mesquita.

The last addition of all nearly doubled the size of the Mosque. Building to the south was impracticable on account of the fall in the land towards the river. Eastwards was the only way out of the difficulty unless the beautiful Court of the Oranges was to be enclosed. Eastwards, therefore, did Almanzor extend his building, and the whole space in this direction from the transepts or *Crucero* of the present church, in a line north and south, was due to his initiative.

The Mesquita at one time contained twelve hundred and ninety columns. Sixty eight were removed to make room for the *Coro*, *Crucero* and *Capilla Major*, which is the portion reserved for service now. In the *coro*, the extremely fine *silleria*, are some of the best in Spain. The Lectern is very good Flemish work in brass of the sixteenth century. The choir books are beautifully illuminated missals, especially those of the "Cruci-

CORDOVA. THE CAMPANARIO TOWER

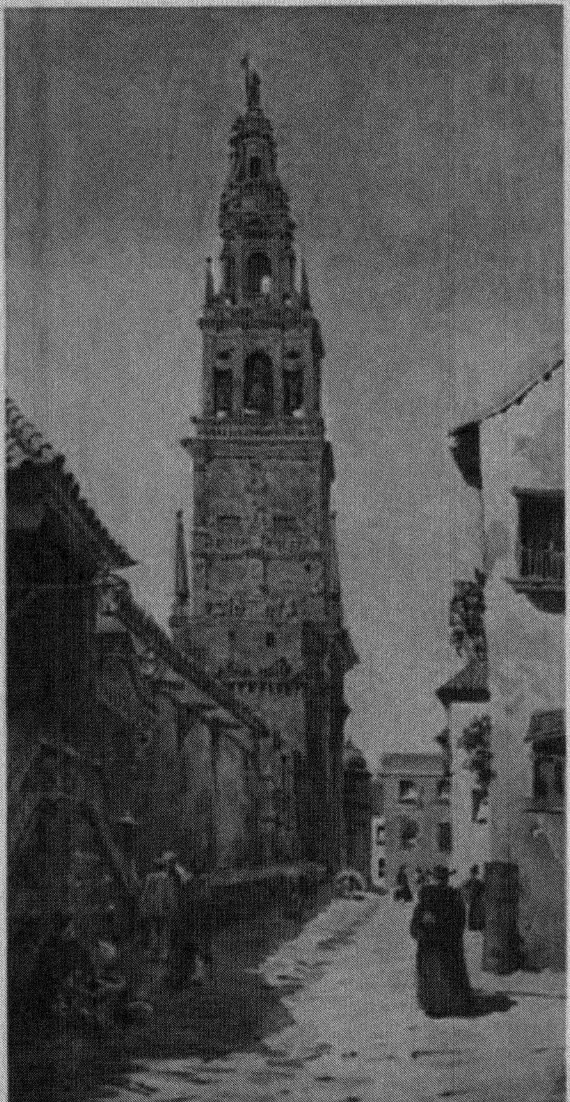

fixion," and the "Calling of the Apostles." All this does not, however, compensate for the partial destruction of the Mosque. So thought the people of Cordova, who petitioned Charles V. in vain against the alterations which have destroyed the harmony of the wonderful building. When passing through the city at a later date and viewing the mischief that had been done, the King rebuked the chapter thus: "You have built here what you, or any one, might have built anywhere else; but you have destroyed what was unique in the world."

Eight hundred and fifty columns now remain out of the above number. The odd four hundred and forty occupied the place where now stand the rows of orange trees in the courtyard, one time covered in, which is known as the Patio de los Naranjos, or Court of the Oranges. The fountain used for the ablutions of the Holy still runs with a crystal stream of pure water, and is to-day the meeting place of all the gossips in Cordova.

Of the five gates to this enchanting court, that of the Puerta del Perdon, over which rises the great Tower, el Campanario, is the most important. It is only opened on state occasions. Erected in 1377 by Henry II. it is an imitation of Moorish design. The immense doors are plated with copper arabesques.

CATHEDRAL CITIES OF SPAIN

The exterior of the Mesquita is still Moorish despite the great church which has been thrust through the centre and rises high above the flat roof of the remainder of the Mosque. A massive terraced wall with flame-shaped battlements encircles the whole, the view of which from the bridge over the river is more Eastern than anything else I saw in Spain.

This fine bridge, erected by the Infidel on Roman foundations, is approached at the city end by a Doric gateway, built by Herrera in the reign of Philip II., that Philip who married Mary of England. It consists of sixteen arches and is guarded at its southern extremity by the *Calahorra* or Moorish Tower, round which the road passes instead of through a gateway, thus giving additional security to the defence.

The mills of the Moslem's day still work, both above and below bridge, and the patient angler sits in the sun with his bamboo rod, while the wheels of these relics groan and hum as they did in days gone by. More cunning is Isaac Walton's disciple who fishes from the bridge itself. A dozen rods with heavily weighted lines, for the Guadalquiver runs swift beneath the arches, and a small bell attached to the end of each rod is his armament. And when the unwary fish impales himself on the hook and the bell gives warning of a bite, the

CORDOVA. THE BRIDGE

CORDOVA

excitement is great. Greater still when a peal begins as three or four rods bend!

The beggars of Cordova were the most importunate that fate sent across my path in the whole of Spain. I found it impossible to sit in the streets where I would gladly have planted my easel, and it was only by standing with my back to the wall that I was able to make my sketch of the Campanario. These streets are tortuous and narrow, and the houses, built on the Moorish plan with a beautiful *patio* inside, are low. At many a corner I came across marble columns, some with Roman inscriptions, probably from Italica, placed against the house to prevent undue wear and tear. In the narrowest ways I noticed how the load borne by the patient ass had scooped out a regular track on either wall about three or four feet from the ground. Wherever I went, to the oldest quarters of the town in the south-east corner or the modern in the north-west, I could never rid myself of the feeling that Cordova was a city of the past. Her life is more Eastern than that of Seville, and her people bear more traces of the Moor. Decay and ruin are apparent at every turn, but how picturesque it all is!—the rags, the squalor, and the ruin. How I anathematised those beggars with no legs, or minus arms, when I tried to begin a street sketch! The patience of Job would not have helped me, it was the loathsomeness of these cripples that drove me away. Begging is prohibited in Seville and Madrid and in one or two other towns, would that it were so in Cordova.

Away up in the southern slopes of the Sierra de Cordoba stands the Convento de San Jerónimo, now a lunatic asylum. Built out of the ruins of the once magnificent Medînat-az-zahrâ, the Palace that Abderrhaman III. erected, its situation is perfect. In the old days this palace surpassed all others in the wonders of its art and luxury. The plough still turns up ornaments of rare workmanship, but like so many things in Spain its glories have departed.

Yes, Cordova has seen its grandest days, the birthplace of Seneca, Lucan, Averroes, Juan de Mena—the Spanish Chaucer—Morales, and many another who became famous, can now boast at best with regard to human celebrities as being the Government establishment for breaking in horses for the cavalry. Certainly the men employed in this are fine dashing specimens of humanity, and they wear a very picturesque dress. But Cordova like her world-famed sons, sleeps—and who can say that it would be better now if her sleep were broken?

CORDOVA. FOUNTAIN IN THE COURT OF ORANGES

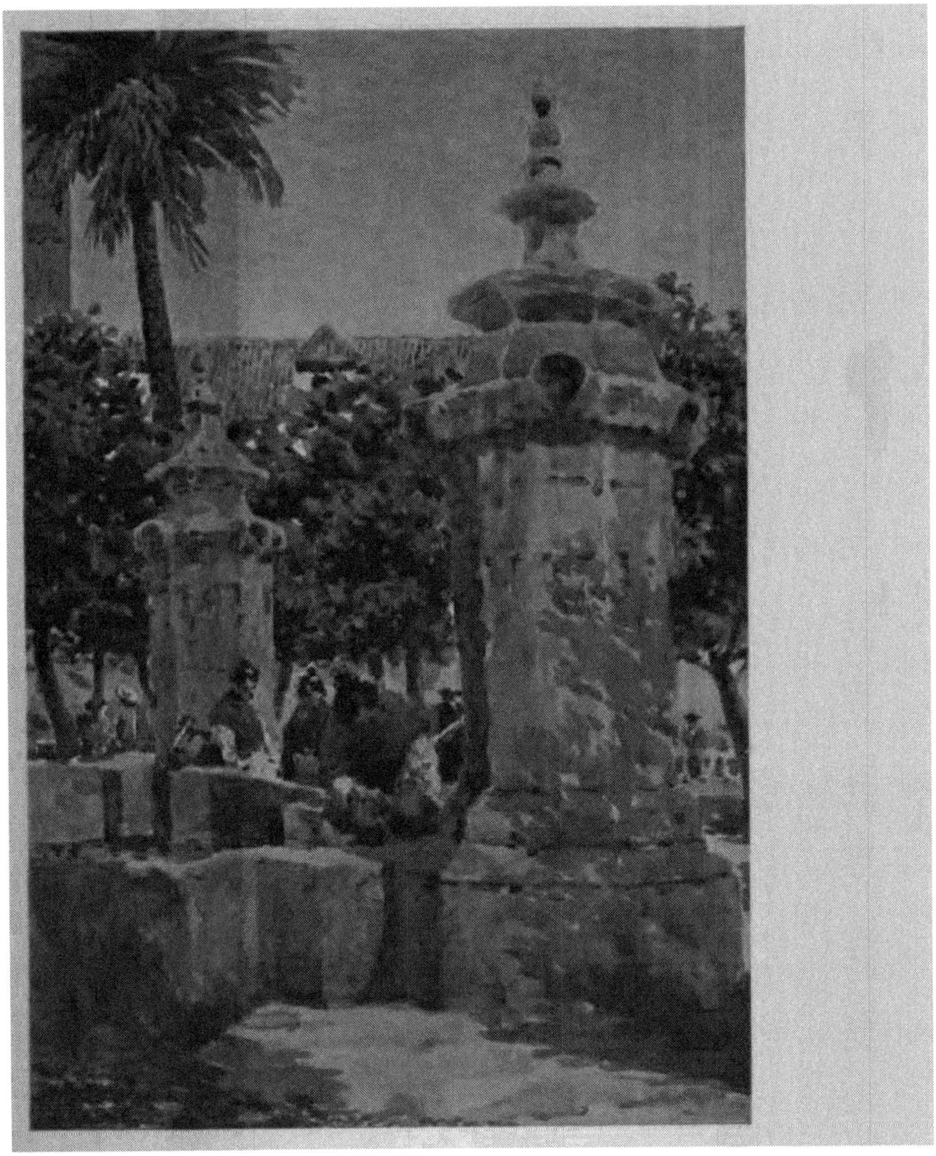

GRANADA

SPREAD out on the edge of a fertile plain at the base of the Sierra Nevada, Granada basks in the sun; and though the wind blows cold with an icy nip from the snows of the highest peaks in Spain, I cannot but think that this, the last stronghold of the Moors, is the most ideal situation of any place I have been in.

The city is divided into three distinct districts, each with its own peculiar characteristics. The Albaicin, Antequeruela, and Alhambra. The first named covers the low ground and the hills on the bank of the Darro, a gold-bearing stream which rushes below the Alhambra hill on the north. The second occupies the lower portion of the city which slopes on to the plain, and the Alhambra rises above both, a well-nigh demolished citadel, brooding over past glories of the civilised Moor, the most fascinating spot in all Spain.

The Albaicin district is practically the rebuilt Moorish town, where the aristocrats of Seville and Cordova settled when driven out of those cities by St. Ferdinand in the thirteenth century. Many traces remain to remind one of their occupation in the tortuous streets which wind up the steep hill sides, and the wall which they built for greater security is still the boundary of the city on the north. The Albaicin is a grand place to wander in and lose oneself hunting for relics and little bits of architecture. At every turn of the intricate maze I came across something of interest, either Moorish or Mediæval. A mean looking house with a fine coat-of-arms over the door had evidently been built by a knight with the collector's craze. He had specialised in millstones; a round dozen or more were utilised in the lower portions of the wall and looked strange with stones set in the plaster between them. A delicious *patio*, now given over to pigs and fowls, with a broken-down fountain in the centre of its ruined arcaded court, recalled the luxuries of the Infidel. The terraced gardens standing behind and above many a blank wall carried me back to those days of old when the opulence of the East pervaded every dwelling in this Mayfair of Granada. Of all these the Casa del Chapiz, though degraded into a low-class dwelling, is with its beautiful garden the most perfect remnant of the exotic Moor.

In the Carrera de Darro, just opposite the spot where once a handsome Moorish arch spanned the stream, stands a house wherein is a Moorish bath

GRANADA. CARRERA DE DARRO

GRANADA

surrounded by horseshoe arcades. The bath is 18 ft. square, and in the vaulted recess beyond is one of smaller dimensions commanding more privacy for the cleanly Eastern whose day was never complete without many ablutions.

Not far away up the hillside, in cave-dwellings amidst an almost impenetrable thicket of prickly pears, live the *gitanas*. I fear they now exist on the charity of the tourist, and make a peseta or two by fortune-telling or in the exercise of a more reprehensible cleverness, a light-fingered dexterity which is generally only discovered by those who " must go to the gipsy quarter" on their return to the hotel. These gipsies no longer wander in the summer months and lie up for the winter as they did of yore. They are not the Romanies of old times, and a nomadic life holds no charm for them now. They make enough out of the tourist to eke out a lazy existence throughout the year, and are fast losing all the character of a wandering tribe and the lively splendour of their race.

Higher up, the banks of the Darro are lined with more cave-dwellings, a great many of which, to judge by their present inaccessibility, are undoubtedly of prehistoric origin. Those that I took to be of later date have a sort of level platform in front of the entrance, from which the approach of a stranger could be seen and due warning taken by those inside of any hostile intent.

The Antequeruela quarter, called thus from the remnant of Moorish refugees who driven from Antequera found here a home, extends from the base of Monte Mauro to some distance below the confluence of the Darro and Genil, Granada's other river. It is the most modern quarter and busiest part of the city.

The life of an ordinary Spanish town passes in front of me as I sit in the sun sharing a seat with an old man wrapped closely in a *capa*. It is April. We are in the Alameda, a broad promenade which leads to the gardens of the Paseo de Salòn and de la Bomba. On either side are many coloured houses with green shutters. They are very French, and to this day I try to recall the town in France where I had seen them before. How often this happens when we travel abroad!—a face, a scent, a sound. Memory racks the tortuous channels of half-forgotten things stored away somewhere in the brain, and for days with an irritating restlessness we wander fruitlessly amid the paths of long ago.

I turned to my companion on the seat, he looked chilled despite the warmth of an April sun. "Tell me, sir, to whom does all the fine country of the Vega belong?" "Absent landlords, señor; they take their rents and they live in Madrid, and the poor man has no one to care for him." "But surely he begs and does not wish to work or to be cared for. The beggars in Granada are more numerous than in any place I know." "That is true, señor," and with a shake he relapsed into silence, drawing his capa closer around him. The turn the conversation had taken was not worth pursuing.

New buildings are superseding the old in Antequeruela, and poverty and squalor pushed further out of the sight of El Caballero, his Highness the tourist. Æsthetically we appreciate the picturesque side of poverty, the tumble-down houses, the rags, the graceful attitudes of the patient poor for ever shifting in the patches of sunlight as the great lifegiver moves round. Dinner will be ready for us at 7 o'clock in the hotel, there would be no call to leave home if every town we came to was clean and its people prosperous. "But what about *Los Pobres*, the beggars?" you ask. "Are they really deserving of charity, or only lazy scoundrels?" I cannot answer you. I can only tell you that I have never seen such terrible emaciated bundles of rags as those I saw in Granada.

In Seville, though it is forbidden to beg, it was the one-eyed that predominated; in Cordova he or no legs, who having marked down his prey, displayed great agility as he scuttled across the street with the help of little wooden hand-rests ; but here not only were both combined, but various horrors of crippled and disfigured humanity with open sores and loathsome disease thrust themselves before me wherever I went. It was disgusting—but oh ! how picturesque ! If only, my good *Pobres*, you would not come so close to me !

They say Spain is the one unspoilt country in Europe. Personally I think she is the one country that wants regenerating. Her girls are women at sixteen, old at thirty, and aged ten years later. Her men take life as it comes with very little initiative to better themselves. Very few display any energy. Their chief thoughts are woman, and how to pass the day at ease. Luckily for the country, at the age when good food and clean living helps to make men, her youth is invigorated by army service. True it is not popular. In the late war they died like flies through fever and ill-feeding, and many were the sad tales I heard of José and Pedro returning from the front with health ruined for life. It was a sad blow to Spain, that war. Her navy demolished and her colonies lost. It may be the regeneration of the nation, her well-wishers hope so, but it is a difficult thing to change the leopard's spots. The beggar being hungry begs, and well-nigh starves, his children follow his example and probably his great grandchildren will be in the same line of business a hundred years hence—*Quien sabe?* who knows?

I still sit in the sun rolling cigarettes; it is extraordinary how soon the custom becomes a habit, and think of all this. A string of donkeys passes with baskets stuffed tight with half a dozen large long-funnelled water cans. They have come in with fresh drinking water from the spring up the Darro under the Alhambra hill, and a little later the water-sellers will be offering glasses of the refreshingly cool contents of their cans. Granada is a city running with water, but the pollution from the drains and the never-ending ranks of women on their knees wringing clothes in its two streams, into which, by the way, all dead refuse is thrown, makes that which is fit to drink a purchasable quantity only.

I watch the peasants from the Vega, who come in with empty panniers slung across their donkeys, scraping up the dirt of the streets which they take away to fertilise their cottage gardens. Herds of goats go by muzzled until milking is over. They make for that bit of blank wall opposite, and stand licking the saline moisture which oozes from the plaster in the shade. The goats of Granada are reckoned the finest in Spain, and, as is the custom throughout Andalusia, graze in the early spring on the tender shoots of the young corn. This not only keeps them in food, but improves the quality of that part of the crop which reaches maturity. I could sit all day here if only the sun stood still. My companion removed himself half an hour ago and it is getting chilly in the shade, so up and on to the Cathedral.

What a huge Renaissance pile it is. Built on the Gothic plans of Diego de Siloe it is undoubtedly the most imposing edifice of this style in Spain. Fergusson considers its plan makes it one of the finest churches in Europe. The western façade was erected by Alonso Cano and José Granados, and does not follow Siloe's original design. The name of the sculptor-painter is writ in big letters throughout the building. To him are due the colossal heads of Adam and Eve, let into recesses above the High Altar, and the seven pictures of the *Annunciation, Conception, Presentation in the Temple, Visitation, Purification* and *Assumption* in the Capilla Mayor. The two very fine colossal figures, bronze gilt, which stand above the over-elaborated pulpits; a couple of beautiful miniatures on copper in the Capilla de la Trinidad; a fine Christ bearing the Cross and a head of S. Pedro over the altar of Jesus Nazareno, are also by Cano. Many other examples from his carving tools and brush are to be found in the Cathedral, of which he was made a "Racione" or minor Canon, after fleeing

GRANADA. INTERIOR OF THE CATHEDRAL

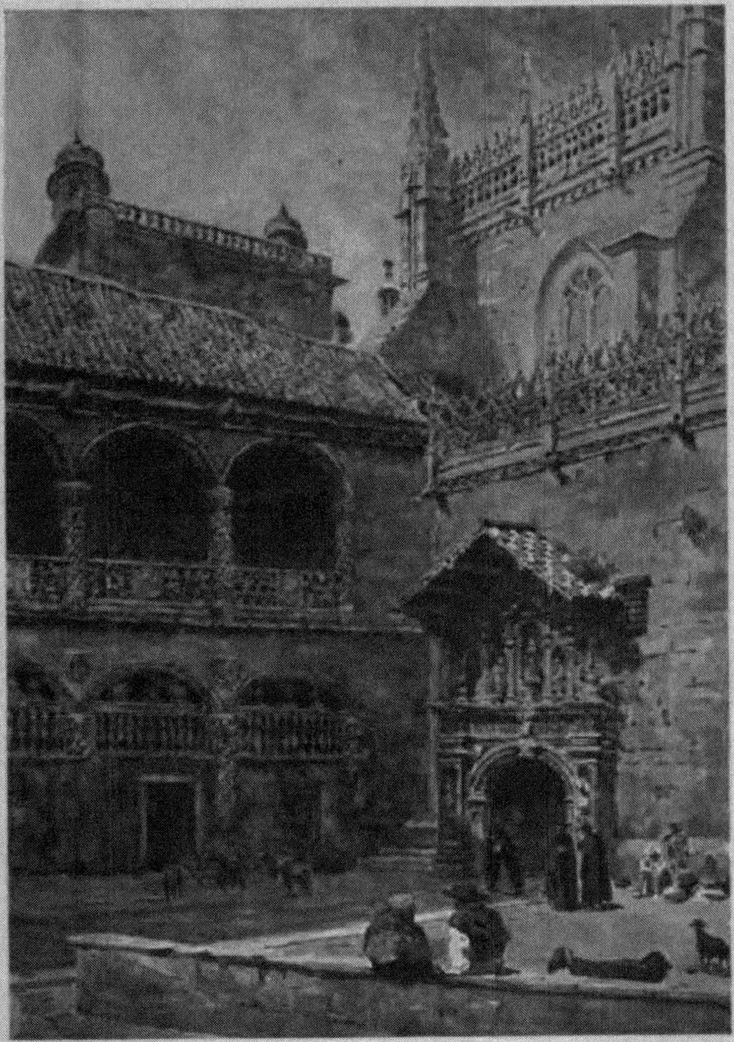

from Valladolid when accused of the murder of his wife. The little room he used as a workshop in the Great Tower may still be visited and his remains lie tranquilly beneath the floor of the cave.

In the Capilla de la Antigua there is that curious little image which, found in a cave, served Ferdinand as a battle banner; and also contemporary (?) portraits of the King and his Queen.

To me the thing of surpassing interest, which ought to be the most revered building in all Spain, was the Capilla Real and its contents. The *reja*, which separates the choir from the rest of the chapel, is a magnificent piece of work, coloured and gilded, by Bartolomé. As the verger unlocked the great gate he drew my attention to the box containing the lock with its three beautifully wrought little iron figures and intricate pattern. We passed in, the gate swung to with a click, the lock was as good as if it had but recently been placed there. These *rejas* throughout the country are all in splendid condition. A dry climate no doubt preserves them as it has preserved everything else, and I very seldom detected rust on any iron work. The humidity of the winter atmosphere is insufficient, I suppose, to set up much decay in metal, and certainly the only decay in Spain is where inferior material has been used in construction, or the negligence of man has left things to rot.

With the gate locked behind me I stood in front of the two marble monuments, the one of the recumbent figures of Ferdinand and Isabella, the other of Philip and Juana la Loca—crazy Jane. Beyond rose the steps up to the High Altar, close at my side those—a short flight—that led to the crypt where the coffins of these four rest. I felt surrounded by the Great of this Earth, and certainly a feeling of awe took hold of me as their deeds passed through my mind and I realised that here lay the remains of those who had turned out the Moor, bidden God-speed to Columbus, and instituted the Inquisition.

They are wonderful tombs these two. Ferdinand wears the order of St. George, the ribbon of the Garter, Isabella that of the Cross of Santiago, Philip and his wife the Insignia of the order of the Golden Fleece. Four doctors of the church occupy the corners of the first tomb, with the twelve Apostles at the sides. The other has figures of SS. Michael, Andrew, and John the Baptist, and the Evangelist. Both tombs are elaborately carved, the medallions in *alto-relievo* being of very delicate work. Next to that magnificent tomb in the Cartuja de Miraflores at Burgos, these are the finest monuments in all Spain.

GRANADA

Above the High Altar is a florid *Retable* with not much artistic merit. My interest was entirely centred in the two portrait figures of Ferdinand and Isabella. They each kneel at a Prie-Dieu facing one another on either side of the altar—the King to the north, the Queen to the south. Below them in double sections are four wooden panels in bas-relief, to which I turned after a long examination of these authentic and contemporary portraits. These panels are unsurpassed as records of the costume of the day and a faithful representation of their subject. On the left is the mournful figure of Boabdil giving up the key of the Alhambra to Cardinal Mendoza, who seated on his mule between the King and Queen, alone wears gloves. Surrounding them are knights, courtiers and the victorious soldiery. In the background are the towers of the Alhambra. To the right is seen the wholesale conversion by Baptism of the Infidel, the principal figures being monks who are very busy over their work, inducing the reluctant Moor to enter an alien Faith.

There is something very impressive about these panels, they render so well and in such a naïve manner the history they record. The surrender of the Moor after 750 years' rule, the end of his dreams, the final triumph of the King and Queen, who devoted the first portion of their reign to driving him out of the country, and the great church receiving the token of submission at the end of last act, they are all here.—The verger touched my arm, my reverie of those stirring times was broken, he had other things to show and noon was fast approaching. Pointing to three iron plates let into the floor of the chapel, he inquired if I would like to see the spot where rest the coffins of these great makers of history. Certainly; I could not leave the Cathedral without a silent homage to those who placed Spain first among the nations. He lifted the plates, and lighting a small taper which he thrust into the end of a long pole, disappeared down the steps, with a warning to mind my head for the entry was very low. I followed, stooping. At the bottom of the steps was a small opening heavily barred. The verger pushed his lighted taper and pole through the bars, and beckoned to me to look. I peered into the dark chamber, there resting on a marble slab were the rough iron-bound coffins of the "Catholic Kings." The taper flickered and cast long shadows in the gloom, discovering the coffins of Philip and Juana. It was all very eerie, a fitting climax in its simplicity to the magnificent monuments above and to the history writ on the walls of the Capilla Real. I shall never forget it.

In the sacristy I was shown the identical banner

GRANADA

which floated from the Torre de la Vela when the Alhambra had surrendered. Isabella herself had worked this for the very object to which it was put. Next to it hangs Ferdinand's sword, with a remarkably small handle. I had thought, from the kneeling effigy in the Capilla Real, that both he and Isabella must have been "small-made" and this verified my guess. Many other personal relics of the two were shown me. The Queen's own missal, a beautiful embroidered chasuble from her industrious fingers, an exquisitely enamelled viril, &c. Time was short, my verger wanted his dinner, and I had seen enough for one morning. He let me out through the closed door into the Placeta de la Lonja and in a sort of dream I carried away all I had seen.

The next morning I returned to the Placeta and stood in the doorway of the old Royal Palace, now used as a drapery warehouse, and commenced the drawing figured in the illustration. The rich late Gothic ornament of the exterior of the Capilla Real is well balanced by the Lonja which backs on to the sacristy. Here Pradas's work has been much mutilated and the lower stage of the arcading built up. The twisted columns of the gallery and its original wooden roof remain to tell us what this fine façade once was.

There is a great deal of interest in this huge

CATHEDRAL CITIES OF SPAIN

Cathedral, which to the tourist is quite overshadowed by the Alhambra. In the north-west corner of the Segrario which adjoins the building on the south, is the Capilla de Pulgar. Herman Perez del Pulgar was a knight serving under Ferdinand's banner. Filled with holy zeal, he entered Granada one stormy night in December 1490 by the Darro conduit, and making his way to the Mosque which then stood where the Segrario now is, pinned a scroll bearing the words "Ave Maria" to its principal door with his dagger. This daring deed was not discovered until the next morning, by which time the intrepid knight was safe back in camp. His courage was rewarded by a seat in the *coro* of the Cathedral, and at his death his body was interred in the chapel which bears his name.

Nearly all the churches of Granada occupy the sites of Mosques. Santa Anna, like San Nicolás, has a most beautiful wooden roof. San Juan de los Reyes contains portraits of Ferdinand and Isabella; its tower is the minaret of what was once a Mosque.

The Cathedral itself is so crowded in by other buildings, that no comprehensive view of the fabric is possible. Unfortunately this is the case, with one or two notable exceptions, throughout the country. Its fine proportions are thus lost, and it is only the interior with its great length and breath, its lofty arches and fine Corinthian pilasters that serve to dignify this House of God.

Taking a morning off, I walked out to the Cartuja Convent. The Gran Capitan, Gonzalo de Cordoba, at one time granted an estate to the Carthusians and on it they erected the convent to which I turned my steps. The Order about this time was immensely wealthy and they spent money with reckless lavishness on the interior of their church. Mother-of-pearl, tortoiseshell, ebony and cedar-wood entered largely into their decorations, as well as ivory and silver. But perhaps the marbles in the church are the most remarkable part of their scheme. These were chosen for the wonderful patterns of the sections, and with a little stretch of the imagination I could trace well-composed landscapes, human and animal forms in a great many of the slabs. The overdone chirrugueresque work, to which add these fantastic wall decorations, makes this interior postively scream. It is nothing more nor less than a vulgar display of wealth. The cloisters of the convent also attest the bad taste of the Carthusians, they contain a series of pictures which represent the most repugnant and bloodthirsty scenes of persecutions and matyrdoms of the Order.

In another convent, San Gerónimo, was buried the Gran Capitan. A slab marks the spot, but his

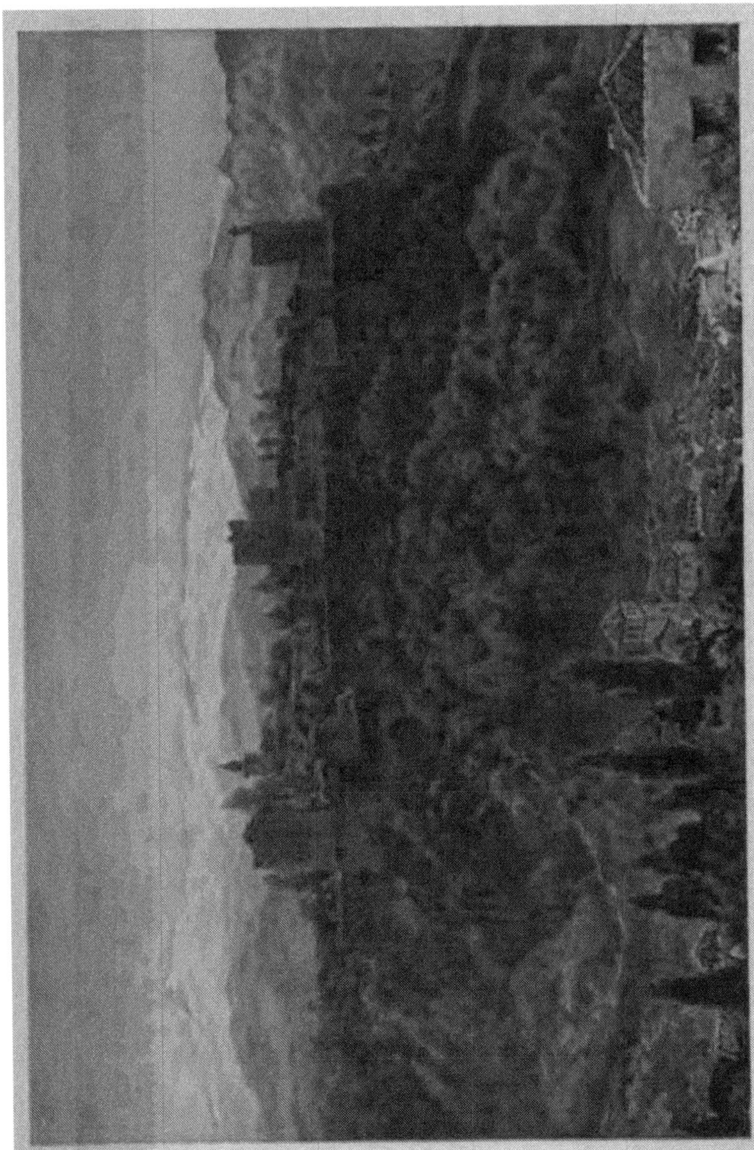

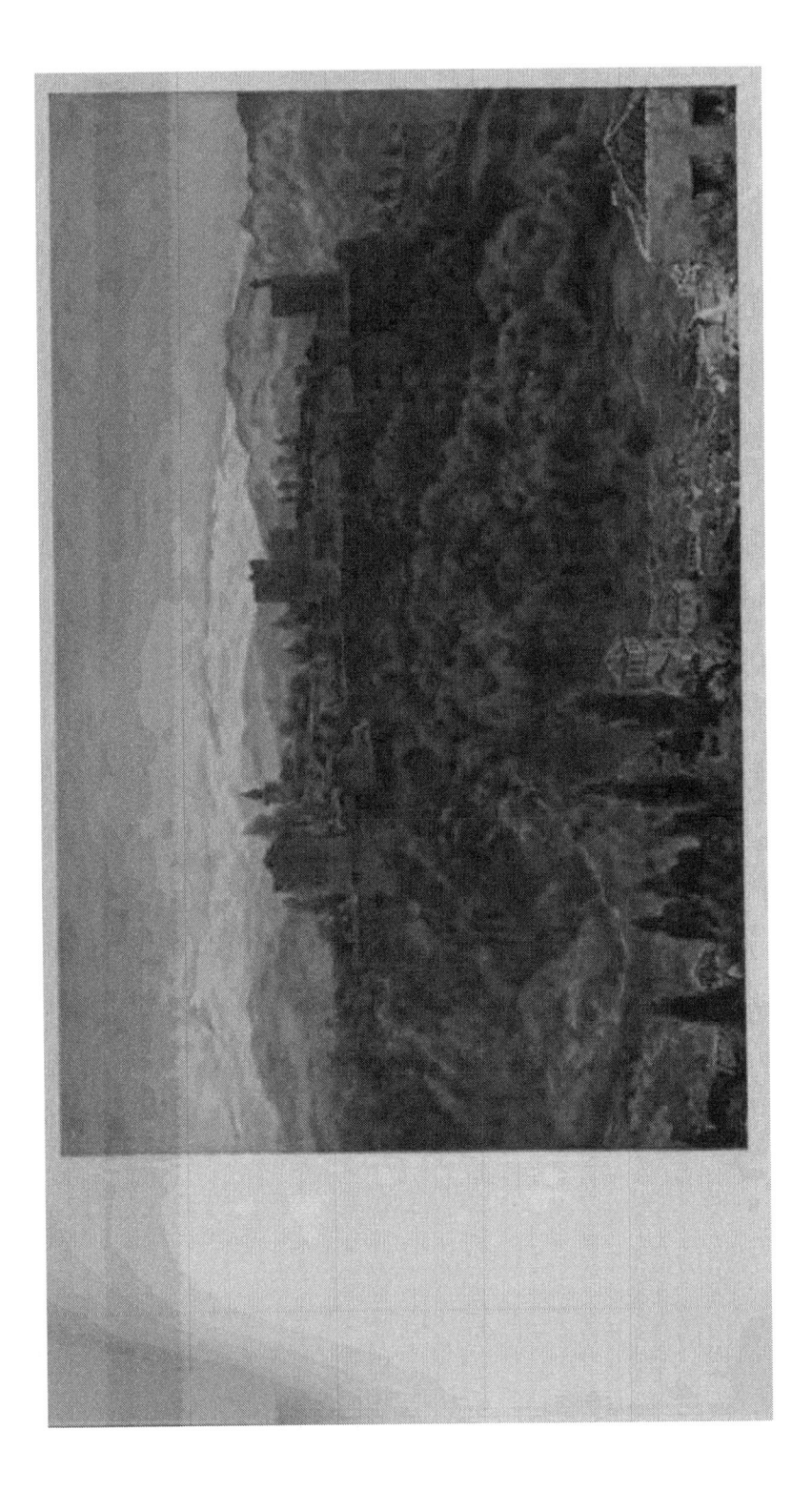

GRANADA

carriage crawled up the steep ascent, in the lulls of the storm, the sound of running water. It was fairyland, it was peace. After that long, tedious journey and the glare of the electric lit streets I had just passed through, I sank back on the cushions and felt my reward had come.

How is it possible to describe the Alhambra? It has been done so often and so well. Every one has read Washington Irving, and most of us know Victor Hugo's eulogy. I had better begin at the beginning, which is the gateway erected by Charles V. under which I passed with such a happy consciousness. Further up the hill, through which only pedestrians can go, is the Gate of Judgment, the first gateway into the Moorish fortress. Above it is the Torre de Justicia erected by Yusuf I. in 1348. On the external keystone is cut a hand, on the inner a key. Much controversy rages round these two signs and I leave it to others to find a solution. In old days the Kadi sat in this gateway dispensing justice. The massive doors still turn on their vertical pivots, the spear rests of the Moorish guard are still attached to the wall, and you must enter, as the Moors did, by the three turns in the dark passage beyond the gate. A narrow lane leads to the Plaza de las Algibes, under the level or which are the old Moorish cisterns. To the right is the Torre del Vino, and on the left the Acazaba.

CATHEDRAL CITIES OF SPAIN

Come with me up the short flight of steps into the little strip of garden. Let us lean over the wall and look out on to the Vega. Is there anywhere so grand and varied an outline of plain and mountain? Do you wonder at the tears that suffused the eyes of Boabdil as he turned for a last look at this incomparable spot? The brown roofs of Granada lie at our feet. Far away through the levels of the green plain, the Vega, I can see the winding of many silver streams. Beyond those rugged peaks to the south lies the Alpujarras district, the last abiding place of the conquered Moor. Further on the mass of the Sierra Aburijara bounds the horizon, west of it is the town of Loja, thirty miles away, buried in the dip towards Antequerra. To the north is Mount Parapanda, the barometer of the Vega, always covered with mist when rain is at hand. Nearer in is the Sierra de Elvira, spread out below which are the dark woods of the Duke of Wellington's property—he is known in Spain as Duque de Ciudad Rodriguez. It is clear enough for us to see the blue haze of the mountains round Jaen, and the rocky defile of Mochin. The Torre de la Vela shuts out the rest of the view. There is a bell hanging in this tower which can be heard as far away as Loja. Now turn and look behind. Right up into the blue sky rise the snow peaks of the Sierra Nevada. Mulhacen, the highest point

GRANADA

in all Spain, is not visible, but we can see Veleta which is but a few feet lower. The whole range glistens in the afternoon sun, but it is the evening hour that brings such wonderful changes of colour over these great snowfields, and, after the sun is down, such a pale mother-of-pearl grey silhouetted against the purple sky.

The entrance into what we call the Alhambra is hidden away behind the unfinished Palace of Charles V. The low door admits us directly in the Patio de los Arrayanes, or court of the Myrtles. Running north and south it gets more sun than any other court of the Alhambra. What a revelation it is! In the centre is an oblong tank full of golden carp. The neatly kept myrtle hedges encircle this, reflected in the clear water they add refreshing charm to a first impression of the Moorish Palace. On the north rises the Torre de Comares, the approach to which is through a beautifully proportioned chamber, the roof of which was unfortunately destroyed by fire in 1890. The whole of the ground-floor of this tower is known as the Hall of the Ambassadors. The monarch's throne occupied a space opposite the entrance and it was here that the last meeting to consider the surrender was held by Boabdil. The elaborate domed roof of this magnificent chamber is of larch wood, but the semi-darkness prevents one realising to the full extent its beauties. From the windows, which almost form small rooms, so thick are the walls of the Tower of Comares, fine views over the roofs of the city and the Albaicin hill are obtained.

The Court of the Lions, so called from the central fountain upheld by marble representations of the kingly beast, is surrounded by a beautiful arcade. At either end this is thrown out, forming a couple of extremely elegant pavilions. Fairy columns support a massive roof, the woodwork of which is carved with the pomegranate of Granada. Intricate fret-work is arranged to break the monotony of strong sunlight on a flat surface. Arabesques and inscriptions, stamped with an iron mould on the wet clay, repeat themselves all round the frieze. Orange trees at one time adorned the court and cast gracious shade on its surface. The fountain threw up jets of splashing water, the musical sound harmonising with the wonderful arrangement of light and shade. I tried to picture all this as I sat making my sketch, but even in April, though hot in the sun, I required an overcoat in the shadow, and I must own that the ever-present tourist with his kodak sadly disturbed all mental attempts at the reconstruction of Moorish life.

On the south side of the court is the hall of the

GRANADA. THE ALHAMBRA, COURT OF LIONS

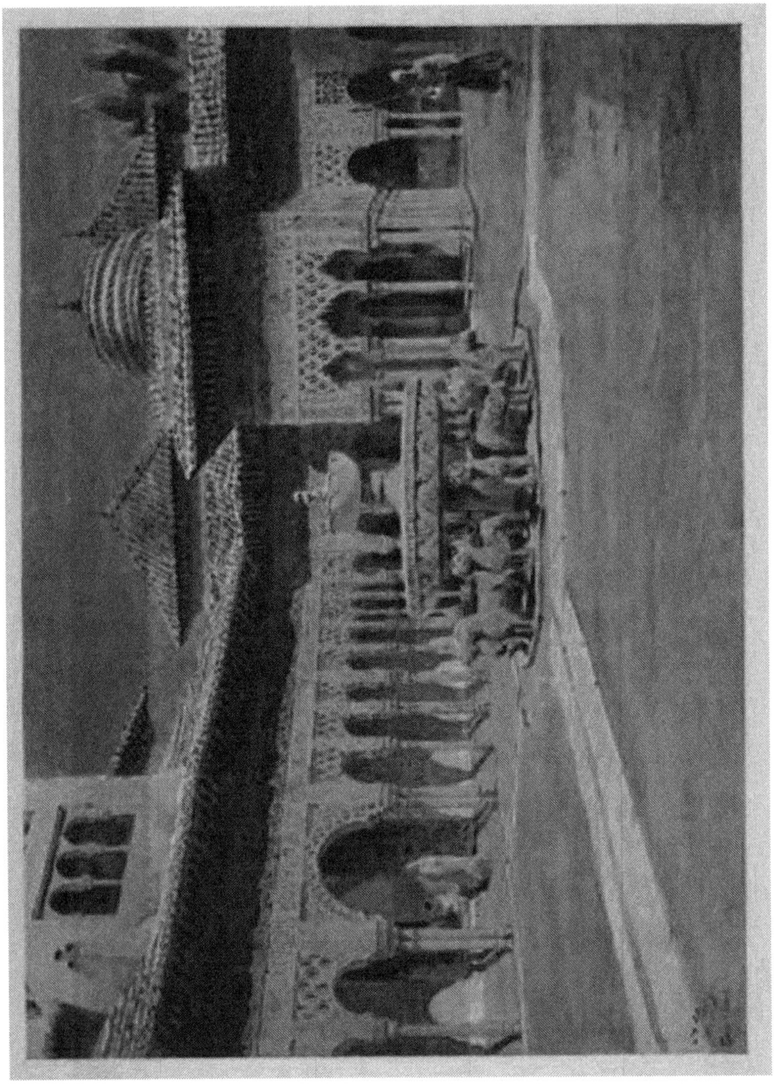

GRANADA

Abencerrages, named after that noble family. The massive wooden doors, which shut it off from the arcade, are of most beautiful design. The hall is rectangular and has a fine star-shaped stalactite dome. The *azulejos*, or tiles, are the oldest that remain in the Alhambra. A passage leads to what was once the Royal Sepulchral Chamber.

On the east side is the so-called Sala de la Justicia divided into several recesses and running the whole length of this portion of the court. The central recess was used by Ferdinand and Isabella when they held the first Mass after the surrender of the Moors. The chief interest of the Sala I found to be in a study of the paintings on the semi-circular domed roofs. They portray the Moor of the period. The middle one, that in the chapel-recess, no doubt contains portraits of Granada's rulers in council. The other two represent hunting scenes and deeds of chivalry. It is supposed that the Koran forbids the delineation of any living thing. The Moor got over this difficulty by portraying animal life in as grotesque a manner as possible, or by employing foreign captives to do this for him. One theory of the origin of the Lion Fountain is that a captive Christian carved the lions and gave his best—or his worst—as the price of his liberation. Personally I think they are of Phœnician origin. Animals and birds in decoration reached the Moor from

Persia, where from unknown ages they had always been employed in this way; and the Môsil style of hammered metal work is replete with this feature.

On the north side of the court lies the Room of the Two Sisters, with others opening out from it, which seems to point to the probability that this was the suite occupied by the Sultana herself. Moorish art has here reached its highest phase. The honeycomb roof contains nearly five thousand cells, all are different, yet all combine to form a marvellously symmetrical whole. Fancy ran free with the architect who piled one tiny cell upon another and on these supported a third. Pendant pyramids cluster everywhere and hang suspended apparently from nothing. In the fertility of his imagination the designer surpassed anything of the kind that went before or has since been attempted. Truly the verses of a poem copied on to the *azulejos* are well set. "Look well at my elegance, and reap the benefit of a commentary on decoration. Here are columns ornamented with every perfection, the beauty of which has become proverbial."

Beyond this entrancing suite of rooms is the Miradoro de Daraxa with three tall windows overlooking that little gem of a garden the Patio de Daraxa. It was here that Washington Irving lodged when dreaming away those delicious days in the Alhambra.

GRANADA

The old Council Chamber of the Moors, the Meshwár, is reached through the Patio de Mexuar. Charles V. turned this chamber into a chapel, and the hideous decorations he put up are still extant. An underground passage, which leads to the baths, ran from the *patio* and gave access to the battlements and galleries of the fortress as well as forming a connecting link between each tower.

The baths are most interesting, but to me were pervaded by a deadly chill. I felt sorry for the guardian who spends his days down in such damp, icy quarters. A remark I made to him inquiring how long his duty kept him in so cold a spot, called forth so terrible a fit of coughing that I got no reply. I was told afterwards that he was only placed there as he was too ill for other duty, and it was expected he would not live much longer! There are two baths of full size and one for children. The *azulejos* in them are very beautiful, as they also are in the disrobing room and chamber for rest.

An open corridor leads from the Hall of the Ambassadors to the Torre del Peinador which Yusuf I. built. The small Tocador de la Reina, or Queen's dressing-room, with its quaint frescoes, was modernised by Charles V. Let into the floor is a marble slab drilled with holes, through which perfumes found their way from a room below while the Queen was dressing.

CATHEDRAL CITIES OF SPAIN

The glamour of the East clings to every corner of the Alhambra, and the wonder of it all increased as I began to grow familiar with its courtyards and halls, the slender columns of its arcades, with their tracery and oft-repeated verses forming ornament and decoration, and the well thought-out balance of light and shade. What must it all have been like when the sedate Moor glided noiselessly through the cool corridors, or the clang of arms resounded through the now silent halls! It is difficult to imagine. The inner chambers were then lined with matchless carpets and rugs and the walls were covered with subtly coloured *azulejos*.

Many are the changes since those days of the Infidel who cultivated the art of living as it has never been cultivated since. Restoration is judiciously but slowly going on, and every courtesy is shown to the visitor. A small charge might be levied, however, to assist the Government, even in a slight degree, with restoration, and I am sure no one would grudge paying for the privilege of sauntering through the most interesting remains of the Moorish days of Spain.

The unfinished Palace of Charles V. occupies a large space, to clear which a great deal of the Moorish Palace was demolished. The interior is extremely graceful. The double arcades, the lower of which is Doric and the upper Ionic, run round

GRANADA. GENERALIFE

GRANADA

a circular court which for good proportion it would be hard to beat.

On the Corre de Sol, a little way out of the Alhambra and situated above it, is the Generalife. It belongs to the Pallavicini family of Genoa, but on the death of the present representative becomes the property of the Spanish Government. A stately cypress avenue leads to the entrance doorway, through which one enters an oblong court full of exotic growth and even in April a blaze of colour. Through a tank down the centre runs a delicious stream of clear water. At the further end of this captivating court are a series of rooms, one of which contains badly painted portraits of the Spanish Sovereigns since the days of Ferdinand and Isabella.

Up some steps is another garden court with another tank, shaded by more cypress trees. One huge patriarch is over six hundred years old, and it is supposed that under it Boabdil's wife clandestinely met Hamet the Abencerrage.

Space will not permit me to tell of the many entrancing excursions I made to the foot-hills of the Sierra Nevada and up the two rivers. I can only add that the valleys disclosed to the pedestrian are a wealth of rare botanical specimens, and if time permits will well repay a lengthened sojourn in the last stronghold of the Moors in Spain.

MALAGA

MALAGA disputes with Cadiz the honour of being the oldest seaport in the country. In early days the Phœnicians had a settlement here, and in after times both the Carthagenians and Romans utilised "Malacca" as their principal port on the Mediterranean littoral of Spain. In 571 the Goths under their redoubtable King, Leovigild, wrested the town from the Byzantines. Once more it was captured, by Tarik, in the year 710 and remained a Moorish stronghold until Ferdinand took it after a long siege in 1487.

It is said that gunpowder was first used in Spain at this siege, when the "seven sisters of Ximenes," guns planted in the Gibralfaro, belched forth fire and smoke.

In the year 709 the Berber Tarif entered into an alliance with Julian, Governor of Ceuta, who held that place for Witiza the Gothic King of Spain. With four ships and five hundred men he crossed the narrow and dangerous straits to reconnoitre the European coast, having secretly in view an independent kingdom for himself on the Iberian peninsula. He landed at Cape Tarifa.

This expedition was so far successful that in two years' time another Berber, of a name almost similar, Tarík to wit, was sent over with twelve thousand men and landed near the rock which received the name of Jabal-Tarík, or mountain of Tarík, the present Gibraltar.

Witiza in the meantime died and was suceeded by Roderic, who, hearing of the invasion of this Moorish host, hastened south from Toledo and met his death in the first decisive battle between Christian and Infidel on the banks of the Guadalete near Cadiz. Tarík then commenced his victorious march, which ended in less than three years with the subjugation of the whole country as far as the foot of the Pyrenees—Pelayo, in his cave at Covadonga near Oviedo, alone holding out with a mere remnant against the all-conquering Moor.

If you ask me, "What is Malaga to-day?" I can reply with truth, "The noisiest town in Spain." Like all places in the south it is a babel of street-cries, only a little more so than any of the others. The *seranos*, or night-watchmen, disturb one's rest as they call out the hour of the night, or whistle at the street corners to their comrades. A breeze makes hideous the hours of darkness by the banging to and fro of unsecured shutters. The early arrival

MALAGA. VIEW FROM THE HARBOUR

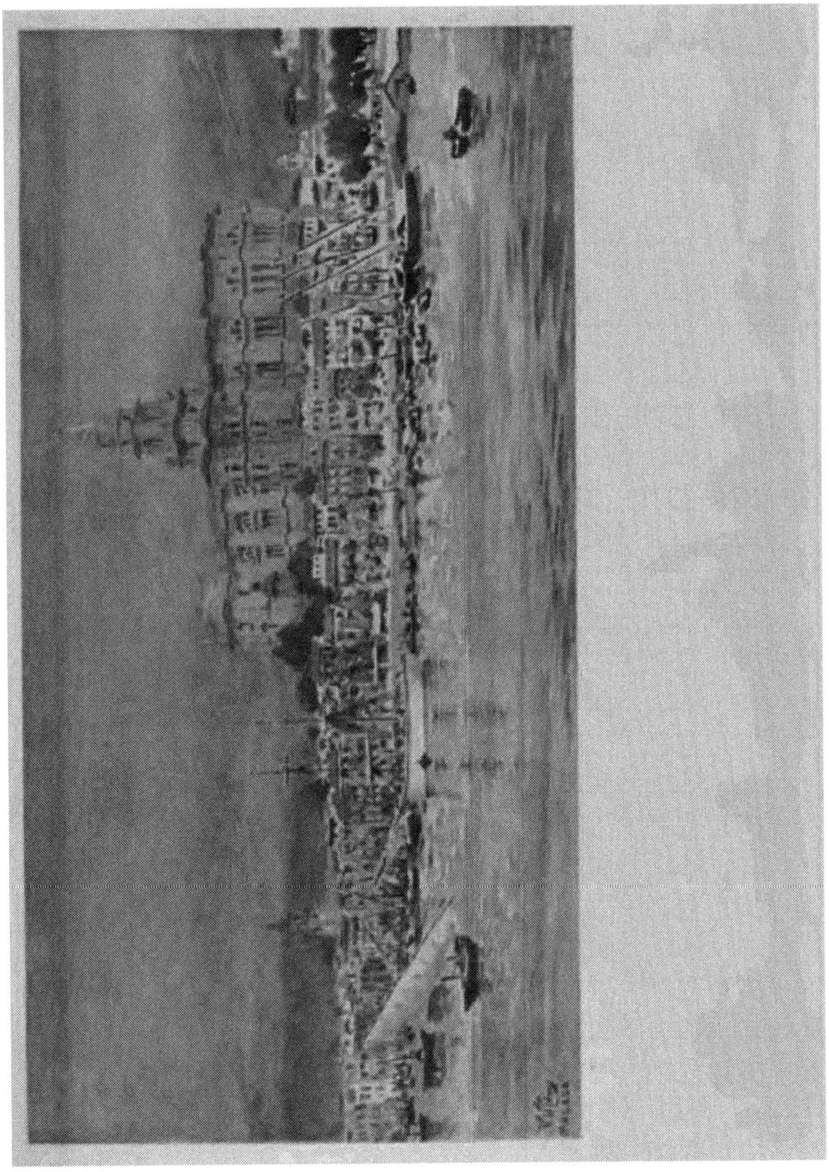

of herds of goats with tinkling bells heralds the dawn, which is soon followed by the discordant clatter of all those, cracked and otherwise, which hang in the church belfries. The noisiest town I visited, most certainly, but for all that a very enchanting place. In a way not unlike Naples, for the Malagueno is the Spanish prototype of the Neapolitan. Lazy, lighthearted, good-natured, but quick to take affront, he gets through the day doing nothing in a manner that won my sincere admiration. "Why work, señor, when you have the sun? I do not know why the English travellers are always in such a hurry. And the North American, he is far worse. I earned two posetas yesterday. To-day I have no wants, I do not work. To-morrow? Yes, perhaps to-morrow I work, but to-day I sit here in the sun, I smoke my cigarette, I am content to watch others, that is life!"—and who can say that the Malagueno is far wrong? Not I.

Malaga's Cathedral, an imposing building of a very mixed Corinthian character, occupies the site of a Moorish mosque which was converted into a church. Of this early church of the Incarnation, the Gothic portal of the *Segragrio* is the only portion remaining. The present edifice was begun in 1538 from the plans of that great architect Diego de Siloe, but being partially destroyed by an earthquake in 1680, was not completed until 1719. It cannot be called complete even now, and the long period over which its construction has been spread accounts for the very many inconsistencies in a building which is full of architectural defects.

The west façade is flanked by two Towers, only one of which has been finished; this is drawn out in three stages like the tower of La Seo at Saragossa, and has a dome with lantern above. The doors of the north and south Transepts are also flanked by towers, but they do not rise beyond the cornice line. The interior, reminding one of Granada's Cathedral, is seemingly immense. The proportions are massive and decidedly good. It was in his proportions that Siloe excelled. The length of this is three hundred and seventy-five feet, the width two hundred and forty, and the height one hundred and thirty feet. The columns which support the heavy roof consist of two rows of pillars one above the other. The vaulting is of round arches.

A picture by Alonso Cano in the chapel of Our Lady of the Rosary, and one of a *Virgin and Child*, in that of San Francisco, by Morales, were the only two objects that I could say interested me, besides the magnificently carved *silleria del coro*, the work of many hands, but chiefly those of Pedro de Mena, a pupil of Cano.

MALAGA

With all its architectural incongruities it is an impressive fabric, and rises high above the surrounding roofs, like a great Liner with a crowd of smaller boats lying around her. So it struck me as I sat on the quayside of the Malagueta making my sketch, sadly interfered with by an unpleasant throng of idling loafers.

Beyond Malagueta lies Caleta, and on the hill above them is the Castilla de Gibralfaro, from which when the sky is clear the African mountains near Ceuta can be seen. Below the Gibralfaro and between it and the Cathedral, lies the most ancient part of the city, the Alcazába, the glorious castle and town of Moorish days. And now?—like so many of Spain's departed glories, it is not much more than a ruined conglomeration of huts and houses of a low and very insanitary order.

At the other end of Malaga is the Mercado, and close by is the old Moorish sea gateway, the Puerta del Mar, washed by the waters of the blue Mediterranean in their day, but at the present time well away from the sea and surrounded by houses.

The everyday market is held in the dry bed of the treacherous Guadelmedina, a stream which rose in the fatal October of 1907 and swept away all the bridges, swamping the lower quarters of the city. Many lives were lost in this disastrous flood and many bodies picked up by fishing-boats far out at sea. However, when I made my sketch there was no chance of such a visitation, and I found the market folk more polite than the loafers on the quay.

The country lying at the back of the city and at the base of the sun-baked and scarred mountains by which it is surrounded, produces almost everything that grows. From this—the Vega—come grapes, raisins, figs, oranges, lemons, water and sweet melons, quinces, pomegranates, medlars, plantains, custard-apples, guava, olives and sugar-cane—a veritable paradise for the fruit grower. Up the hill slopes, where the olive luxuriates, fine woods of sweet acorn and cork trees are passed, and any day you may see large herds of swine feeding on the acorns that have fallen, and routing out other delicacies that their sensitive noses tell them lie hidden beneath the surface. The pork of Estremadura is reckoned the best in Spain, and that from these oak woods a good second. The pig in Spain is a clean feeder, and you can eat him with perfect safety anywhere. Such a thing as the offensive pig-sty, the disgrace of rural England, is absolutely unknown here.

Malaga's climate is delightful, despite the fierce winds and the dust they raise. Though rain

MALAGA. THE MARKET

MALAGA

seldom falls the cool sea breezes in summer bring a refreshing tonic to the dweller up country; and many Spaniards at this season come here for bathing, and obtain a maximum of sunshine without the intense heat of the interior.

VALENCIA

VALENCIA DEL CID is inseparably connected with the hero of Spanish romance, Rodrigo Diaz of Bivar, to give him his real name, "Cid" being a corruption of the Moorish *Seyyid*, and first appearing in historical documents of the year 1064. Rising to great power, Alfonso of Leon appointed him to the command of his army, but through jealousy banished him in 1081. From that date the Cid became a true knight-errant. Barred from the kingdom of Leon, he was ever ready to sell his services to the highest bidder; and after many wanderings found himself with a goodly following of knights, only too eager in those days, when might was right, to be in the train of so redoubtable a champion, *en route* to Saragossa. The Moorish ruler of that city being at loggerheads with the Count of Barcelona accepted the Cid's proffered services, and the result was a battle in which the Catalans were badly beaten.

With no prospects of further service in Aragon, the Cid turned his face south and marched on Valencia, whose Moorish King Yahya was only too pleased to request his protection in advance, instead of succumbing to his conquering arm. Thus began Rodrigo's connection with the city, which with one or two intervals ended only at his death.

It was from the top of the Miguelete Tower, which is pictured in my illustration of the Cathedral, that he showed his wife Ximena and their daughters the fair land he had conquered. This was in 1095, when after having rejoined Alfonso and left him again, he had returned and recaptured the city after a siege of twenty months. Four years later died the man whose name was a terror to the Infidel, and his widow Ximena, following the traditions of her warrior husband, held Valencia against overwhelming hordes of Moors. The story of the bitter end, how she placed his body on his favourite war-horse and drove it through the ranks of the enemy, has always been a theme for the balladmonger of Spain.

It was in 140 B.C. that Junius Brutus founded a small Roman colony on the banks of the river Turia. Pompey destroyed this settlement and rebuilt it. In 413 the Goths took possession. The Emir of Cordova captured it in 714 and Valencia remained a vassal state until the fall of the Omayeh dynasty. Like other provinces, it became merged under the single banner that floated over the

VALENCIA. SAN PABLO

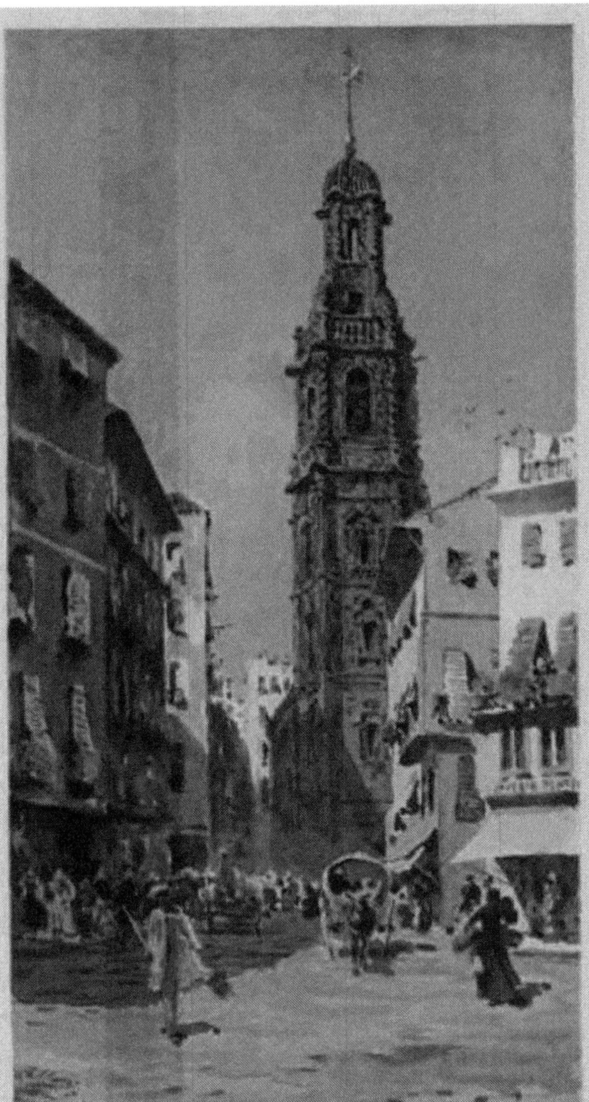

greater part of the Peninsula at the union of Aragon and Castile. Being a coast town and savouring of the south, it was not until the time of the bigoted Philip III. that the industrious and unfortunate Moriscoe was finally expelled from the shelter of Valencia's walls.

Souchet sacked the place in the Napoleonic wars and received the title of Duke of Albufera from his master. Rather an empty honour, Albufera being the large and malarious tract of marshland along the coast a few miles to the south of El Grao, and worth but very little.

El Grao is Valencia's Port, and is three miles distant from the city. The road which connects the two is about the busiest high road I saw in Spain. From sunrise till long after sunset two streams of vehicles pass to and fro. Strings of laden donkeys, waggonettes crammed with good-humoured laughing fisher and country folk pass along, an electric tram carries those who can afford the extra *centimos*, and the carriages of Valencia's well-to-do citizens take them to the harbour for a breath of sea air out on the breakwaters. Everything seems alive, and though there is that balmy feeling in the air which one gets in Andalusia, there is none of the indolence and seductive *dolce far niente* of that enchanting province. No! quite the other way in Valencia. The peasants are extremely industrious. The soil of the *Huerta* bears them three crops during the year. The system of irrigation, the old Moorish system by-the-way, is perfect, and though the product of a soil which is forced to bear more than it naturally can, is reinforced at sowing time, in the case of corn, by Russian grain, it cannot be said that Valencia depends on any outside help for her prosperity. The swamps bordering the coast grow the finest rice in the world. The wines of the province are good and cheap, held in much esteem by French merchants to fortify the lighter produce of their own country. So cheap are they in fact, that in some parts of the province it costs more to get a drink of water than a glass of wine. Yet drunkenness is unknown. If a Valencian took a drop too much, he would be promptly boycotted by his neighbours, and for ever after looked upon as a disgusting and outlandish boor, a disgrace to his village and a man to be shunned.

The peasant is very illiterate and scrupulously honest—the one follows the other. Like the Andalusian, he is absolutely trustworthy in all his dealings, which are conducted by word of mouth. In buying and selling no signatures to documents pass between the contracting parties. If any paper is ever signed, it is confirmed by certain scratches or marks known to belong to so and so—the

VALENCIA. DOOR OF THE CATHEDRAL

signed. His word is his bond, it is generally all he can give, but it is enough and is worth more than signatures sometimes are. Further north, where modern ways of life are more in vogue, and where all is more "advanced," there are ten lawyers to the one in Valencia and the south.

The Cathedral was originally a Gothic structure, but one fashion following another, has been at different times so altered and robbed of all architectural beauty that there remains but little of interest in the building. It was founded in 1262 and finished two hundred years later. El Miguelete, the celebrated Bell Tower, is so named because the bells were first hung on St. Michael's Day. Like the Torre de Vela of the Alhambra, a bell is here struck which regulates the irrigation of the *Huerta*.

In this connection, and as an exemplification of the peasant's trustworthiness, once a month, on a Thursday, the Tribunal de Aguas sits in the Plaza de la Seo outside the Puerto de los Apóstoles or north door of the Cathedral. Its presiding members are chosen by their fellow peasants for their integrity and general standing in the community. They exercise absolute control over the seven different irrigation districts. The Government has once or twice interfered with this, but unsuccessfully. Plaintiffs and defendants appear before this primitive tribunal seated in a public square. The case is stated, *pros* and *cons* weighed, and judgment given fairly on its merits. Any one passing can stop and hear the arguments of both sides. As a proof of the shrewdness the peasants possess and the confidence they have in their dealings with one another, no appeal is ever made from the judgment of their elders.

This north door has good sculptured figures in the jambs and archivolt. Above is a fine rose window. These are among the remains of the first building. Another relic of the early structure is the octagonal *cimborio* erected about the same time as the doorway, *i.e.*, 1350. The lancet windows over the Puerta del Paláu, which is surmounted by a round arch with carvings in the jambs, are all of the same period. The third doorway, the Puerta del Miguelete, is florid and overdone, and dates from the eighteenth century. Its bronze doors however are extremely fine.

The best features of the much-spoilt interior are the octagon and the very beautiful Corinthian *silleria del coro*. The original *retablo* over the High Altar was set on fire by the lighted cotton attached to a pigeon let loose at a religious ceremony in 1469. The side panels alone were saved from the results of the terrified bird's erratic flight. Close by on a pillar is hung the armour of James I. of Aragon.

VALENCIA

Over the sacristy door is a good painting by Ribalta of *Christ Bearing the Cross*, and in the ante-room an *Adoration* by Ribera, besides five good examples of Juanes' brush.

Among the treasures of the Cathedral is an extraordinary piece of goldsmith's work, a Calix, showing four different periods of this art, *i.e.*, Roman, IXth, XVth and XVIth centuries. It figures in the picture of the *Last Supper* by Juanes, which is now in the Prado at Madrid. An interesting trophy also belongs to the Cathedral in the shape of the chain which at one time closed the old Port of Marseilles.

The many different varieties of marble used in the decoration of the building form a very pleasing series, and go some way towards compensating the disappointment one experiences with the much-altered style of what ought to be a grand interior.

I saw a good procession one evening wending its way through the crowds which lined the narrow street near the church of Santa Catalina. The balconies were filled with occupants who showered rose leaves down as the effigy of St. John passed by. The light from the torches carried by some boys flickered upwards and caught the faces of those peering over from their vantage posts above. The crowd knelt as the saint passed, and once more the vitality of the Church, which I could not but feel wherever I went in Spain is the thing that lives, was again in evidence.

Over the door of the church of San Martin is a good equestrian group in bronze. San Domingo has some very beautiful cloisters of late Gothic date, and San Salvador possesses Valencia's miraculous image. Nicodemus is reputed to have made this, the Christ of Beyrout. The marvellous relic navigated itself from Syria across the waters of the Mediterranean and reached Valencia against the river's stream. A monument on the bank marks the spot where the wonderful voyage ended by the safe landing of the Christ. It is much visited by the devout. In the chapel attached to the Colegio del Patriarca hangs Ribalta's fine *Last Supper*. Every Friday morning at ten o'clock the *Miserere* is celebrated here. The impressive ceremony commences with the slow lowering of this picture from its place above the High Altar. The void is filled by a dark cloth, which, as the service proceeds, is gently drawn aside disclosing a second cloth, this is again repeated, followed by another, and when this, the fourth cloth, is parted asunder a fine painting of *Christ Crucified* is revealed. Meanwhile chants appropriate to the solemn service have been filling the church and increasing the tension of the congregation. The whole ceremony is a very good piece of stage

VALENCIA. RELIGIOUS PROCESSION

management and certainly most thrilling and inspiring. The black *mantilla* for ladies is *de rigeur*.

Valencia's walls, erected in 1356, were demolished in 1871 to give work to the unemployed, and the spacious *Paseo* made in their stead. The trees planted along this carriage drive have added materially to the health of the city.

Of the two remaining gates, the Torres de Serranos is much the better. Built in the second half of the fourteenth century on Roman foundations, its massive construction and great height are very grand. It is one of the best gates I know. The archway itself is rather low. The double floors above have fine Gothic vaulting and are approached by a flight of steps. The gallery is supported on heavy corbels, and the cornice has deep machicolations. The whole rises in isolated grandeur and and may perhaps gain, from the painter's point of view, by the absence of flanking walls.

The Torre de Cuarto is another enormous gateway with two huge round towers on either side. It still bears the marks of Souchet's artillery—whose round shot did apparently no damage whatever. Not far from this gate lies the Mercado situated in the middle of the old quarters of the city. Valencia is quite a modern town, it is rapidly losing everything of any age, and changing its narrow insanitary streets for spacious well-built thoroughfares.

The Mercado is by far the largest and most attractive market in Spain. Fruit and vegetables, wicker goods of all sorts, baskets, chairs, toys, leather-work and harness, brightly coloured mule trappings, every description of wood and metal-work, the usual assortment of old iron, lamps antique and modern, oleographs and chromos, saints and virgins jostling the latest cheap reproduction of a famous *Torrero* or *Bailarina*, furniture, worn-out field implements and new cutlery, lace, everything, in fact, including smells, the variety of which I found unequalled anywhere. Strong garlic assaulted my nostrils—in three more steps I was in the midst of roses and carnations, half a dozen more and a horribly rank cheese made the air vibrate; and so it continued from one end to the other of this most fascinating kaleidoscopic throng, to study which I returned every day of my sojourn in Valencia.

On one side of this wonderful market-place stands the Lonja de la Seda. It dates from 1482 and occupies the site of the Moorish Alcázar. Perhaps of all the examples of Gothic civil architecture in Europe, the Lonja de la Seda can claim the first place. The west façade, facing the Mercado, has a double row of square-topped Gothic windows, above which is a traceried gallery running round the entire building with gargoyles and a frieze of heads below the embattled parapet.

In the centre is a Tower with a couple of Gothic windows. There are two separate buildings in this "Silk Exchange," one of which has a beautiful court. The whole of the other is occupied by the Exchange Hall. The rich star vaulting of the interior is borne by two rows of spiral columns without capitals; they branch out to the roof like the leaves of a palm tree and it is very evident that this beautiful treatment was suggested by the growth of the tree.

Valencia has always been celebrated for a certain style or school of painting, and in the Museum, which occupies the buildings of the old Convento del Carmen, Ribalta, Espinosa and Juanes are seen at their best. The school is noted for the peculiar deep red undertone of the shadows, which is very markedly apparent in the works hanging on these walls. There are also some beautiful examples of native faience and pottery, for Valencia is still the home of Spanish lustre ware.

The Valencians are great bird fanciers, and very keen pigeon shots. Numerous lofts built on the roofs for these birds cut the sky-line in the old quarters of the city. Sunday sees the dry bed of the Turia full of competitors in shooting matches, when toll is taken of the feathered inhabitants of these airy dwellings.

If it were not for the rather bad drinking water and the malarious marshes, the breeding-ground of a most particularly venomous mosquito, Valencia would be as pleasant and lively a spot for residence as any in Spain. The climate is good and it is near the sea. It stands on the edge of a veritable fruit garden, and its people are pleasant and friendly.

TORTOSA

JOURNEYING to Valencia from the north one is carried along a grand bit of coast with glimpses of the blue Mediterranean rolling in on stretches of yellow sand, and breaking into spray on the rocks above which the train runs. The *rapido* stops for lunch at Tortosa, and I got out intending to stay if there was anything in the famous old city or its Cathedral which might bear illustrating in this book.

I reached the best *fonda* in the place, and was heartily welcomed by its lively little landlord, who immediately handed me one of his cards, whereon was set out, amongst many superlatives, the news that an interpreter was attached to the house. "Gone away for the day, señor," was the reply when I asked for an interview. He was always away I fear; however, I did not need his services and my host and I became fast friends. So friendly indeed that I only just avoided an embrace at parting on the day I left. He took great interest in my doings, and on his side gave me much information. He explained to me how the mighty

Ebro, on which Tortosa is situated, and to which it owes its existence, had risen in flood during the disastrous October of 1907. "Right up to here, señor"—this while I was having lunch—and he pointed to a spot a couple of inches off the floor of the *comedor*, which was on the first floor of the house—" A terrible flood that !"—" Yes, señor, the streets were for weeks full of mud and all sorts of things. Hundreds of poor people lost everything and many were swept out to sea."

Another day I remarked on the gas that lit the *fonda* and asked my host why he had not put in electric light. "It is too expensive, señor; some people have it, and the Market Hall is lit by it; but you must understand that Tortosa long ago did away with oil lamps and was one of the first places in Spain to use gas. And now ?—well it is enough for us, and the electric light is too expensive."

Elsewhere in Spain I have been told with pride that the country is still in the foremost rank of civilisation—whatever the Progressive Press says —and the almost universal use of electricity has been pointed out to verify the boast. But Tortosa, which led the van when gas was a novelty, is the only place of any importance that I know which is still lit by this means.

Local tradition has it, that the city dates back to

the time of St. Paul who, I was told, settled here and built himself a nice little house. Whatever the saint did it is on record that before his day the town was an important Iberian port of the Ilercaones tribe, and in later years under the Romans, possessed a mint of its own, being then known as Julia Augusta Dertosa. Strategically the key of the great river, Tortosa was subject to repeated attempts at capture by those not in occupation. During the time when it was held by the Moors, Charlemagne's son Louis, after an unsuccessful attempt, gained possession, only to be driven out in the year 810. It was not until 1148 that the Infidel's reign was finally terminated by Ramon Bereuguer, Count of Barcelona.

In the following year a desperate attempt was made by the Moors to retake their stronghold, and the inhabitants, reduced to the last stage of despair, contemplated the sacrifice of their women and children, and then a final sortie to end their own lives. The women, however, showed a true militant spirit, they courted death, but not in this mean manner. Mounting the hardly defensible walls with every and any weapon they could lay hands on, the men were directed to sally forth. The gates were opened, and cheered on by their wives and daughters, the sterner sex rushed out. So determined was the onslaught that the Moorish host was beaten back and fled leaving all the plunder in his camp behind.

Ramon, to show his appreciation of the heroism displayed by the fair ones, invested them with the Order of the Axe (La Hacha) and decorated them with the red military scarf. Also decreeing that at their marriage they should precede mankind, and to this added the privilege of duty-free dress materials. What more could woman want?

The Cathedral occupies the site of a mosque erected in 914 by Abderrhaman. A Cufic inscription in the wall at the back of the sacristy relates this with the date. Bishop Lanfredo dedicated the building to the Virgin in 1158, but the present structure dates from 1347. It is extremely good Gothic, with a heavy baroque west façade, ugly and ill-proportioned. Of the exterior but little is visible, and my sketch simply includes the upper part of the façade, visible over the roofs of the quaint old town, with the river flowing in front.

The interior is very simple and dignified. The slender columns of the nave rise to a great height; the light that filters through the few clerestory windows that are not blocked subdues the garishness of a bad *trascoro*, and finds its way amongst the tracery of the arches of the double apse. In

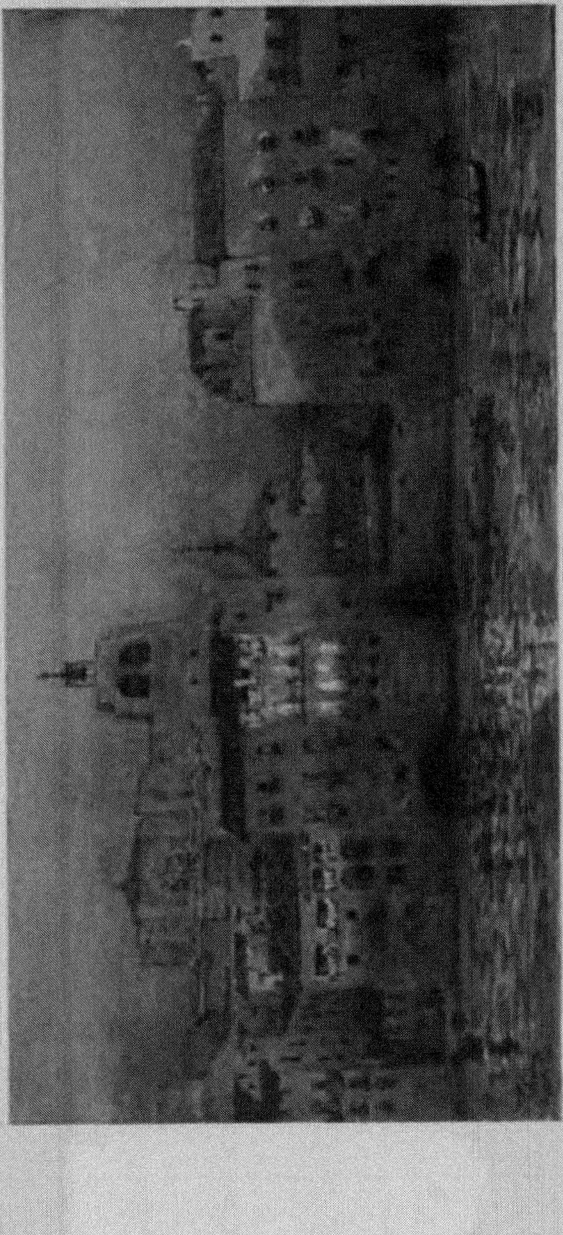

Avila Cathedral this same feature prevails. A double aisled apse with open-work tracery between the arches and below the vaulting of the aisles.

The *silleria* of the *coro* were carved by Cristóbal de Salamanca in 1588, and are really beautiful. The two pulpits are covered with interesting iron bas-reliefs, and the High Altar encased in a mass of plateresque silver work. The *retablo* is a good specimen of early Gothic work, and I could not help thinking how much better such an one is than the many overdone chirrugueresque atrocities met with in more famous places.

Tortosa is the centre of a district the mountains of which yield many different kinds of marble, and the Cathedral is especially rich in these. Perhaps the chapel of Cinta contains the best; the most used is the *broccatello di spagna* a purple colour with tiny marine molluscs embedded in the hard clay. The Cathedral is adorned at certain festivals with a series of splendid tapestries, and amongst many relics overlooked and left by the French is a fine Moorish casket of ivory.

Pope Adrian IV., the Englishman, was at one time Bishop of Tortosa, a fact which added interest to this beautiful little Cathedral.

The cloisters are early pointed Gothic, now much dilapidated and uncared for. On the encircling walls are many highly interesting mural tablets, a few of which have recumbent figures cut in low relief with their backs to the wall, as is the case in the earliest Gothic effigies of this sort.

TARRAGONA

MY recollections of Tarragona can be summed up in three words—blue sea, sunshine, and peace.

Some fifteen or twenty years ago the quays of its fine harbour were full of life and bustle, ships entered the port and ships went out. The trade with France in light wines was good, and with England and America in those of heavier quality, better still.

Nowadays it is cheaper to send wines by rail. Reus, a railway centre a few miles inland, has captured a great deal of Tarragona's trade, and modern history repeats itself once more. Cheap and quick delivery are the watchwords. Hurry and hustle are leaving the old trading towns behind. Barcelona is not far away. Centralisation is everything, and thus it happened that I found very few places in Spain so reposeful as Tarragona. And I might add so beautifully situated as this old city which climbs and crowns a hill that rises from the very edge of the blue Mediterranean.

Very few cities in Spain can boast of prehistoric

walls still extant. Tarragona can do so. The huge uneven blocks of granite, which may be seen in my sketch of the Archbishop's Tower, occupy the lower portion of the old Roman walls. On the north side of the city they are even more visible than in the sketch. Some of the blocks measure thirteen by seven by five feet. Three of the ancient portals, the stone of which is faced inside, still exist, but apparently no records do, to tell us who placed these Cyclopean defences where they stand to-day.

Many remains of Roman days may be seen built into the houses of the old and higher town, tablets, mural inscriptions, bits of columns, &c. The Cathedral possesses numerous plinths and pillars of marble from the quarries at Tortosa, built into its walls, and the Font in the Baptistery is an old Roman basin. What a glorious city it must have been when the Emperor Augustus made it his capital! and the overland trade met the sea-going in the harbour below.

Twenty miles away at Gayá the Romans tapped a continuous supply of fresh water, and their aqueduct, a good deal of which remains, ranks next to that of Segovia in size, and stands as an example of how the Romans built. Roman villas with incomparable views out to sea, dotted the hillsides; temples to every god and goddess rose

TARRAGONA

[...] which contained a million inhabitants, [...] a mint of its own, and, favoured by [...] and art, became known as "Colonia victrix [...]territa."

[...] Moslem sacked Tarragona, and for four [...] one of the glories of Colonial Rome lay a [...] of ruins. In 1089, at the commencement [...] building of the Cathedral, the see, much [...] disgust of Toledo, was raised to metropolitan [...]. Thenceforth, between the two cities, [...] disputes have arisen as to the Primacy of [...].

[...]hough begun at the above date, most of the [...]thedral is of twelfth and early thirteenth-century [...]. It is not known who designed this magnifi-[...] church, the finest example of Transition in [...]. The interior is very simple and very [...]ified. The roof is borne by grand piers, thirty-[...] in circumference. Their bases are broken [...] four seats, one in each corner, placed thus to [...] the line of the composition, and break [...] otherwise too great severity of the foundations. [...] is no triforium; but an early pointed [...] of large bays, and a superb rose window [...] west, of date 1131, admit a flood of light. [...] could well be simpler than the pairs of [...] columns which carry the centre arches of [...], nor finer than the delicate single attendant at their sides from which spring the transverse sections. All these are capped with square Romanesque capitals.

The chancel is pure Romanesque and very beautiful. The semicircular end of the Capilla Mayor and the two small apses are the oldest part of this noble building. The *retablo* of the High Altar is alabaster, and carved with reliefs of the martyrdom of Santa Tecla, Tarragona's patroness. The delicate tapering finials and the figures under canopies below, are carved in wood. Behind the High Altar is a very interesting urn which contains the ashes of Cyprian, a Gothic archbishop.

The fine *cimborio* which rises above the crossing has eight windows of three and four lights alternately, which contain fragments of very brilliant coloured glass. In the transepts are two magnificent wheel windows full of good glass, indeed I know of no better scheme of colour than that which adorns this window on the south side.

The *silleria del coro* are the work of Francisco Gomar and date from 1478. The body of James I. of Aragon lies in a tomb at the west end of the *trascoro*, having been brought here from the ruined Monastery of Poblet—the Escorial of Aragon. A ruin where still lie under their much despoiled and

TARRAGONA. THE ARCHBISHOP'S TOWER

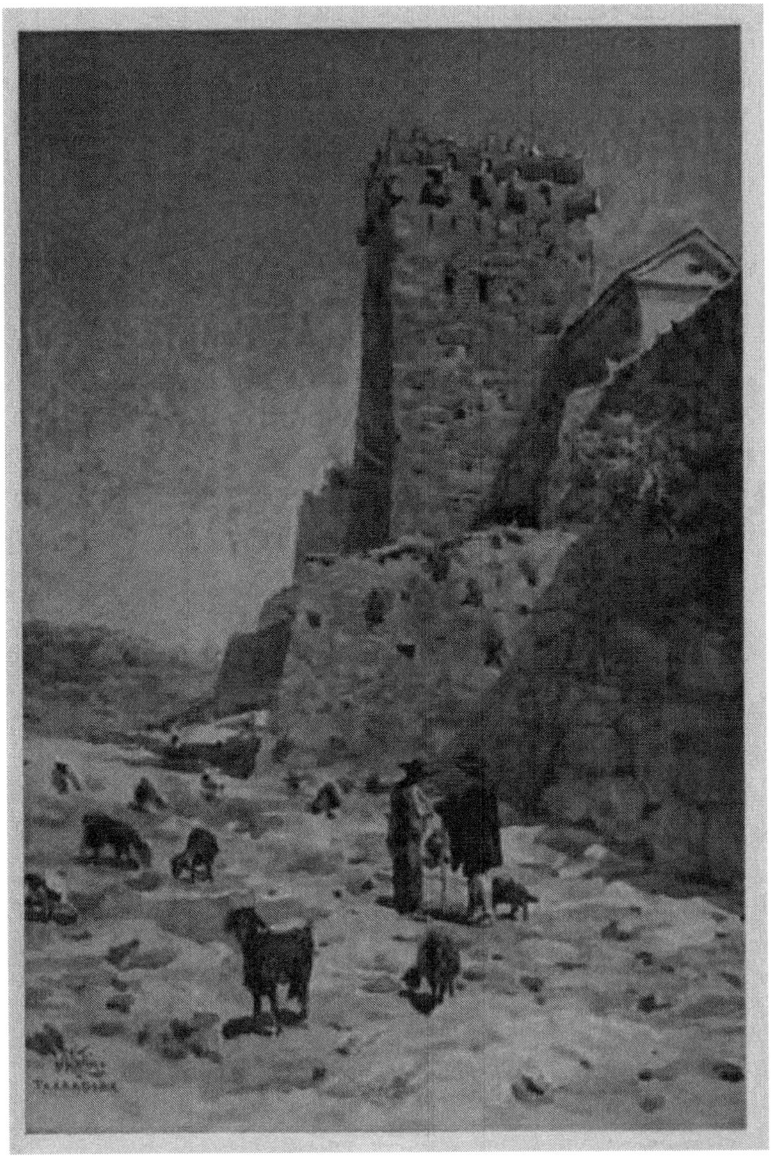

mutilated tombs some of the rulers of that kingdom.

This grand Cathedral is not dependent on gloom or subdued light for its great impressiveness. On the contrary it is the best lit of any of Spain's Cathedrals, and it is on its excellent proportions and scale alone that its reputation for solemnity will always rest, and its majesty be ever remembered.

The west façade, commenced in 1248, is constructed of a light-coloured stone, which time has improved into a very beautiful sienna brown. The upper portion is unfinished. In the centre is a fine and deeply recessed Gothic portal, flanked by two massive buttresses. Under Gothic canopies stand statues of the Apostles and Prophets, the lintel of the doorway is supported by a Virgin and Child, above which is the Saviour, and a row of figures rising out of their tombs on the Judgment Day. Above all is the already-mentioned rose window. So well does the mass of the building rise above the adjacent roofs that this window is visible from the breakwater of the harbour. The two doorways on either side of the façade are pure Romanesque. Each is surmounted by a small wheel window. The iron work which covers the doors is of a very intricate design; and the huge iron knockers with grotesque heads, the hinges of the doors, and the copper work as well, gave me many pleasant moments in marvelling at the skill of the smiths of days gone by.

It was in the cloisters however that I found the greatest charm of the whole Cathedral. The court is a veritable garden, where date palms, fig trees and oleanders crowd one another in the neatly arranged beds behind box hedges. I spent many pleasant hours in this delightful spot, my solitude broken by occasional visits from the Sacristan, who, in his faded and patched purple cassock, came in at odd times for a chat. Very proud of his Cathedral was this quiet custodian, and I shall never forget his soft voice and winning smile, nor the great interest he evinced in my sketch. The swifts rushed screaming past, the bees hummed from flower to flower, the scent of the plants was delicious, the warm sun and the splash of the fountain—turned on for my benefit—all went to help the welcome repose and forgetfulness of the outer world that overcame me as long as I was at work in this little Paradise.

The double doorway in the north transept through which one enters the cloisters from the Cathedral, is the finest of all. The capitals of its detached shafts are wonderfully carved. They represent the Awaking of the Three Kings by an Angel, the Nativity and the Journey of the Magi.

TARRAGONA. THE CLOISTERS

TARRAGONA

The arcading of the cloisters consists of six bays on all four sides, these bays are subdivided into three round arches, with a couple of circular openings above and enclosed within the arch. Some of these openings contain very beautifully carved tracery.

The capitals of the columns are a museum of quaint fancy and good carving. In one set, all the incidents of a sea voyage are cut, in another, mice are seen carrying a cat to his grave, who, shamming death, turns and devours some of them before his obsequies are complete. There is a Descent from the Cross, where one of the Faithful wields a pair of pincers much longer than his own arms, so determined is he to pull out the nails that cruelly wound Christ's hands.

Many fragments of Roman sculpture are let into the walls; and a lovely little Moorish arch, with a Cufic inscription and date 960, reminds one of the Infidel's rule over the city.

To reach times nearer our own, there are two inscriptions telling of the occupation by British troops, which run—*5th Company* and further on *6th Company*—obviously pointing to the fact that these lovely cloisters sheltered some of our own troops during the Peninsular War. Like many other Cathedrals, Tarragona's possesses a grand series of tapestries, which are hung round the columns and walls during certain festivals. They are mostly Flemish and not in any way ecclesiastical. One indeed that I saw was anything but this. Cupid was leading a lady, who was in *déshabille*, into her chamber, wherein, by a four-post bed, stood a gentleman with a lighted taper in his hand !

It was pleasant in the evening to stroll down to the harbour and out along the mole, to watch the deep-sea fishing fleet race home with the long sweeps out in every boat as the wind dropped and the sea became an oily calm. I must own it was with great regret I left this now peaceful spot—a city that once boasted of a million inhabitants, and prior to that was a great Phœnician port ! Of all the Cathedral Cities of Spain I would rather return to Tarragona than any other, hold converse with my friend the Sacristan, who knows and loves his Cathedral so well, and end the day as the sun goes down watching the boats return from long hours of toil.

BARCELONA.

BARCELONA the Progressive, the finest port of Spain, with its large harbour, its wide boulevards, splendid suburbs, good hotels, huge factories and modern prosperity has well earned the title of first city of the New Spain.

Amilcar Barca in 225 B.C. founded the Carthagenian city which occupied the Taber hill on which the Cathedral now stands, and twenty years later it became a colony of Rome. Remnants of the old walls can still be traced in the narrow streets which centre round the Holy Fabric. Under the Goths, Barcino, as it was then called, rose to some importance, money coined here bears the legend "Barcinona." The Moors were in possession of the sea-washed fortress for about one hundred years, and then the reign of the Counts of Barcelona, independent sovereigns, began.

Count Ramon Berenguer I., who ruled from 1025 to 1077, instituted the famous " Códego de los Usatjes de Cataluña," an admirable code of laws, to which was added in the thirteenth century the " Consulado del mar de Barcelona." This latter code obtained in the commercial world of Europe the same authority as the old "Leges Rhodiæ" of the ancients.

When at the height of its prosperity, Barcelona, the centre of commerce, received a severe blow by the union of Cataluña with Aragon, on the occasion of the marriage of Count Ramon Berenguer IV. to Petronila daughter of Ramiro II. King of Aragon. When Aragon and Castile were united Barcelona became subject to the "Catholic Kings," and ever since, in language, in habits and enterprise has shown her dislike for and her struggle against the ways of Castile.

To-day Barcelona is far in advance of any other city of Spain. I felt I was once more in Europe when the comfortable hotel 'bus rattled along through the well-lit streets. Perhaps I was getting tired of life in the Middle Ages, and was obsessed with Mediæval Cities! At any rate, a clean bed in a modern hotel was a luxury I thoroughly appreciated, and I started the next morning to explore, with a mind at ease and a consciousness that there would be no irritating little pin-pricks, no *mañana* for a couple of weeks at least.

The Cathedral stands on the site of a Pagan Church converted by the Moors into a Mosque. The present edifice replaced the Christian Church

BARCELONA. IN THE CATHEDRAL

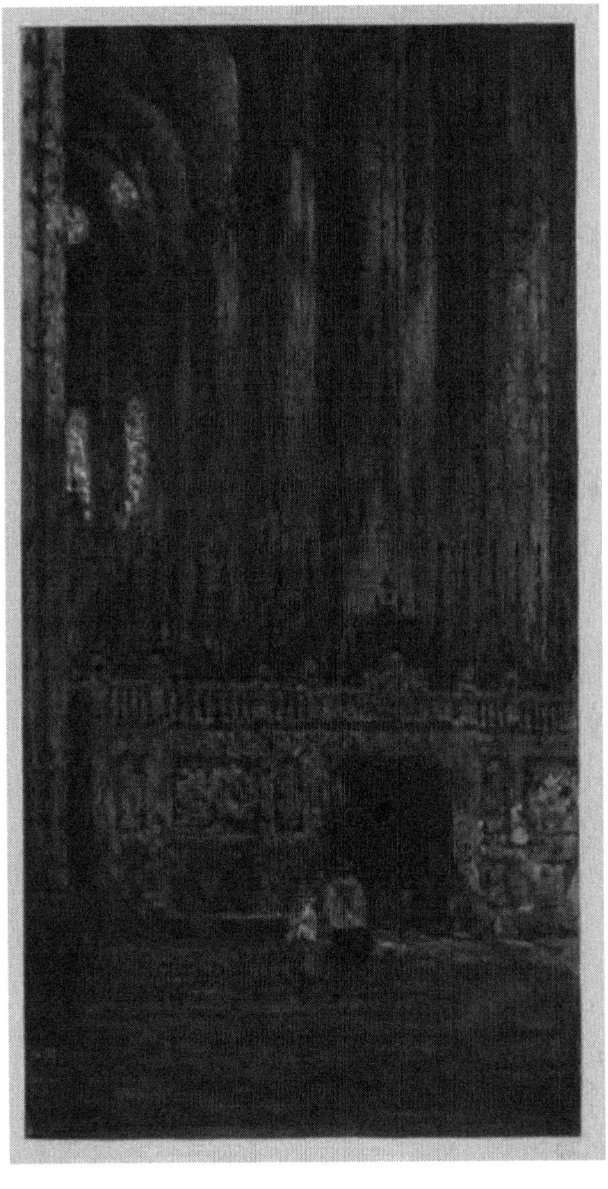

which superseded this Mosque, and was begun in 1298. The crypt was finished in 1339 and the cloisters in 1388. The west façade was covered with scaffolding while I was there, and so may perhaps be completed in another thirty years.

The interior of this splendid Gothic church is very dark. The pointed windows are all filled with magnificent fifteenth-century glass. At the sunset hour, when the rays of light strike low and filter through the many colours of these windows, the effect in the gloom of this solemn building is most beautiful. As the orb of day sinks lower and lower the light lingers on column after column right up the lofty nave to the High Altar until he suddenly disappears, and all within is wrapt in deep twilight.

The nave is very narrow and very high. The clustered columns seem to disappear into space, and the vaulting is almost lost in the darkness. There are deep galleries over the side chapels in the aisles, which have a rather curious arrangement of vaulting. From the roof of the aisles at each bay depend massive circular lamps which catch the light and heighten the effect of mystery which is omnipresent throughout the Cathedral.

A flight of steps in front of the High Altar—an almost unique feature—leads down to the crypt, where rests the body of Santa Eulalia, Barcelona's patron saint. Her alabaster shrine is adorned with reliefs of different incidents in her life.

The *retablo* of the High Altar is richly ornate with tapering Gothic finials of the fifteenth century; below it is a sarcophagus containing the remains of St. Severus.

Above the Gothic *silleria del coro* hang the coats-of-arms of the Knights of the Golden Fleece. Among them are those of Henry VIII. of England. The only installation of the Order was held here by Charles V.

The side chapels contain very little of interest, but the cloisters are otherwise. Entered either from the street or the south door of the Cathedral their beauty is very striking. In the centre palms and orange trees rear their heads, and the splash of the fountains, in one of which the sacred geese are kept, is refreshingly cool after the bustle of streets outside.

San Pablo del Campo, now a barrack, is the most interesting of Barcelona's ecclesiastical remains. This church, built by Wilfred II. in 913, is more like the ancient churches of Galicia than those of Catalonia. Very small and cruciform, a solid dome rises from the centre. Its cloisters are perfect, the arcading is composed of double shafts with well-cut figures on the capitals.

The peculiarity of Catalonia's churches is well

BARCELONA.

illustrated in the aisleless Santa Maria del Mar, San Just, and Santa Maria del Pi. The first named has some magnificent glass and four good pictures by Viladomát, and in the crypt beneath the High Altar a curious wooden figure of San Alajo. San Just has the belfry common to the churches of Catalonia, an open iron-work screen, from which depend the bells, and Santa Maria del Pi contains a fine wheel window and more magnificent glass.

A relic of Loyola, the sword that he offered on the Altar of the Virgin at Montserrat, is still preserved in the old Jesuit Church of Nuestra Señora de Belen.

Among the many notable buildings in Barcelona is the Casa Consistorial, or Town Hall. It was built in 1378, and has a very original Gothic front. A beautiful *patio* with slender arches and twisted columns adds to the interest of the interior.

The Casa de la Diputacion opposite contains the picture on which Fortuny was at work when he died. The *patio* here is perhaps better than that in the Casa Consistorial. It is in three stages, from the topmost of which huge gargoyles of all sorts of devils and monsters rear their ugly heads.

In the old quarters of the city, where the five- and six-storied houses almost touch, the streets are very tortuous and not considered safe at night.

In this respect, however, Barcelona does not stand

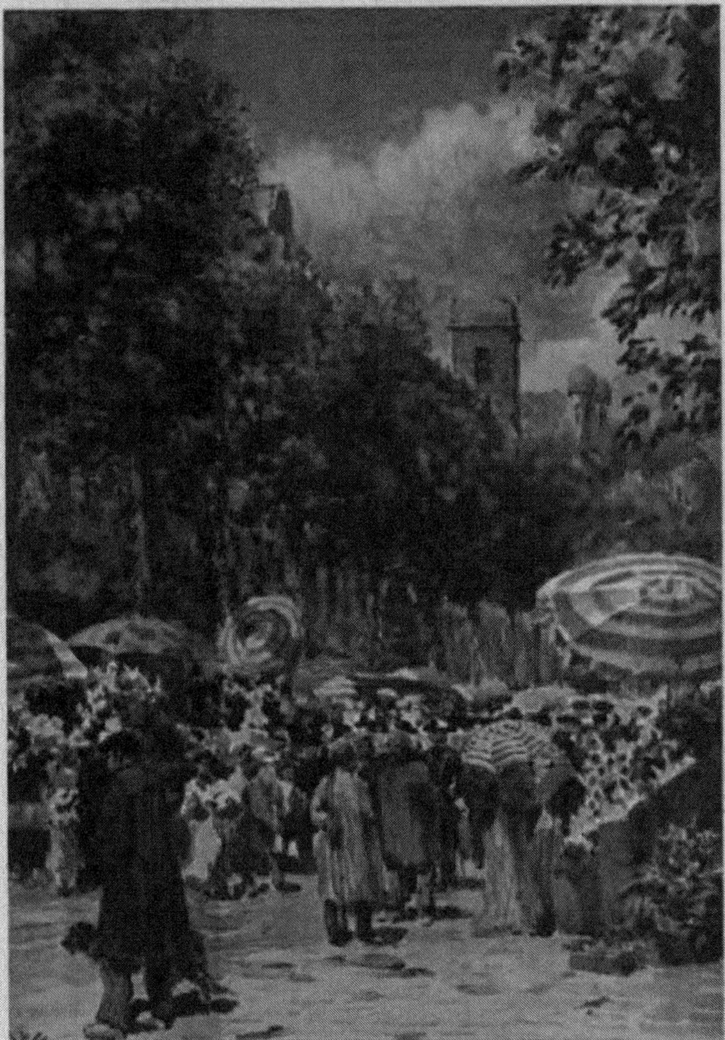

local talent in glaring vermilion and green. I watched the holiday-makers sitting in ramshackle booths, rapidly putting away all sorts of curiosities of the shell-fish order, and I wondered if they would survive the day. Perhaps the copious draughts of wine they took was an antidote, at any rate their laughter and good humour gave point to my unspoken thought—"let us eat and drink, for to-morrow we die."

Going on, I often spent some time comparing the drill of artillery recruits, whose instructors marched them up and down on a quiet bit of the roadway, with those at home, and I generally finished my walk and sat me down on the glorious stretch of sand that runs away north as far as eye can follow. The evening would then draw in, and the twinkling lights on the ships in the harbour warn me it was time to return. While twilight lasted I retraced my steps homewards along the quay-side, invigorated by an afternoon of sea breeze and salt spray.

The focus of Barcelona's life is the celebrated Rambla. The derivation of this word is Arabic— "Raml-sand"—a river bed, for a small stream at one time meandered down to the sea where now is the liveliest street in the north of Spain.

On either side of the central promenade, under the shade of stately plane trees, are the carriage drives. The broad walk itself is thronged, especially in the morning when marketing is done, with an ever-changing crowd. Boys distribute hand-bills, dog-fanciers stroll about bargaining with dealers, itinerant merchants cry their wares. A family of father, mother, and children cross the stream of promenaders, followed by a pet lamb. Acquaintances meet and gossip away a good ten minutes.

At the top end of the Rambla are situated the stalls of the bird-sellers, who also deal in mice, a great place this for mama and her small daughters. Lower down, the flower-sellers congregate under their red-striped umbrellas. It was here that I made my sketch, in which luckily, for a bit of colour, I was able to include the blue-bloused porters in their red caps who wait about for a job with the rope of their calling slung over their shoulders. Here too all the odd job men stand awaiting hire. House painters in white blouses with insignia of their trade—a whitewash brush on the end of a pole—held high, and others—an endless variety.

Barcelona, being a business town, is democratic to the core, it is also to the core, Catalan. The names of streets are displayed in Catalan as well as Spanish. The animals in the Zoological Gardens also are known by their Catalan, and Castilian as well as Latin names! Barcelona will have no deal-

BARCELONA

ings with Castile, its people speak their own language and address the foreigner in French. Barcelona is go-ahead. In the houses of the new suburbs l'art nouveau screams at one, and everything is up-to-date!

The Spaniard is well-known to be lazy, not so the Catalan. I have never seen a Spaniard running, but I have seen a Catalan walking fast!

The city then, without a leader, its inhabitants starving, at length surrendered.

So ancient is Gerona that its early history is lost in the mist of ages. Charlemagne drove the Moors out when they were in possession, but it soon passed back into their hands again. The Counts of Barcelona ruled over the place until the union of Catalonia and Aragon, an event which gave birth to the Crown Prince's title of Principe de Gerona. Hence we know that in the twelfth century it was a city of great importance. In consequence of its adhesion, at the end of the War of Succession, to the house of Hapsburg, Gerona was deprived of its privileges and university, since which time it has steadily gone down hill.

Down hill it may have proceeded, but I found it a very pleasant, quaint old-world city set in the midst of verdant hills and running waters. Shady walks are taking the place of now useless fortifications; and have not I sat in one of the most delightful rose gardens you could wish to rest in, and heard the note of the nightingale trilling on the perfumed air? Most of Spain has gone down hill, and most of Spain is nothing but enchanting.

Gerona is bisected by the river Oñar, and from its waters which wash them, the houses rise tier above tier up the hill side. In the summer when the river is running low, and if it happen to be a

GERONA

THE siege of Gerona is as celebrated in the Spanish history of the Napoleonic wars as that of Saragossa. Both exemplify the bravery and tenacity of the Spaniard of the north. In the first siege in 1808, three hundred men of the Ulster Regiment, under their gallant leader O'Daly, helped to garrison the place against two ferocious attacks by Duchesne and his French soldiery. The first failed and the second ended in the utter rout of the besiegers with the loss of all the artillery and baggage train.

In the following year three French generals with an army of thirty thousand men invested the city. Alvarez, the Spanish Governor, was almost without any means of defence, and the women of Gerona enrolled themselves under the banner of Santa Barbara, the patron saint of Spain's artillery, and took their places on the ramparts side by side with their husbands and sweethearts. Alvarez, ably seconded by a few English under Marshall, held out until he was struck down by disease and death.

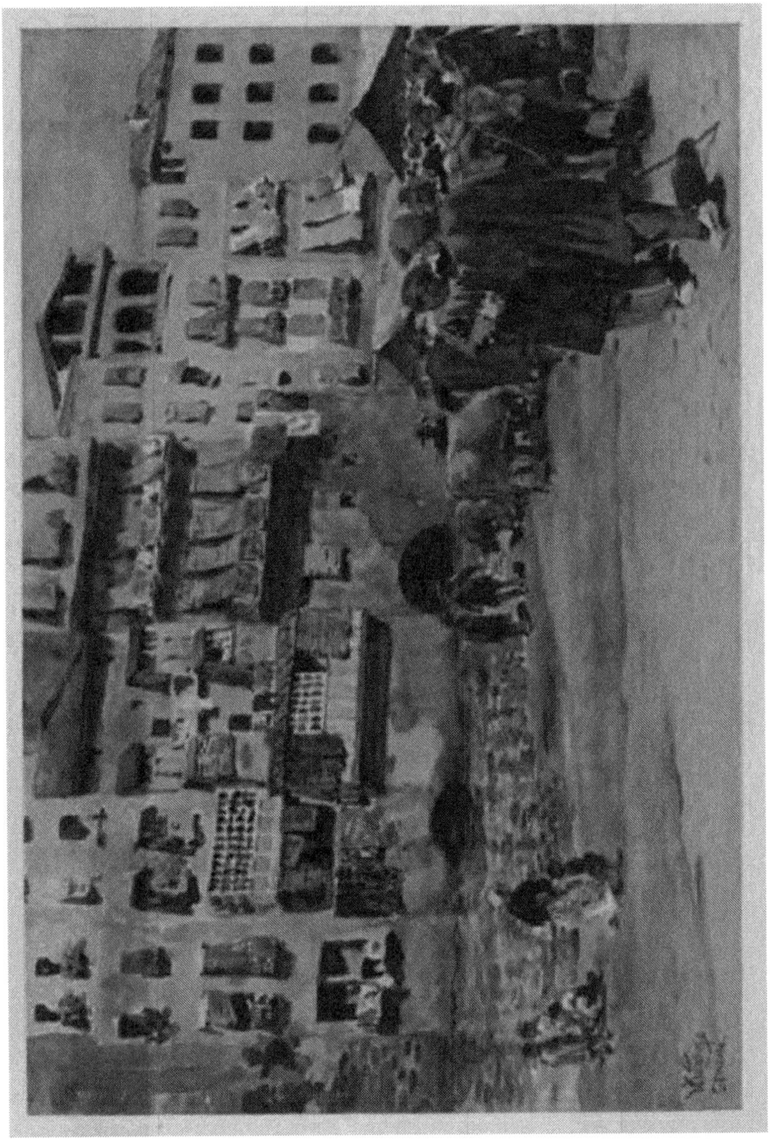

GERONA

Saturday, you will see one of the most remarkable sights that Spain can boast of. Under and around the arches of the the old bridge are congregated hundreds of brown and fawn-coloured cattle. The background of ancient houses, yellow, grey, white, brown—every tone, rises up above this throng. Coloured garments, the week's washing, flutter in the breeze, green shutters and blinds hang from the creeper-clad balconies.

It is market day. The lowing of oxen, mingled with the hum of bargaining humanity in red caps and Prussian-blue blouses, surges up like the sound of breakers on a distant shore. You who enter Spain by the east route, go to Gerona at the end of the week—you will never regret its Saturday market.

The Cathedral stands well. The west façade, a Renaissance addition, is approached from the Plaza below by a grand flight of ninety steps in three tiers. In the unfinished jambs of the south door are a series of interesting terra-cotta figures dating from 1458.

There is nothing else in the exterior worthy of note, but directly I entered I stopped in amazement at the daring of an architect who could build so enormous a span as that under which I found myself. This span is seventy-three feet, the clear width of the nave, and unsupported by any pillars. No flying buttresses outside give additional strength to the thrust of the roof. The stonework is perfect and the vaulting inside simple. So bold and hazardous were the plans of Guillermo Boffy that the chapter at first refused to sanction them. Being in doubts as to his sanity, they sought the opinion of twelve other architects, who were examined separately. As they all approved and passed Boffy's plans, the construction of this marvel was commenced, and the first stone laid in 1416.

The apsidal chancel had been begun a century earlier and finished in 1346, pretty much on the same lines as this part of Barcelona's Cathedral.

Unfortunately—how often does one have to acknowledge this!—the *coro*, with its hideous *respaldos*, painted to imitate Gothic arches in perspective, almost ruins this splendid and solemn interior. Among the seats of the *silleria del coro* there are still preserved some that date from the fourteenth century.

Early carved work ot the same period is found in the elaborate *retablo* over the High Altar, which is surmounted by three fine processional crosses. The *baldaquino*, also of wood, is covered like the *retablo* with plates of silver. It is a mass of precious metal, enamelled coats-of-arms and gems, and is an extremely interesting relic of that century.

Over the sacristy door are the tombs of Count Ramon Berenguer II. and his wife Ermensendis,

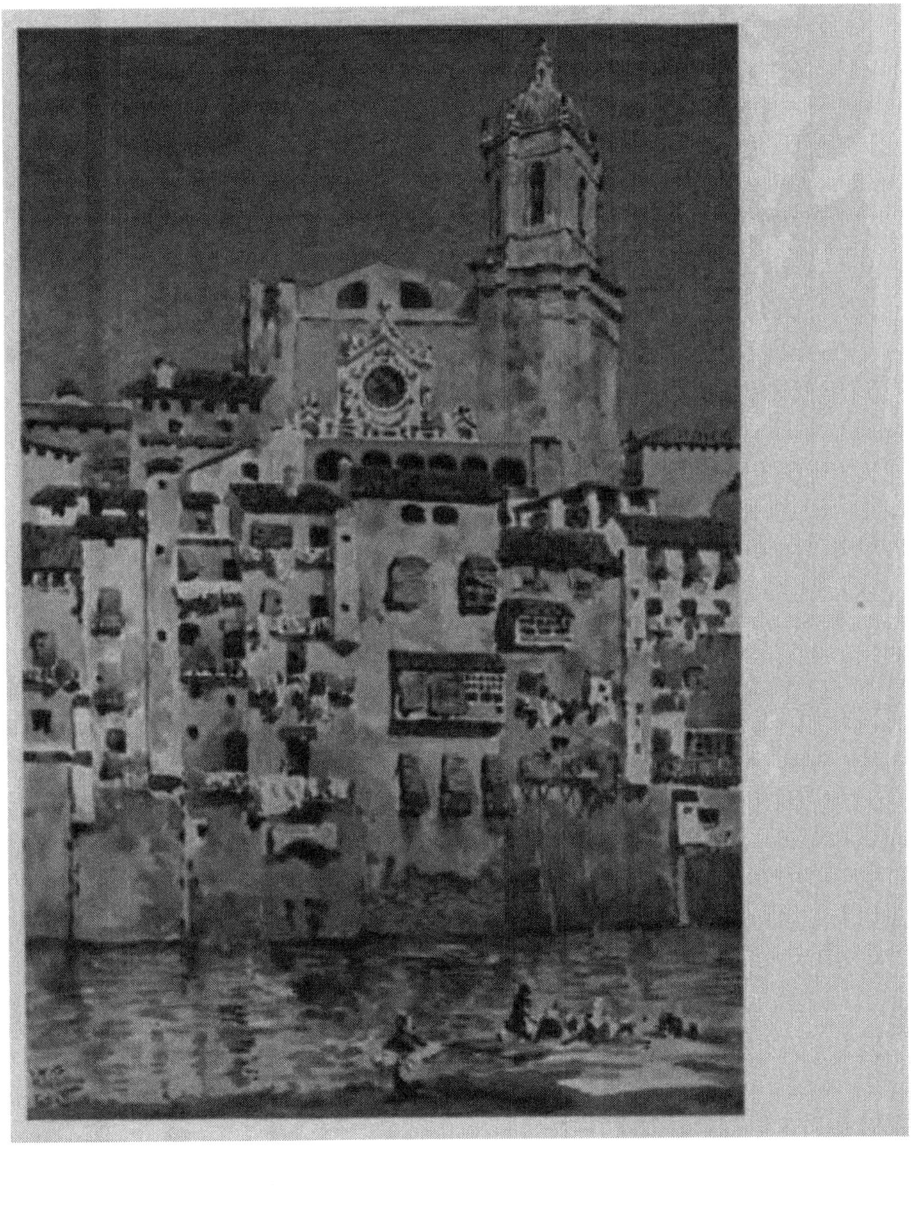

who died in 1314, predeceasing her husband by twenty-four years. The sacristy itself contains a remarkable piece of twelfth-century crewel work, said to be the earliest known specimen in existence. It is covered with figures of a type similar to those of contemporary MSS. The Romanesque cloisters form an irregular trapezium. The columns are doubled and about a foot apart, not unlike those of Tarragona.

The finest Romanesque example that Gerona possesses is the church of San Pedro de los Galligans. The apse, little damaged during the siege, forms a tower in the town wall. There is no doubt of the great antiquity of this building, which dates probably from the early part of the tenth century. The east end is mostly constructed of black volcanic scoria. The nave and aisles, the bays of which are very simply built, are almost prehistoric in their roughness.

In the cloisters attached to the church is the Museo Provincial. Many relics of Gerona's heroic defence can here be seen, as well as some early Christian and Hebrew remains.

GERONA

who died in 1058, predeceasing her husband by twenty-four years. The sacristy itself contains a remarkable piece of twelfth-century crewel work, said to be the earliest known specimen in existence. It is covered with figures of a type similar to those of contemporary MSS. The Romanesque cloisters form an irregular trapezium. The columns are doubled and about a foot apart, not unlike those of Tarragona.

The finest Romanesque example that Gerona possesses is the church of San Pedro de los Galligans. The apse, little damaged during the siege, forms a tower in the town wall. There is no doubt of the great antiquity of this building, which dates probably from the early part of the tenth century. The east end is mostly constructed of black volcanic scoriæ. The nave and aisles, the bays of which are very simply built, are almost prehistoric in their roughness.

In the cloisters attached to the church is the Museo Provincial. Many relics of Gerona's heroic defence can here be seen, as well as some early Christian and Hebrew remains.

TOLEDO

STANDING high above the yellow Tagus, which, confined in a deep gorge, rushes and swirls far below between precipitous granite cliffs, Toledo was always an ideal position for a fortress before modern firearms rendered Nature's defences of little avail.

Its name is associated with the great Cardinals of the Rodrigo, Tenorio, and Foncesca families, as well as scions of the houses of Ximenes, Mendoza, Tavera, and Lorenzana. The wealth of these Prelates was immense, and their power, Ecclesiastical and Temporal, proportionate. They practically had no rivals, they certainly feared none, they ruled kings as well as countries, and their allegiance to Rome was purely nominal. They made wars and fought in them. For their patronage of art and literature future generations have had good cause to be grateful. They built schools and improved the means of communication throughout the land. Under their influence the Church was omnipotent, and they have written their names deep in the pages of Spanish history.

In fact, so great was the power of Toledo's clergy that it grew to be the cause of the foundation of the Capital at Madrid. Philip II., who removed the Court from Valladolid to Toledo, found it better, after a short residence here, to take himself and his Court to a town where he no longer encountered the arrogance of Ecclesiastical rule.

Under the Romans, who captured it in 193 B.C., "Toletum" became the capital of Hispania. Leovigild removed hither from Seville, and his successor, Reccared, who embraced the orthodox form of Christianity, made it the ecclesiastical as well as political capital of his dominions.

For nearly four centuries, from 712, when the Moors took Toledo, it was under their rule; but divided counsels and the treachery of the downtrodden Hebrew enabled Alfonso VI. to enter in triumph with the Cid. The King then styled, himself Emperor, and promoted the Archbishop to the Primacy of Spain. Under Alfonso's rule the city grew rapidly in every way. Churches and convents were built, defences strengthened, and Toledo knew no rival.

With far-seeing wisdom, Moor and Christian were allowed to intermarry, and lived together in peace for wellnigh one hundred and fifty years. The advent in 1227 of that ecclesiastical firebrand, St. Ferdinand, however, altered this. One of his

TOLEDO. THE CATHEDRAL.

first acts was to pull down the Mosque, wherein the Moors of the city, by Alfonso's royal prerogative, had been allowed to worship, and commence the building on its site of the great Cathedral.

For two hundred years and more did the architects who followed Pedro Perez add bit by bit, leaving their mark on its stones. Partly constructed of granite it is immensely strong. A softer stone has been used with great discretion in the decorative portions of the building.

No comprehensive view of the Cathedral is obtainable, so closely do the houses surround it on the south and east, and creep up the hill on which it is built, on the north. The west front is best seen from the Plaza Ayuntamiento, a pleasant little garden which the Town Hall bounds on one side. I managed a sketch from the narrow street below this garden.

Only one of the two towers of the west façade is finished as originally intended. The other is capped by a dome, designed by El Greco, that painter of the weird, and under which is the chapel wherein the Mozárabic ritual is celebrated daily at 9 A.M.

The great west door, La Puerta del Perdon, is enriched with embossed bronze work. Flanking on it either side are the doors of Las Palmas, and de los Escribanos. The arches of all three have

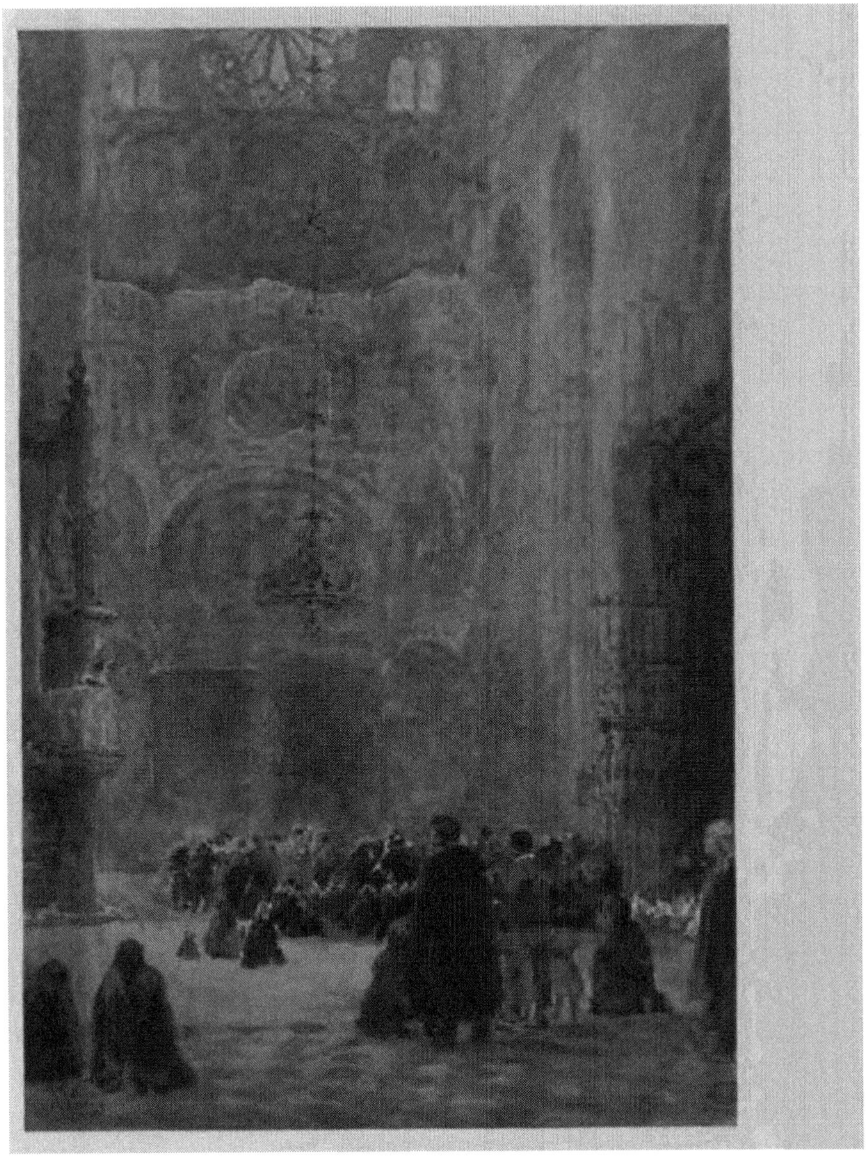

in each bay is a rose window forming a clerestory, and the colours in the glass of these shine like jewels in a crown.

There are in all twenty chapels, every one of which contains something worth study. The lofty *retablo* in the Capilla Mayor is of the richest Gothic. Above is a colossal Calvary of later workmanship. Cardinal Ximenes built this chapel, among the many monuments of which are the tombs of Spain's earliest kings. Separating it from the *crucero* is a magnificent Plateresque *reja*, on either side of which stands a gilded pulpit.

Behind the *retablo* is the *transparente*, much admired by Toledans, but the one jarring note in the finest of Spain's Cathedrals. This theatrical mass of marble figures, in the midst of which the Archangel Rafael kicks his feet high in the air and squeezes a gold fish in one hand ! is lit from a window let into the roof of the apse.

The Capilla de Reyes Nuevos contains the tombs of the kings descended from Henry II. His tomb and that of his wife, as well as the spouse of Henry III., a daughter of John of Gaunt Duke of Lancaster, are among the many that crowd the walls.

The Capilla de San Ildefonso is an extremely beautiful example of early Gothic work. The much-mutilated tomb in the centre of Cardinal

Albornoz is a masterpiece of the same style. Many other great Ecclesiastics rest in this elegant octagon, notably Inigo de Mendoza, Viceroy of Sardinia, who was killed at the siege of Granada.

The Capilla de Santiago was erected in 1435 by Alvaro de Luna, the man who saved Spain for Juan II. by repressing the turbulent nobles, and who for his fidelity was rewarded by disgrace and execution in the Plaza Mayor at Valladolid. The scallop shells which decorate the walls represent de Luna's office of Grand Master of the Order of Santiago.

Cardinal Ximenes re-established the Mozárabic Ritual, which is celebrated in the Capilla Mozárabe, as a reminder to the Pope that Spain did not owe implicit allegiance to Rome.

The small detached Capilla de la Descension de Nuestra Señora stands against the second pier in the north aisle. It marks the spot where the Virgin came down and presented San Ildefonso with the *casulla* or chausable.

The Salle Capitular is a grand example of early sixteenth-century work, with a Plateresque frieze and gilt *artesonado* ceiling by Francisco de Lara. It contains a series of portraits of the Cardinal Archbishops of Toledo, and frescoes by Juan de Borgoña. The work of this painter is to be met with throughout the Cathedral.

TOLEDO

The *coro* occupies two bays of the nave and is a veritable museum of carving and sculpture. Its *silleria* are in two rows. The lower is of walnut and enriched with scenes representing the campaigns of Ferdinand and Isabella. The upper of the same wood is a perfect classical contrast and is inlaid not carved. Berruguete, whose work may be best studied in Valladolid, executed the seats on the south side, and Vigarney those on the north. A small figure of the Virgin in blackened stone looks really ancient. It stands in the middle of the *coro* on a pedestal. Nicolas de Vergara was responsible for the two reading desks, which are masterpieces of gilded metal work.

The Gothic cloisters enclose a delightful garden, and have an upper cloister reached by a door in the Archbishop's Palace. From this pleasant *claustro alto* a very good idea of the size of the Cathedral is obtained.

Space does not permit me to enlarge on the manifold works of art which this noble building contains. The pictures, the iron work—though I must just mention a beautifully fanciful knocker of two nude nymphs hanging downwards from the head of a satyr whose hands clasped together, form the handle, which adorns La Puerta de la Presentacion—the sculpture, notably that on the *respaldo*, or outer wall of the *coro*, and the many relics in the

Treasury, would all occupy more than I can afford. Suffice it to say that nowhere in Spain is there a Gothic building of such well-proportioned dimensions, such simplicity in its leading features, such a fine idea in the interior of the spacing out of light and shade, as in this magnificent Cathedral—the grandest of the three due to French influence.

And Toledo's churches? There are nearly sixty still remaining, every street seems to contain one! And Toledo's convents? There are almost as many. Of the former, San Juan de los Reyes, on the high ground above the bridge of Saint Martin, the last remnant left of a once wealthy Franciscan convent, was built by Cardinal Ximenes in commemoration of the "Catholic Kings" victory of Toro. On its outer walls still hang the manacles and chains of the captive Christians who were set free at the conquest of Granada, and the interior is embellished with the arms of Ferdinand and Isabella, and covered with sculptured heraldry.

Santa Maria la Blanca, originally a Jewish synagogue, is in the *Mudéjar* style, and has some charming arabesques, with a fine cedar ceiling said to be of wood from the trees at Lebanon. Almost opposite—we are in the Juderia, or Jews' quarter, to the south-east of San Juan de los Reyes—is another synagogue, el Transito. Built in 1366 by Samuel Levi, Pedro the Cruel's treasurer, in the Moorish

TOLEDO. THE ZÓCODOVER

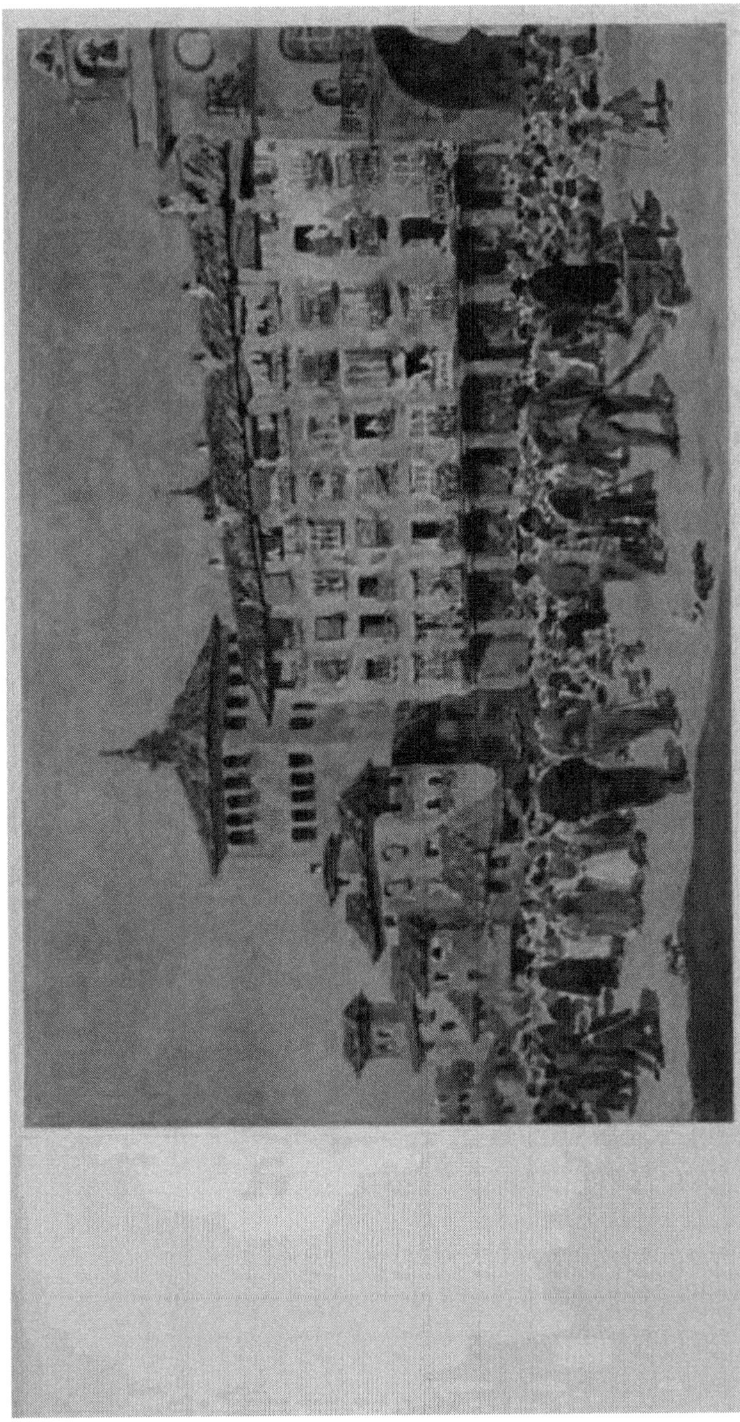

On its eastern side a fine Moorish arch leads down the hill by a footpath to the Bridge of Alcántara. Immediately the arch is passed on the left lies the old Hospital de Santa Cruz. It is one of the best examples of the Transition to Renaissance in Spain. The portal is deeply undercut and elaborately carved in soft "white rose" stone and marble. The inner gate is plateresque and only surpassed by San Marcos at Leon and the gateway of the university at Salamanca. Cardinal Mendoza's arms adorn the beautiful *patio*, which has a double arcade of great elegance, and the stone work on the balustrade of the staircase leading out of this is very fine. Opposite, on the other side of this steep descent, are the Military Governor's quarters which are dominated by the huge Alcázar, now the Military Academy for Infantry Cadets. Destroyed by fire in 1886, the present edifice, rebuilt soon after, is seen in the illustration of the Alcántara Bridge rising a great square mass on the top of the hill. It was the fortress and palace of Moorish days. Alvaro de Luna had a share in its alteration and Herrera completed it to the present size by additions executed for Philip II. Many a time has it been sacked by the conquerors of Toledo and many a prisoner of note passed his last hours within its gloomy walls, before being led out to death in the Zocodovér.

TOLEDO. THE ALCÁNTARA BRIDGE

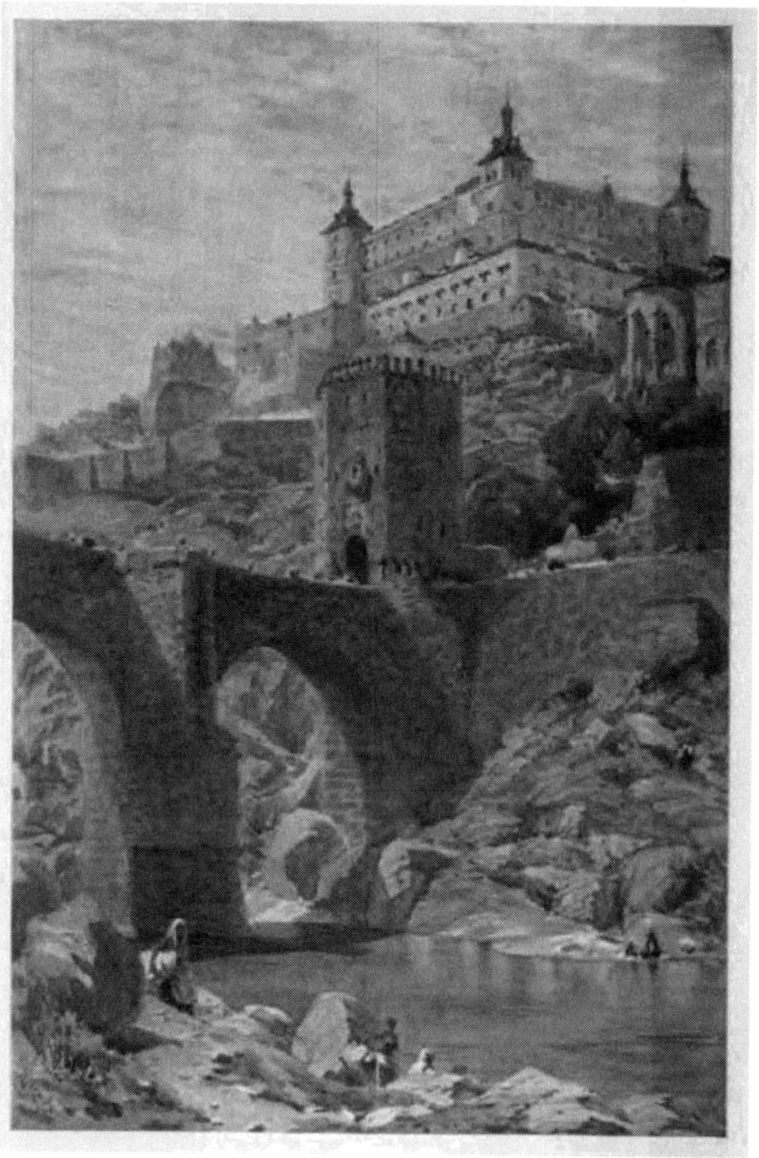

TOLEDO

Both Toledo's bridges are magnificent. The Alcántara, crossed on the way from the station, has but a couple of arches which span the mighty river at a great height. It is defended by a gateway at either end, that on the inner side being the Moorish Tower in my sketch. The Bridge of Saint Martin has one arch of enormous span with four smaller, which carry it over the rushing Tagus. Between these two bridges from the opposite bank of the river one gets the best idea of Toledo's strength. Nothing in Spain surpasses the grim majesty of the city, which rises above the sunbaked and wind-blistered crags that form the gorge below through which the river has cut its way. No spot could have been better chosen for defence than the hill enclosed in this "horseshoe" of mad waters. Small wonder that within its encircling walls grew up a race of Prelates whose rule spread far beyond the borders of Castile, and whose powerful hand was felt in countries of an alien tongue.

Of the eight city gates the most interesting is the Puerta del Sol, a Moorish structure with two towers on either side of a horseshoe arch. It is close to the little church of el Cristo de la Luz, and from either of the towers a very good idea is obtained of Toledo's defences. Near the Puerta del Cambon, another of the gates, is the site of the old palace of the last of the Spanish Goths, Roderic, who lost his life on the banks of the Guadalete near Cadiz when giving battle to Tarik and his Berbers.

My whole impression of Toledo was that of a city of gloom. Its larger houses were forbidding in the extreme. In these a huge portal, with armorial bearings and massive pillars, defended by a stout iron-bound door, opens into a dark porch, from which one enters the *patio* through an equally strong entrance. The windows that look on to the street are heavily barred and none are within reach of the pedestrian. Its streets, too narrow and steep for vehicular traffic, are as silent as the grave (most Spaniards wear shoes made of esparto grass or soft leather), save when a young cadet from the Alcázar passes along rattling his sword, and attracts the attention of the señoritas who sit high up in those inaccessible balconies. Built on the Moorish plan, these tortuous thoroughfares twist and turn like a maze, and it seemed to me that the sun never entered them.

Houses and streets, walls and towers, still remain as they were in the great Cardinal's days, and stand, even now, as symbols of the iron rule of the Church. The Cardinal's hat is to be found graved in stone over many a door, and the "Sheaf of Arrows," the arms of the "Catholic Kings," is still to

TOLEDO

be seen over the entrance of what was once the palace of Pedro the Cruel.

Toledo blades are still made and proved in the ugly factory a mile outside the city. Toledo ware (made in Germany) is sold by most of the shops. The growing trade in liquorice is a modern industry, but if it were not for another recent innovation, the Military Academy, it would take no stretch of the imagination to carry one back again into the Middle Ages and to sink one's individuality and become a human atom under the rule of the great Church.

SALAMANCA

BEFORE I ever thought that Fate would take me to Spain, I had formed in my mind, as one is apt to do, a Spain of my own, a Spain of glorious romance. I had been in many cities throughout the country, but it was not until I reached Salamanca that, "Surely," thought I, "the Spain of my imagination is now realised."

Here in the middle of the plain, with which one's thoughts are somehow familiar, rises the great Cathedral, its towers are landmarks for miles round. Here is a beautiful river winding through valleys deep cut in the ochre-coloured soil, its banks are clad with verdure and it is spanned by an ancient bridge. Away over the plain, just visible in the haze, are the blue mountains of the south. In the midst of all, the dull mud and yellow walls of the city, the many-hued roofs of red and brown, with deep shadows under their eaves, rise tier above tier to the Cathedral above. And this, the prototype of Spain's greatness, her Church, the ever-present reminder that in days gone by its princes led her armies to victory and placed her in the van of nations.

I am standing on the noble bridge, half of which is even now as it was in the days of the Roman occupation. Those massive walls up there of monasteries and convents always formed part of the picture of my imagination. They bake under a September sun, just as all Spain ought to do. A long string of heavily laden mules trots past, their bells jingling merrily, their drivers shouting and cracking their whips. A well set-up peasant with his head in a handkerchief and broad-brimmed hat, cut-away tunic, red sash and tight knee breeches, canters by seated on a high peaked saddle. His well-bred horse shows a good deal of the Arab strain, across its quarters are a couple of rugs and its rider carries an umbrella. A beggar stops before me, and prays that, for the love of the Holy Mary, I will give him a *perro chico*. Two wizened old cronies go by chattering about Manuelo's wife. One carries a couple of fowls tied together by their legs, the poor birds are doing their best to hold their heads in a natural position. Some little urchins are throwing stones at the washerwomen by the riverside below. An old man seated on a donkey's rump ambles past. Yes, this is what I imagined Spain to be. I turn my steps towards the city. I wander by the Cathedral and reach

the great university of the middle ages. What would Salamanca have been without its university! I pass many fine houses, with coats-of-arms emblazoned over their portals. I gaze at their high walls and windows barred to keep the intruder from the fair sex. Most of them seem falling into decay, but this only adds to the romance. At length I reach an arcaded square. The columns of the arcades are wooden, they are at all sorts of angles, but the houses above still stand. The sun blazes down on scores of picturesque market folk, who sell almost everything from peaches and fowls to little tinsel images and double-pronged hoes. Dogs are sniffing about picking up stray scraps. Children run in and out, fall down and get up laughing. Every one is busy. The animation of this little square, as I suddenly come upon it out of a deeply shaded and aristocratic street, is just the Spain I had always thought of—a Spain of contrasts. Brilliant sun and grateful shade. Seclusion behind high walls, and a strange medley of noisy folk, for ever bargaining, buying and selling. Certainly in Salamanca it is all here. I hear the click of the castanets and the sound of the guitar in the evening, I see the ardent lover standing at those iron bars whispering soft raptures to his mistress, and the picture is complete.

Salamanca is a sleepy old city which the world

seems to have left behind. In the summer it is a veritable furnace, in the winter it is swept by icy blasts. Before the Christian era it was known as Salmantica. Hannibal came and captured it in B.C. 247 and under the Romans it was the ninth military station on the great road which they built connecting Cadiz and Merida with Astorga and Gijón. Alfonso IX. of Leon founded the university, which reached its zenith as a seat of learning during the sixteenth century. Philip II., having transferred his Court from Valladolid to Toledo, made Salamanca's bishop suffragan to that city's, since when it seems to have been left out in the cold and slowly but surely proceeded down hill. This is the reason, I think, why it attracted me so much. It is essentially a city with a Past and of the Past. The French under Thiébaut pulled it to pieces and used the material from its demolished buildings to fortify the place. This was in 1811. The following year saw Marmont's troops utterly routed by Wellington, three miles south of the fortifications. It was this victory that gained him his Marquisate and a grant from Parliament of £100,000.

Like Saragossa, Salamanca possesses two Cathedrals. The older intensely interesting in every way, the later, a huge late Gothic pile begun in 1513 and finished in 1733. This immense structure affords a good study of the changes of architectural

SALAMANCA: THE OLD CATHEDRAL

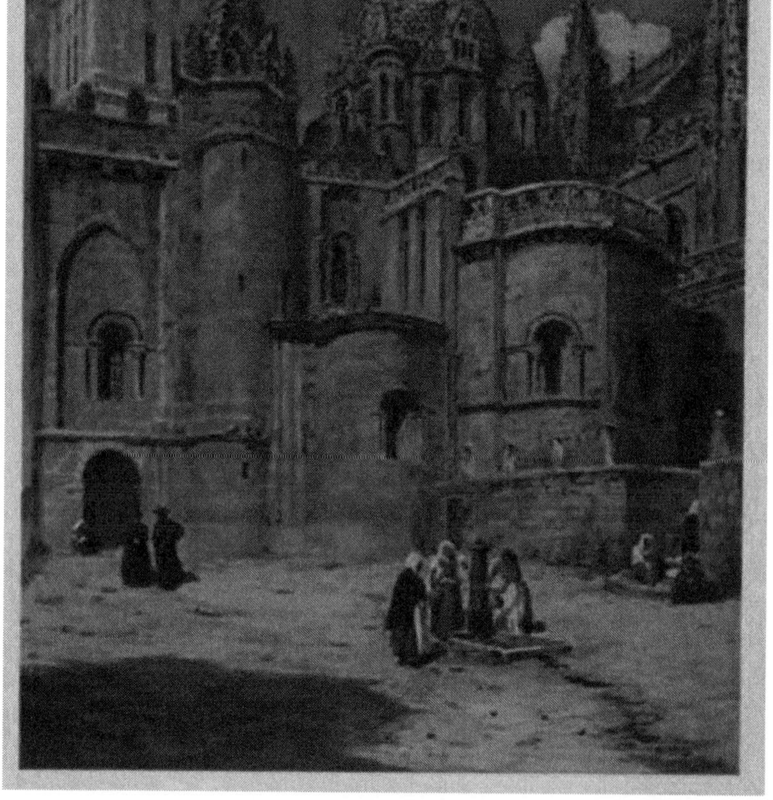

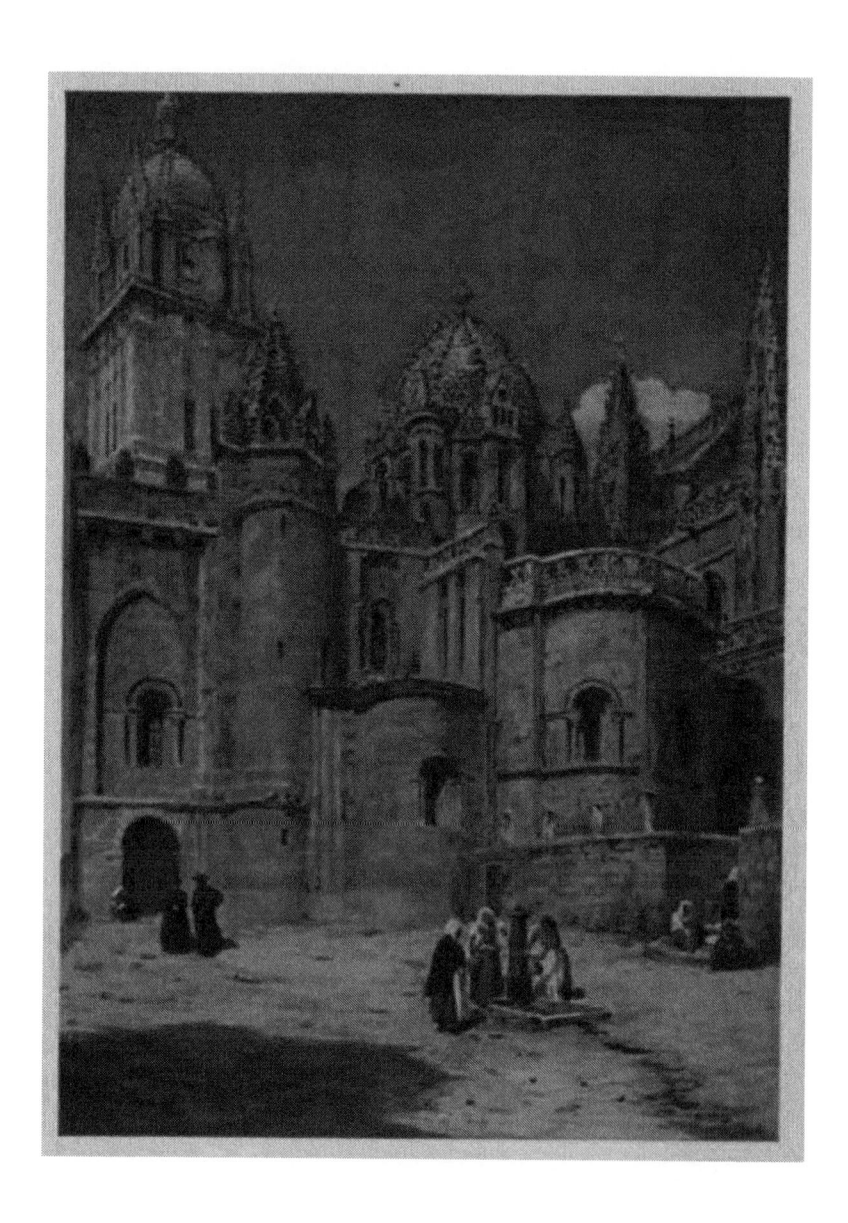

SALAMANCA

taste spread over the years which intervened between these two dates.

The west façade is a marvel of intricate sculpture in the richly-coloured soft stone that has been used as if it were plaster or wax. Late Gothic predominates amidst a deal of Plateresque and Barroque ornament. Despite its incongruities it is extremely fine, but would look even better if some of the numerous niches had not lost their statues, and if little boys did not find a pastime in lodging stones amongst those that are left, greatly I fear to their detriment. Over the double doorway are high reliefs of the Nativity and Adoration of the Magi, a negro prince being an especially good figure in the latter subject. Above is a Crucifixion.

The north porch is also very fine and gains in effect, as indeed does the whole of this side of the Cathedral, by the raised piazza on which it is built. The approach is up some dozen steps, the whole of the piazza being surrounded by pillars as at Leon and Seville.

Juan Gil de Hontañon, who designed this and the sister Cathedral at Segovia, surpassed himself with the Great Tower and its finely-proportioned dome, the top of which is 360 feet high. The crocketed pinnacles, the flying buttresses, the dome over the crossing, and the wonderful deep yellow of this huge church, whatever may be one's opinion about the architecture, make it one of the most impressive of Spain's Cathedrals.

I was disappointed with the interior on first acquaintance, but it has only to be known to be appreciated. The imposing proportions, it is 340 feet long, 158 feet wide and close on 100 feet high, gradually asserted themselves, and before I left Salamanca I was much in love with Hontañon's masterpiece. A pierced balustrade takes the place of a triforium, flamboyant Renaissance in the aisles and classical in nave. It runs round the whole church and in the transepts and choir these two occur together. Medallions in the spandrils of the arches add to the rich effect.

Many details in this interior I found to be worth a second and third visit. The Chapel of Dorado, a veritable museum, contains the tomb of the builder, Fransico de Palenzuela. Its walls are covered with a profusion of coloured saints on gilt pedestals. There is a very curious old organ, standing at the back of an also curious old minstrel's gallery. A sad-looking skeleton, with " Memento Mori " cut on a slab at his feet, occupies a dark hole in one of the walls. Fine *azulejos* decorate the chapel, and many other antiquities too, which I cannot enumerate.

In the Capilla del Carmen rest the remains of Gerómino, the Cid's bishop and confessor. An ancient wooden crucifix stands over the altar, it is the identical one carried by the bishop in the wars of the Cid. Another relic of the great Campeador is to be seen in the Relicario. A small Byzantine bronze, "el Crucifijo de las Batallas," studded with chequer work—a fine specimen of early Limoges enamel.

All this interested me muchly, but the "Catedral Vieja," a grand example of late Romanesque style, interested me more. Fortis Salmantica, as it was called, on account of the thickness of its walls, has not been used for service since its huge neighbour was erected.

I made a drawing of the only view which can be obtained of the exterior from the Plazuela chica. The central lantern is surmounted by the emblem of nobility, a cock, and is formed by an octagonal tower with a stone dome. The tower is arcaded and has four domed turrets and dormers at the corners similar to those at Zamora. Street considers that, he has "never seen any central lantern more thoroughly good and effective from every point of view than this is."

To reach the interior one has to retrace one's steps to the "Catedral Nueva" and from its south aisle pass through a doorway into the other building. This was erected on a lower level than its big neighbour and with the attendant verger I

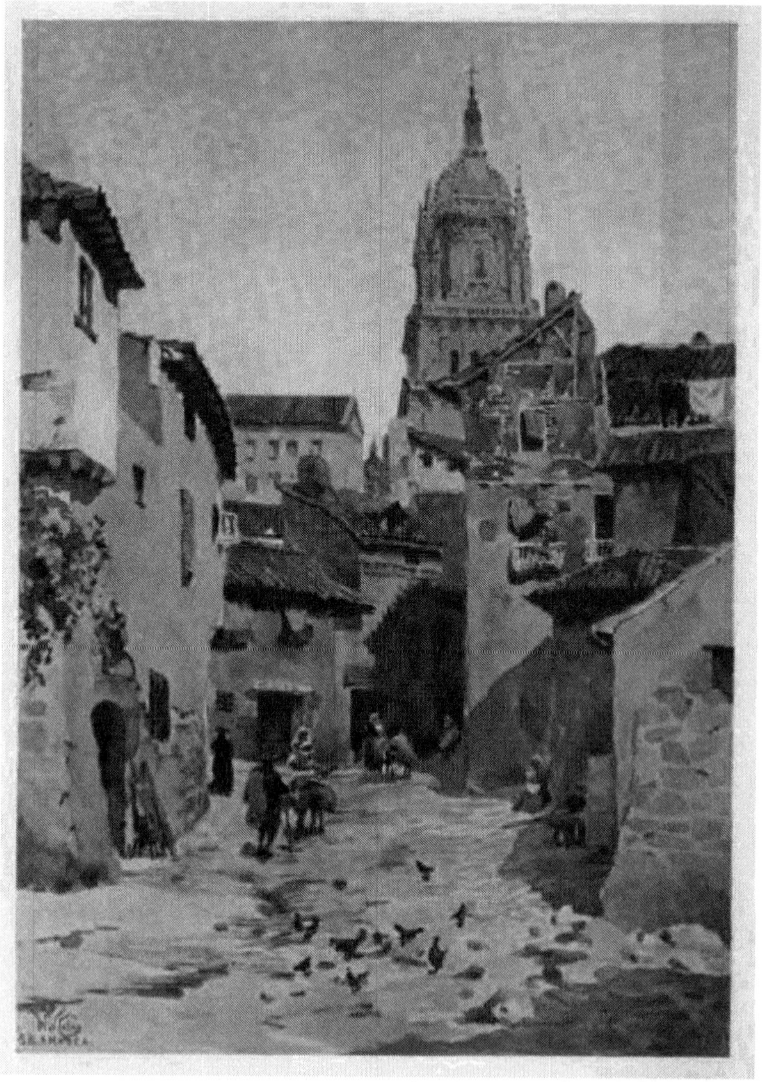

partly modernised and totally disfigured by a coat of whitewash. An uncared-for garden filled with rubbish occupies the centre. Surely some one might be found to tend this little secluded patch of quietness and make it a place for delightful repose instead of the disgrace it now is!

Before the French occupation Salamanca was a city of churches and monastic buildings. To build their fortifications they destroyed thirteen convents and twenty colleges besides many churches. The south-west corner of the city is still an empty desert full of rubble and stone strewn about everywhere, the remains of the now dismantled fortress which overlooked the valley of the Tormes.

Among the churches left, that attached to the now suppressed Dominican Convent of San Estéban is by far the finest. It is a miniature Cathedral in itself. The Gothic exterior is extremely good. The great west façade is highly enriched with Plateresque ornament. An elliptical arch of great dimensions roofs the porch. Below it is a realistic group illustrating the martyrdom of St. Stephen, with the date 1610 cut upon a stone which one of the figures is picking up to hurl at the saint. The cave is over the west end, and for once the whole of the interior is visible. This is very lofty, and the view up to the immense High Altar, executed by Chirriguera himself, superb. There are two more altars in the church by the same hand, and although his flamboyant style is not to my liking, I could not help admiring the way in which he had evidently allowed himself all the licence he was capable of in their sumptuous design.

To the south of the little *plaza* in which San Estéban stands are the cloisters of the convent, in the upper storey of which is Salamanca's museum. Unfortunately it contains nothing of interest; Columbus was lodged by the Dominicans in this convent, and propounded those schemes to the monks, which the learned members of the university had pronounced worthless and crack-brained. He found in Fray Diego de Deza and the other brothers warm supporters.

The once magnificent Convent of las Agustinas Recoletas, founded by the Count of Monterey, has a beautiful church in the shape of a Latin Cross. Over the High Altar is one of Ribera's masterpieces—*The Immaculate Conception*. Monterey was known as "the good slow man" and was Viceroy of Naples in Philip IV.'s reign. He accumulated great wealth during his Viceroyalty and built himself the fine palace which stands close to the convent. There is an anecdote current in Salamanca that when a peasant woman craved an audience of the King, which he granted, she prayed "God might make him also Viceroy of Naples."

SALAMANCA

The University which made Salamanca famous was united with that of Palencia by Ferdinand, and very soon took the foremost rank as a seat of learning in Europe, though at the Council of Constance in the year 1414, Oxford was given precedence, a ruling which much disgusted the patriotic Spaniard.

The building was entirely altered by the "Catholic Kings," who erected the marvellous west façade, one of the best examples of Plateresque work in the country. Like that of the Cathedral and San Estèban, it is a wonderful example of what can be done with soft stone, and how well the most delicate modelling has survived in this dry climate. Some of the Moorish ceilings of the interior have been restored. The grand staircase leading to the upper floors and cloister is especially well carved with dancers and foliage. Over the door of each *aula*, or lecture room, is a tablet denoting the science taught within. The fine library is rich in theological lore and early editions of Aristotle, &c.

The little square on to which the west façade opens also leads through a good doorway into the Grammar School, with a delicious cloister and shady garden.

The four sides of the square and the walls of the Cathedral are covered with numerous hieroglyphics and names in Roman characters. They are the initials, signs, and names of the numerous scholars who have distinguished themselves in different walks of life. A custom now followed in all our own schools on boards of honour.

The Collegio Mayor de Santiago Apostol is a seminary for Irish priests. The number in training is generally about twenty. This building, originally founded in 1592 by Philip II. and dedicated to St. Patrick, is a very good example of cinquecento architecture.

Among the many fine houses still left after French depredations, that of La Casa de las Conchas is the most celebrated. It dates from 1512, and is so named on acount of the scallop shells which decorate the exterior walls. The window grilles are exceptionally fine. The Spanish proverb " La mujer y el vidrio siempre estan en peligro "—" a woman and glass are always in danger," evidently held good when these intricate and beautiful guards were let into the stone. The house has a lovely *patio* and a very fine staircase. La Casa de Sal is another house with a good court, the gallery above being supported by life-size figures. La Casa de las Duendes, or Ghosts, built by Archbishop Fonseca, was supposed to be haunted, hence the name. The Torre del Clavero is a good specimen of the Castilian keep. It was built in 1488 by a

Sotomayer who was Clavero or Key-bearer to the Alcántara Order, and is still in the possession of this noble family.

Throughout the churches, in these houses, and the convents which remain unsuppressed are many fine pictures, and except for Seville, I found here more of interest than in any other city of Spain. In the convents of course mortal man is forbidden entrance, and I could only look at their lofty walls and wish myself a nearer acquaintance with the artistic treasures which I was told lay buried behind them.

Perhaps the best example of a square in the whole of the country is the Plaza Mayor. A lofty colonnade runs around the four sides and every evening the beauties and others of Salamanca make it their promenade. The men stroll round in one direction and the women in the opposite. The social life of a Spanish town passed in view before me, with all its fan and language of the eyes, as I sat at one of the small tables of a café and got this cheap and harmless entertainment for one *real*. The square dates from 1720; the houses are four storeys high and on the north and south sides bear medallions of kings and celebrated men. The Ayuntamiento, with its chirrigueresque façade, occupies the centre of the north side and adds greatly to the appearance of this fine Plaza where up to fifty years ago bull fights took place.

CATHEDRAL CITIES OF SPAIN

My work over, I nearly always found myself wandering on to the desert created by the French at the south-west angle of the city, and with my pipe spending half an hour or so meditating on the Salamanca of the Past and its contrast with the Present. The rock stands high here over the road and river below, and there is a drop of 100 feet or more down on to the former. It is but a narrow lane hedged in by a high wall and this forbidding-looking rock. When walking along this lane one day I noticed many crosses cut in the wall and chalked red. On inquiry I was told that each cross represented a suicide. From the height above, those tired of life or disappointed in love hurl themselves down and it is the unwritten law or prerogative of him who finds the mutilated body to carve a little cross on the wall at the spot where the unhappy mortal has ended his days. But it was not to prevent suicides that I wandered there and sat smoking my afternoon pipe. No, I fear it was something inglorious, it was to get away from the stenches and filth of the town and breathe the fresh air of the plain. I do not think that anywhere, unless it be in Tarragona, were my olfactory nerves so insulted as in Salamanca. Flies in thousands settled on my colour box and paper wherever I sat sketching. I can now appreciate

SALAMANCA

fully the torture of the Egyptians during the plague.

Add to the flies beggars innumerable, with horrible sores, offal and filth in the streets and some of the romance vanishes. Yet Salamanca still remains the Spain of my imagination, for was not all this part and parcel of my dream?

AVILA

AVILA is one of the most perfectly preserved towns in Spain. It gave me the impression of having been dropped from the sky,—complete as it is—so desolate and barren is the boulder-strewn waste that surrounds it. A sort of suburb pushes its mean houses straggling beyond the walls, but Avila itself lies snugly within them. They are perfect—these walls that entirely encircle the old portion of the town. Forty feet high, twelve thick, with eighty-six defensive towers and bastions, and ten gates, they are constructed of slabs of granite set end upwards, and were always a hard nut for invaders to crack.

The Roman Avela afterwards fell into the hands of the Moors, who for long held it as a fortress of the first class. Alfonso VI., the conqueror of Toledo, drove them out after a lengthy siege, and Avila was rebuilt by his son Ramon of Burgundy. It was then that the present walls were built, being erected under the supervision of two foreigners, a Frenchman and an Italian, Florian de Pituenga and Cassandro. Since their day Avila has played an important *rôle* in the history of the country and witnessed many strange events.

In 1465 an extraordinary scene took place on the plain outside the city. That unpopular king, Enrique IV., was reigning at the time, and the hatred of the people towards him reached its height when his effigy was dragged from the city and set upon a throne which had been prepared for the ceremony of degradation. The Archbishop of Toledo having recounted the people's grievances, removed the crown from the effigy's head, others high in the land insulted it and at length pushed it off the throne, the people then kicked it about and a game of "socker" ensued. Prince Alfonso, a mere boy, was raised to the unoccupied seat, and hailed King by the Archbishop, nobles and people, amidst a blare of trumpets and general rejoicing.

Avila is an intensely cold place, frosts often occur here in May, but the summer months are delightful. Every street, every house almost is of interest, and in the old days of its importance there could have been few strongholds in the country so safe as this.

The Cathedral is almost a fort in itself. The east end forms part of the city walls, the apse abutting in line with the next two towers on either side forms part of the defensive works.

Commenced at the end of the eleventh century by Alva Garcia, a native of Navarre, this early Gothic

ÁVILA

AVILA

building is still unfinished. Not much is, however, of this early date, for the general style of the building is of the end of the next century, and many alterations have followed this in later years.

The west front has but one tower, the north—the other, the south, does not rise above the roof. The favourite ball decoration of late Gothic Spain is in evidence, and guarding the doorway are a couple of uncouth mace-bearers. Very terrible are these hairy granite men, but not so dangerous looking as the two lions which stand on pedestals and are chained to the Cathedral walls. Always on guard, these four strange figures have no doubt many a time struck a holy terror into the hearts of would-be evil-doers as they entered the church, and I daresay kept the thoughts of others in the straight line.

The north door is early pointed and carries figures in each jamb, the tympanum is decorated with reliefs of the Betrayal and Last Supper, but all the figures are sadly mutilated.

The third entrance is at the south-east corner of the Cathedral, and is a later addition, opening outside the walls of the city on to the Calle de S. Segundo.

The interior of the Cathedral is very simple and massive, partaking more of strength than elegance. A fitting inside to the severity of the fortress-like exterior. The nave is narrow and lofty, and so are the aisles. The large clerestory windows have their tracery above blocked up, and the lower lights have been treated in the same way, thus giving a certain resemblance to a triforium, a feature the church does not possess.

The aisles in the apse are double, like those at Tortosa, and although the single columns in the centre are very beautiful, these aisles have not the elegance of those in the other Cathedral. The apse is very dark, the stone work at one time was painted red and the little that remains of this colour adds to the religious gloom of its double aisles.

The columns throughout the Cathedral were built to bear great weight, their capitals are simple and their bases the same. The little light that glimmers through the windows adds greatly to the sombre strength of this fine building, which, more than any other of its size, reflects the life of the Spain of those days in which it was erected. Street thinks it less influenced by outside art than any other building in the country, and instances the unique method of laying the stone of the roof as supporting this opinion.

The transepts contain some good glass, as also do the windows in the chancel. There are many good early tombs throughout the Cathedral. Judging from their style Avila was left alone when Chirriguera was erecting monstrosities elsewhere, and to me it is the most homogeneous of Spain's Cathedrals. The *retablo* over the High Altar rises in three stages and contains pictures by Berruguete, Santos Cruz and Juan de Borgoña. On this account my last remark might be criticised, for the whole piece is a jumble of styles. The chancel is, however, too narrow for a view of this medley from the body of the church, and wherever one roams in the building nothing attracts the eye or disturbs the mind by being too flagrantly incongruous.

So dark is the apse that the Renaissance *trassegrario* does not obtrude in the early Gothic of its surroundings. The very fine tomb of Bishop Alfonso de Madrigal, the Solomon of his day, is fortunately illumined by a little light, and I could see the effigy of this wise Prelate seated at his desk busily engaged with his pen and scroll, while above him the Magi and Shepherds are adoring in a good relief.

There are some early paintings in most of the chapels, the *retablo* in that of San Pedro being perhaps the best.

The work of Cornielis, a Flemish sculptor, *circa* 1537-47, is admirably displayed in the very beautiful carving of the *silleria de coro*, and there is no better example of Spanish metal work of the fifteenth century to be found than in the two iron-gilt pulpits.

The sacristy contains a splendid silver monstrance by Arfe, and an Italian enamelled chalice of the fourteenth century by Petrucci Orto of Siena. The cloisters are disappointing, having been much mutilated and the fourteenth-century tracery of the arches blocked up.

Avila, like its neighbour Segovia, contains some of the best examples of Romanesque work, and its many churches are archæologically as interesting as the Cathedral.

Sheltering from the keen north wind under the arcade of San Vicente I made a sketch of the gateway of that name. The church was founded in 1307 and dedicated to three martyrs who were put to death on the rock which may still be seen in the crypt below. The west façade has two incomplete towers, between which is a most elaborately carved Romanesque doorway, standing in a deeply recessed arch.

The pure Romanesque nave has both triforium and clerestory and the unusual feature of pointed vaulting. The proportions of this noble church are very fine, but the interest of the non-architectural visitor will be centred in the Tomb of San Vicente and his two sisters SS. Sabina and Cristeta. A metal work canopy resting on twisted

AVILA. PUERTA DE SAN VICENTE

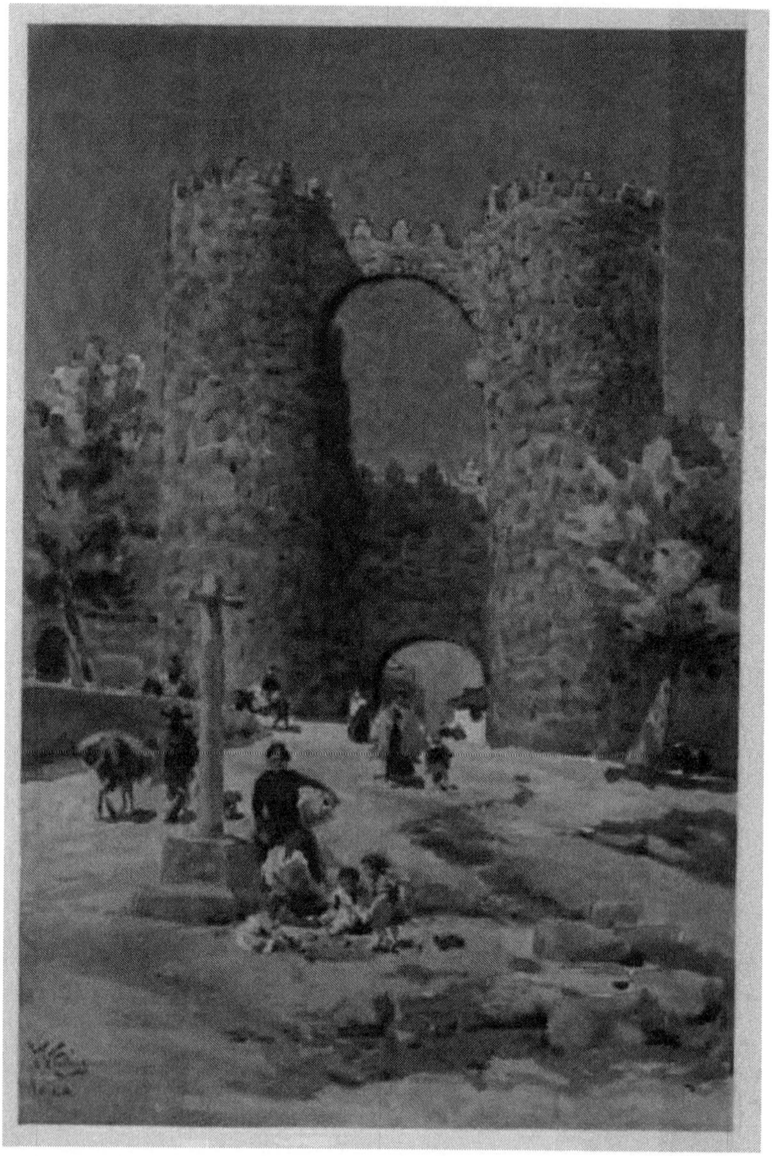

columns surmounts the tomb which is a sarcophagus of the thirteenth century. The legend tells how, after the martyrdom of these three, the body of the first-named was cast out to the dogs, and that a serpent came out of the hole in the rock (still visible) and watched over it. A Jew who mocked was smitten unto death by the reptile and lies buried in the south transept.

The transept choir and three semicircular apses are Transitional, and carry a barrel vaulting.

Outside the city wall, a little way down the hillside and beyond the dirty suburb that intervenes, is the late Gothic church of San Tomás. It possesses a fine *retablo* of the patron St. Thomas Aquinas. The High Altar is placed in a gallery above a low elliptical arch, this feature being repeated at the west end with the *coro* above. At the crossing of the transepts is the beautiful but greatly mutilated tomb of Prince Juan, the only son of Ferdinand and Isabella, by whose untimely death the crown of Spain passed to Austria. Two other tombs of great interest are those of Juan de Avila and Juana Velasquez. Messer Dominco, the Florentine, executed them both.

San Pedro, standing at the east side of the Mercado Grande, is another Romanesque church of great beauty. Over the west door is a fine wheel window. The interior is pure Romanesque and rich in ornament, and the north portal is replete with the same.

Santa Teresa was born of noble parents in Avila. In her early youth her heart hungered for saintly adventures in the broiling sun of Africa and her mind was set upon martyrdom at the hands of the Moors. Fate, however, decreed otherwise. At twenty years of age she took the veil and within a few years had founded seventeen convents of barefooted Carmelite nuns. A favourite saint of Spain, the date of her death, August 27, is kept all over the Peninsula and her festival celebrated with great honour in Avila on October 15.

SEGOVIA

DIRTY, dilapidated and sleepy, but the most enchanting town in Spain. What a treat it was to find myself once more in the Middle Ages after the bustle and noise of Madrid!

The springs of a Spanish 'bus are good. I never entered one without great misgivings as to how long I was fated to remain in this world. To drive into a town such as Segovia is a grand test for the nerves. Crack goes the whip, off start the sorry-looking horses with a jerk. I am flung violently against my neighbour. I hasten to apologise. A disconcerting jolt knocks the hat over my eyes, before it is adjusted I find myself in an attitude of prayer with my head buried in the lap of the stout lady who pants opposite, another bump and she is embracing me, we disentagle ourselves, we apologise, every one in the 'bus is doing the same. The Jehu on the box fears no obstacles, a rock or a rut, they are all the same to him, he takes them all with utter disregard to everything in his way. We fly along, and somehow we land safely. We always do. Yes, the

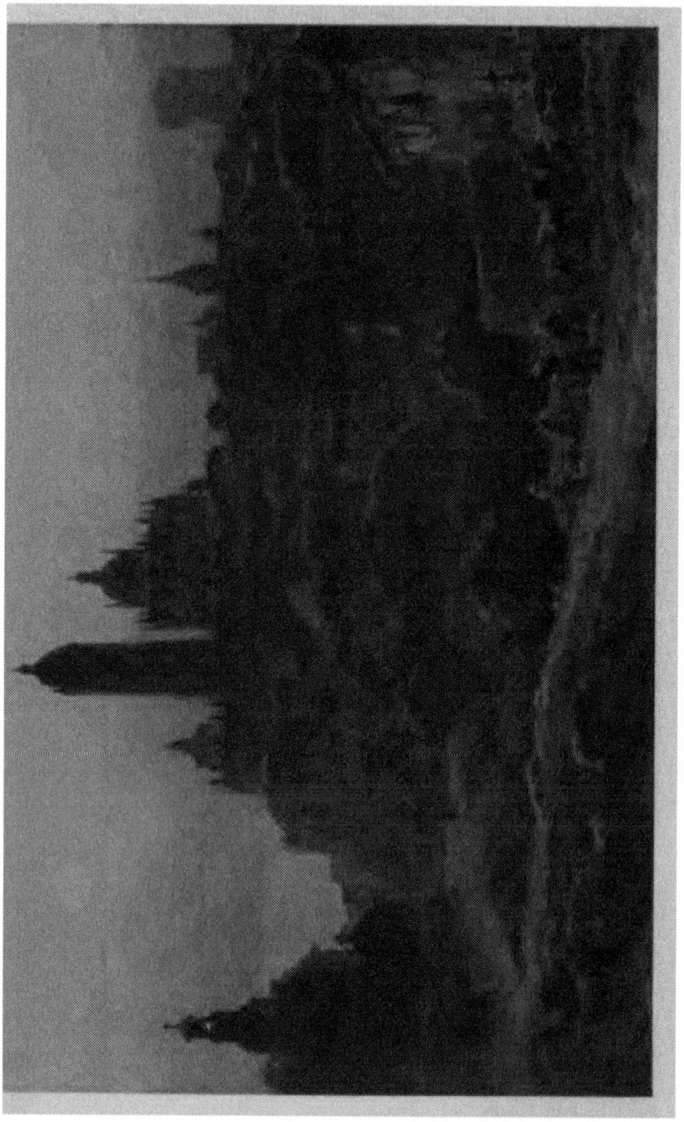

all the trees they found, because trees harbour birds, and birds destroy all fruit and grain!—a truly ingenious theory, quite worthy of the fertile brains of the French, but surely a most ridiculous solution. The Moor brought the orange and the lemon to Europe; he was a lover of shade, he was also a great gardener. No, the reason why Spain has apparently no trees, is that very few have been planted for hundreds of years. Wood is necessary for fires in a country where there is practically no coal. The peasant has always been poor, he has always taken anything that came to hand. He helped himself to the wood of the forests around him. His betters did the same. All the trees near Madrid are known to have been ruthlessly cut down and sold to defray the expenses of Philip II.'s Court; and it is only of recent years that any replanting has been taken in hand.

When the present King was a boy of four years old, a ceremony, now repeated every year at the Fiesta del Arbol, was inaugurated. The Queen Mother took him to Guindebra outside Madrid, where he planted several trees. At every anniversary the day is devoted by school children all over the country to this same object. As many as 10,000 saplings have been put into the ground in a single day, thus laying by a store of wealth for future generations.

Segovia is surrounded by trees. Hidden from the great plain in which the town lies, they cover the banks of the two streams which join issue below the city, thus forming the mass of rock on which it stands. These valleys, eaten out by the running water, are among the great charms of this romantic place. Nothing can exceed the beauty of early spring. Fruit trees in full blossom, tall poplars bending their graceful heads in the breeze and chestnuts bursting into leaf. The air is filled with the twitterings of nesting birds, the sloping banks covered with the tender green of young grass; all nature is alive, the sun is warm and the sound of rushing waters brings peace to the soul. Perched high up, hanging apparently on mighty rocks, the Alcázar broods grimly over the gorge below. Still further up and beyond, rises the mass of the Cathedral, towers, domes and pinnacles. Three hundred and thirty feet high, the great tower rears itself like a sentinel, a landmark for many miles. Round the base cluster the houses of the town like chickens seeking shelter under the wings of a mother hen. No place in all Spain appealed to me so much. No town was so replete with subjects for my brush, and nowhere else did I feel the romance of this marvellous country as in Segovia.

A town of Iberian origin and name, under the Roman rule it was of some importance. The

SEGOVIA. THE AQUEDUCT

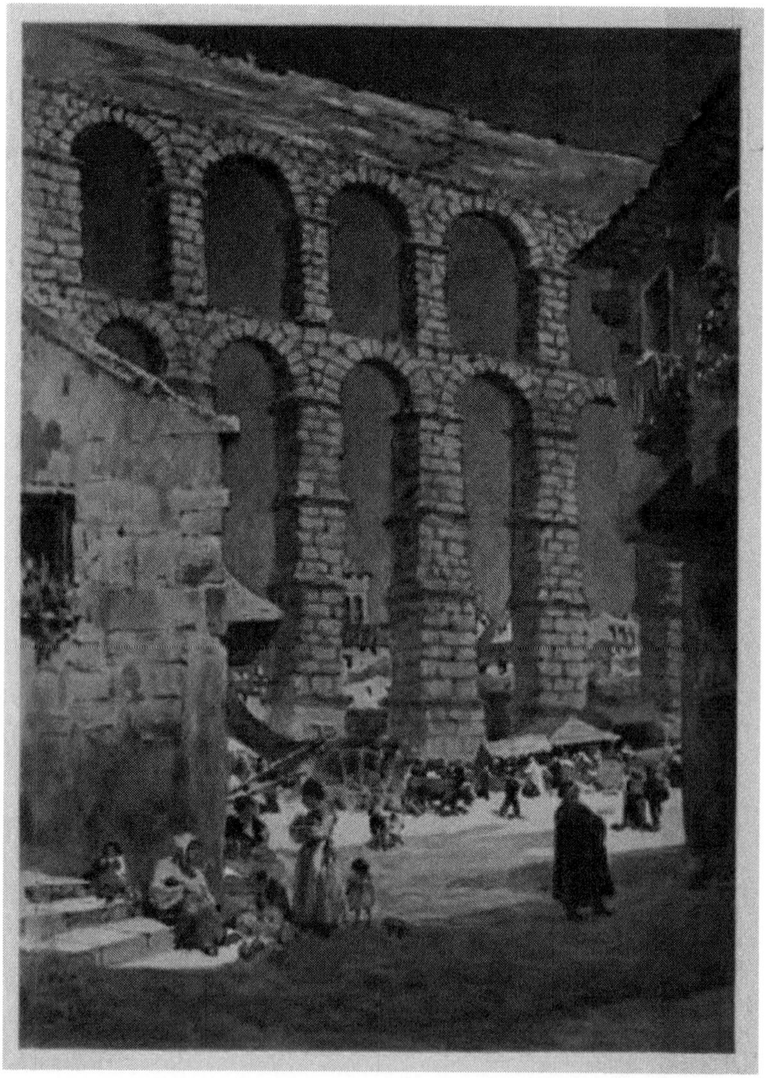

great aqueduct, which spans the valley that divides Segovia in the Plaza del Azoquéjo, brought pure water from a mountain torrent, the Rio Frio, ten miles away. It does the same to-day. Constructed of granite blocks, laid Cyclopean fashion without mortar or cement, it commences near San Gabriel. To break the force of the rushing stream the conduit has many angles. Without doubt it is the most important Roman remain in Spain, for this alone Segovia would be famous.

Once upon a time his Satanic Majesty fell desperately in love with a beautiful Segovian. To further his suit, an offer was made to do anything she might require. Her home was on a hill; her work, to fetch water from the stream below. Finding the continual tramp down and up rather irksome, this daughter of Eve bethought herself of a request to mitigate her toil. "Done," said the Evil One, and the aqueduct was built in one night! In terror she fled to the church, and the church discovered that one stone had been left out, also that the aqueduct was extremely useful. The contract was declared void and the maiden freed from the rash promise she had playfully given his majesty. The country folk still know it by the name of the Puento del Diabolo.

During the siege of Segovia, the Moors destroyed thirty-five of the arches, but these were cleverly rebuilt in 1493 by Juan Escovedo, a monk of El Parral, who received the scaffolding in payment for his work. More recently, extensive repairs in the same way have been successfully carried out. The most imposing view is in the Plaza del Azoquéjo, from which it towers upwards in a double line of arches one above the other, and its length is best grasped from El Calvario, a hill to the south of the town.

The Cathedral is a late Gothic pile, built of a warm yellow stone, and looks particularly impressive from the shady walk among the rocks on the left bank of the Clamores, the stream which cuts off Segovia from the southern plateau. It was begun in 1525 by the builder of Salamanca's Cathedral which it greatly resembles, Juan Gil de Hontañon, and continued at his death by his son. The weak point in the exterior, which masses very grandly, is the western façade. The interior is very striking. The wide span of the arches, the richness of the admirable vaulting, the splendid late Gothic windows and the feeling of light and space are fine examples of the last stage of Gothic work, just before the influence of the oncoming Renaissance took hold of the architects of that day. The floor is beautifully laid with red, blue and white diamond-shaped slabs of marble; and the very necessary notice—" No escupir, la religiosidad

SEGOVIA

y higiene la prohibur"—keeps it clean and decent.

In the *coro*, which occupies nearly the whole of the centre of the nave, there is a *retablo* by Sabatini. The *silleria* are very fine. They were rescued from the old Cathedral, which was destroyed in Charles V.'s time by the Comunéros, who started business by pulling down churches, appropriating all they could lay hands on, plundering the wealthy and generally behaving as a mob that has the upper hand always does. The outer walls of the *coro* are stucco, painted to represent different species of marble; described, by the way, in a reputable guide book — "beautifully coloured marbles"!

Most of the *rejas* which shut off the side chapels are good gilded iron work. In that of la Piedad there is a good *retablo* with life-sized figures by Juan de Juni, 1571; and in the chapel of the Segragrio a wooden figure of Christ by Alonso Cano. Through a fine Gothic portal in the Capilla del Cristo del Consuelo I entered the cloisters in company with a verger, who took great pride in his Cathedral. These cloisters are surpassingly beautiful; a very good example of flamboyant Gothic. In vain did I search for a corner from which to make a sketch. The courtyard was overgrown with shrubs, tall cypresses and

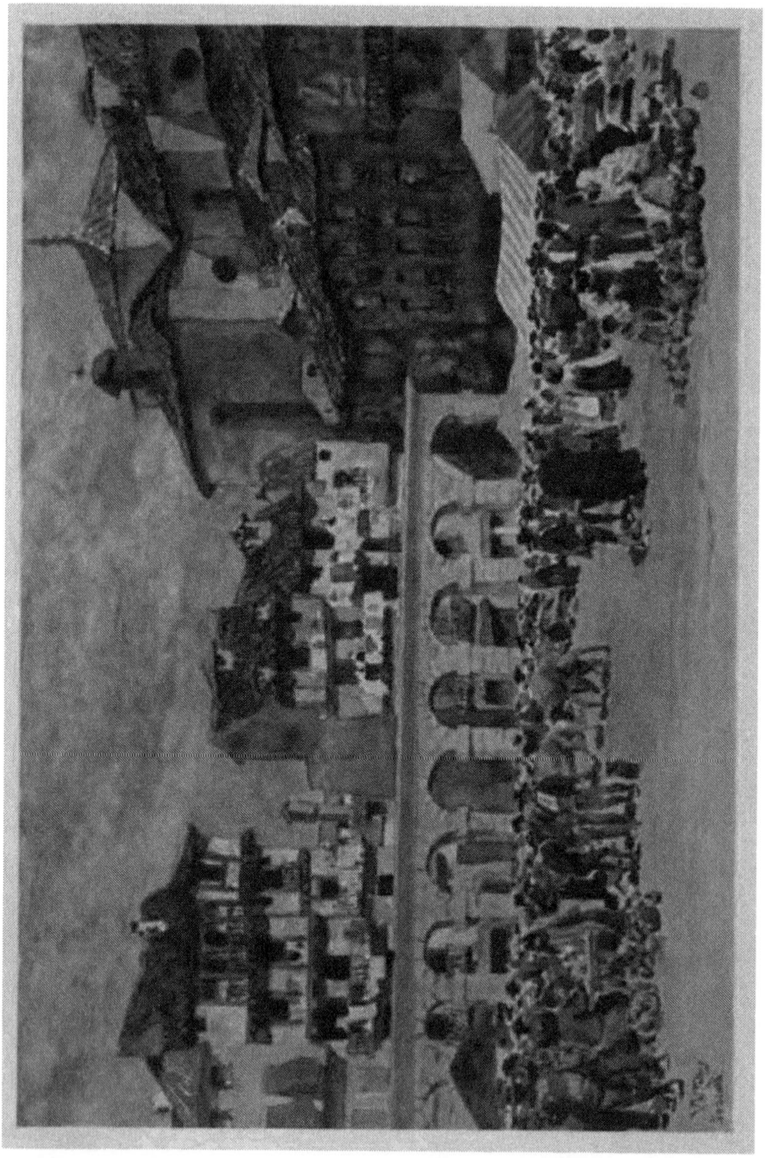

SEGOVIA

San Millan, a Romanesque structure of the twelfth century, is the best preserved church in Segovia. The exquisite arcades on the north and south sides have coupled columns with elaborately carved capitals. Like most of the buildings of this period solidity rather than grace was the effect aimed at by their architects. It possesses a triple apse; the piers supporting the roof are very massive, the capitals to the columns are formed of semi-grotesque figures of man and beast. The two doorways are good. In the church of San Martin there is a carved wooden Passion. Four life-sized figures take the place of shafts in the great doorway, and again a cloister forms the exterior of the south and west walls.

In the Dominican convent of Santa Cruz, founded by Ferdinand and Isabella, is still to be seen a sepulchral urn of one of the original companions of St. Dominic. "Tanto monta" the motto of the King and Queen is cut both inside and out on the walls. Over the west portal are good reliefs of the Crucifixion and the Pietà. La Vera Cruz, a church built by the Templars in 1204, is difficult of access. I procured the key after much trouble, and found the twelve-sided nave forming a sort of ambulatory round the central walled-in chamber. It is an imitation of the Holy Sepulchre at Jerusalem. The Templars were suppressed in

1312, so this gem had but a short exsistence as the house of prayer.

Nestling amidst a grove of acacia trees, hidden away under the rock, is the Santuario de Fuencisla. Built to commemorate the miraculous rescue of Maria del Salto, a beautiful Jewess, this little sanctuary is much affected by pilgrims. The rock which overshadows it is known as La Peña Grajera, or "Crow's Cliff," taking this name from the multitude of carnivorous birds who always assembled here for a meal after a victim had been hurled down to expiate his crime in a death below. Maria, accused of adultery, was led to the top and pushed off the edge to find the fate of so many before her. With great presence of mind she called loudly on the Virgin, who hearing, came to her assistance; and so retarded her downward flight that she alighted gently, escaping unhurt. Here in days long gone by lived a hermit, whose good life and deeds are still a much-reverenced legend among Segovians.

The monastery of El Parral, once a wealthy and powerful house of the brotherhood of San Gerónimo, contains a very good *retablo* by Diego de Urbina. It was founded by a member of the great Pacheco family, who fought three antagonists one ofter another and came off successful. He vowed to build a church on the spot where his skill and prowess gave him so splendid a victory, and to endow it as well. It is now a convent of Franciscan nuns.

Next in importance to the Cathedral is the comparatively new building of the Alcázar. Standing high up on the crags, below which the Eresma and Clamores meet, it occupies an unrivalled position. A fine view of this truly Castilian fortress is obtained from the beautiful walk which encircles the city on the further bank of each stream. Above the tall poplars and thick scrub rise its turrets and spires. The massive walls go sheer up from the rock on which their foundations rest. The huge embattled tower and drawbridge assist the feeling of strength; and it only requires the weathering of years, adding broken colour to the somewhat new-looking exterior, to make this a perfect specimen of mediæval architecture.

The building was originally Moorish, but the many vicissitudes of troublous times saw it in a bad state when Henry IV., "el Impotente," repaired and made it his residence. Within its walls Isabella was proclaimed Queen of Castile in 1474. Cabrera, the husband of her greatest friend, Beatrice of Boabdilla, held the fortress and its treasure, and it was mainly through his valour that Isabella succeeded to the throne. During the Comunéros insurrection the Alcázar held out for Charles V.

CATHEDRAL CITIES OF SPAIN

At the quelling of the revolt Charles did all in his power to thoroughly restore the building and furnish it with great splendour. His son Philip added much that the father's death had left unfinished. Our own King, Charles I., was here entertained, and Gil Blas confined a prisoner. The great fire, originated by some of the students of the military college, almost entirely destroyed the whole castle in 1862. The present edifice dates from shortly after that year and is now used as a storehouse for military archives and an academy for artillery officers.

A very good gateway spans the road that leads out past the Santuario de Fuencisla along the right bank of the Eresma. The river here is an ideal looking trout stream, but alas! fish are not as plentiful now as when Charles I. was entertained and fed on "fatte troute" in the Alcázar. Follow the path over the bridge to the left, it soon narrows into a mere goat track as it skirts the rock; a few steps farther on and the wonderful position of the fortress-castle bursts into view. How fascinating it looked as I saw it one night in the moonlight with the silver beams glinting on its spires. All was very still as I entered the wood of stunted pines beyond. Across the ravine rose the mighty Cathedral silhouetted against a dark starladen sky. A light here and there shone from a window in the houses beneath. I heard the distant cry of the watchman on his rounds. A faint scent from the heavy dew rose to my nostrils, a scent of mother earth. It was with unwilling steps I crossed the stream and sought my bed that night. Such moments are rare.

On the left bank of the Eresma, almost hidden in the trees, stands a building which once was the mint of Spain. Up till the year 1730 all Spain's money was coined here, the proximity to the impregnable Alcázar, which was used as the Treasury, affording security against untimely raids. The old mint is now a flour mill, but still bears the royal arms over its gateway.

At one time Segovia was the great Castilian mart for wool. The church, and monasteries of El Parral, El Paular, and the Escorial owning immense flocks. These were driven to the pure waters of the Eresma, to be cleansed before being shorn. After the sheep-washing, the animals were put into the sweating house, and their legs tied together. The shearer then commenced operations, and as each sheep passed out of his hands it was branded; the shepherds standing by made a selection of the older animals for the butcher, the remainder being taken away to their mountain pastures. Even now there are many flocks in the country around, particularly on the lower hills near La Granja, where I noticed a large number not at all unlike the Kentish breed of Romney Marsh.

Seven miles from Segovia the summer Royal Palace of La Granja lies in the midst of beautiful woods and clear streams. At the foot of the Sierra, the highest peak of which, La Peñalara, raises its crest a few miles off, this elysium is a beautiful spot for those who have earned a holiday from the cares of State. The gardens are most charmingly arranged, and the fountains with a never ending supply of water, better than those at Versailles. Built by Philip V., whose tastes and inclinations were thoroughly French, La Granja has been the scene of important events in the history of the country. The treaty which handed Spain over to France in 1796 was here signed by Godoy. In 1832 Ferdinand VII. revoked the decree by which he had abolished the Salic law, and summoned Don Carlos to the palace as heir to the throne, a call which plunged his unhappy country into civil war. Four years later the Queen Regent was compelled within its walls, by the leader of the revolutionary soldiery, to accept the constitution of Cadiz.

Every corner of Spain holds history, but none can compare with Segovia and its surroundings in romance and old-world charm.

SARAGOSSA

SARAGOSSA lies midway on the railway between Madrid and Barcelona, and, having about it a touch of both these, can qualify as one of Spain's progressive cities. The unsightly factory chimney is beginning to sprout up in the suburbs; old and narrow streets are making way for broader and better; and insanitary quarters giving place to modern hygiene.

Aragon is the poorest portion of this fair land, and Saragossa is its capital. In every age this little kingdom has been torn by war and has suffered heavily, but its people have never wavered in their faith, and are still among the most pious and superstitious of the many different races that people the Iberian Peninsula. They possess that strong attachment for their sterile plains and barren mountains so common to those who wring from Nature a bare existence.

The Emperor Augustus, in the year 25 B.C., vastly improved "Salduba," and gave it the title of Cæsarea Augusta. When in the occupation of Rome it was a free city and had a coinage of its

CATHEDRAL CITIES OF SPAIN

own. The first place in Spain to ... Paganism, Saragossa has always been a city of great holiness. When besieged by the Franks under Childebert in 540, the inhabitants carried the stole of San Vicente round the walls—and the invader fled.

The Infidel, however, proved less susceptible to a Christian relic, and the city fell to the weight of his arms in the eighth century. Being a ... Infidel he recognised no Kalif of Cordova, and between the two there soon began one of those internecine conflicts that in the end led to the termination of Moorish rule.

It was in this connection that Charlemagne was implored to assist the Northern Moor against the Andalusian and crossed the Pyrenees with an eye, no doubt, in the long run, to the acquisition of new territory. No sooner had he reached the plains of Aragon than he was recalled to quell a rising in his own dominions. His back turned, and he being presumably in retreat, the ungrateful people, eager for plunder, followed and inflicted on his rearguard a terrible defeat in the most famous Pyrenean Pass, the Pass of Roncesvalles, a defeat in which Roland, that hero of romance, lost his life.

Thence onward, as the centuries went by, Saragossa was the scene of many a fight. Alfonso I.

SARAGOSSA. LA

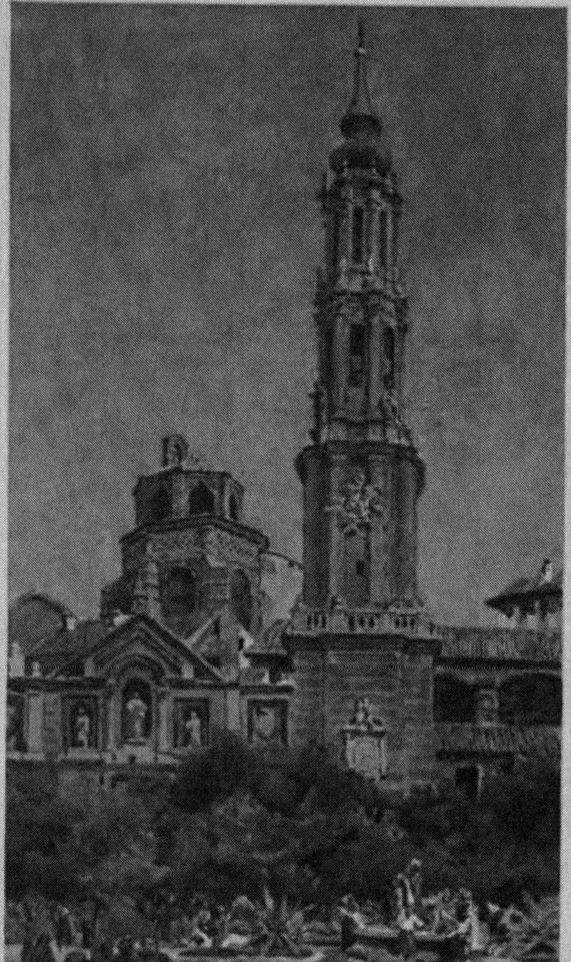

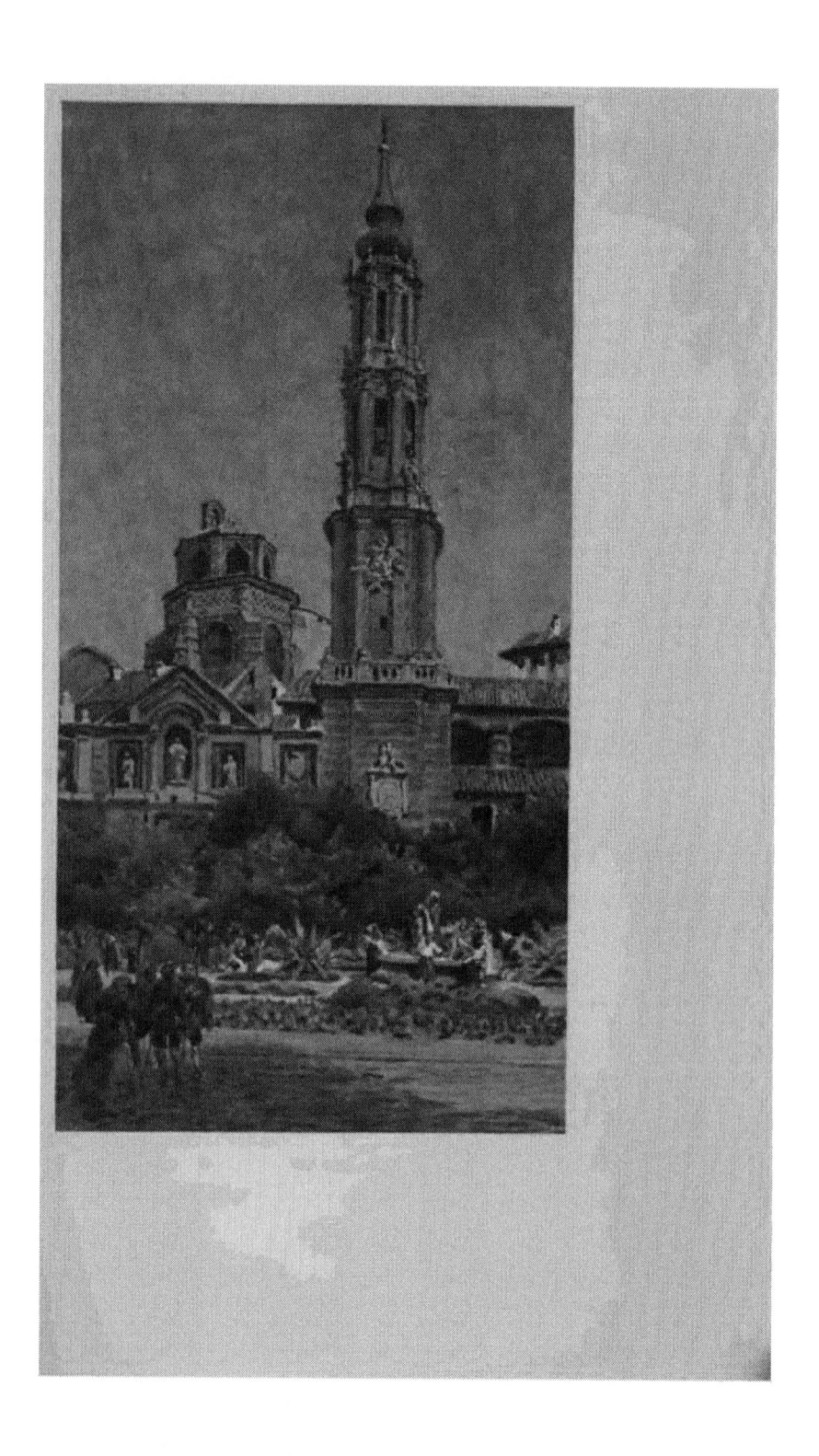

in 1118 recovered it from the Moor after a long siege, and Moslem rule was ended.

Saragossa is best known in the annals of its warfare for the heroic defence, immortalised by Byron, in the war with France. In the month of May 1808, the invader was close at hand, and the citizens organised themselves for defence. A young aristocrat, José Palafox, was chosen as the nominal leader, and had at his right hand the redoubtable peasant, Tio Jorge Ibort —Gaffer George. His two lieutenants were Mariano Cerezo and Tio Marin, while the courageous priest Santiago Sas assisted greatly, through his influence with the populace, to keep things together and prevent petty squabbles. One hundred *duros* supplied the sinews of war! Sixteen cannon, a few old muskets and two hundred and twenty fighting men were all that the leaders could count upon to repel the army of Lefebvre.

The siege began in June and was abandoned in August, in consequence of the disaster to Dupont at Bailén. In the following December four Marshals of France, Junot, Lannes, Mortier and Moncey, with eighteen thousand men, invested the city, but it was not until February of the next year that, having driven the defenders out of the Jesuit convent across the river, the French were able to establish a foothold in the outskirts of the city itself.

Every one knows how the Maid of Saragossa took the place of her dead artillery lover who was killed at his gun; an episode that has since become a theme to instil the young with heroic ideals. Such was the spirit that gained for the city the proud title of *siempre heróica*. Her citizens fought from house to house, every street had barricades, and it was only that when decimated by pestilence and famine, with half the place a smoking ruin, one of the most celebrated sieges of history came to end.

As in Cadiz and Salamanca, there are two Cathedrals in Saragossa, La Seo and El Pilar. The former occupies the site of a church which stood here before the Moors took possession of the place and turned it into a mosque. A year after the advent of Alfonso I., Bishop Pedro de Lebrana reconsecrated La Seo, and its walls have witnessed many historical events in the life of Aragon before the kingdom became merged into one with Castile. It was before the High Altar that her Kings were crowned, and at the font many a royal babe baptized.

La Seo is constructed almost entirely of the dull brown brick with which the older part of the city is also built; the interior piers and vaulting alone being of stone. On the north-east wall, which faces the gloomy palace of the archbishop, there is still extant the most elaborate arrangement of brick work, inlaid with coloured glazed tiles, blue, green, red, white and yellow, forming a very harmonious and attractive scheme.

From the centre of the north-west façade, which is extremely ugly, rises a well-proportioned tower arranged in four stages, with Corinthian columns, the top of which is surmounted by a red tiled cupola and spire. The colour of this took my fancy, it "sang out" so much against the blue of the sky—a contrast I thought worthy of an illustration.

Entering the building by the door in the façade, I was immediatley nonplussed as to the orientation of the Cathedral. To add to the puzzle, for the structure is almost square, four rows of columns seemed mixed up in endless confusion, and the dim light admitted from the few windows only accentuated the mystery. Very beautiful, however, is this Gothic interior which runs north-east and south-west, and I soon found a spot from whence to make a sketch. The columns rise from marble bases of a rich crimson; the vaulting above was lost in gloom, the light coming in from the south-west window struck vividly on portions of the Renaissance *respaldos*, the niches of which are

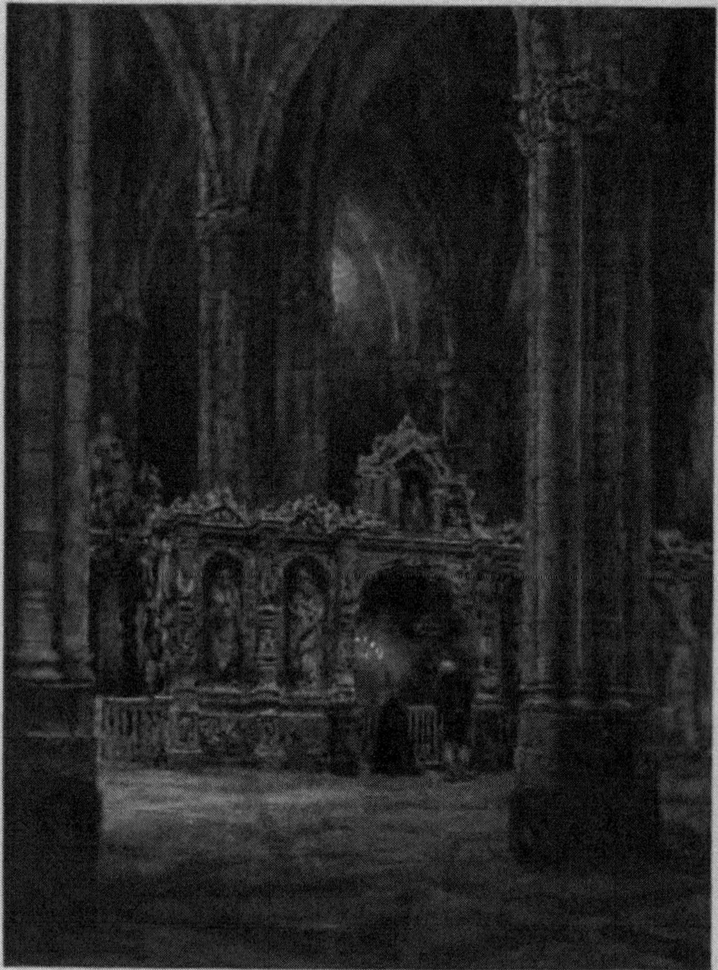

up devils who are roasting in Hades. Among the vestments is an extremely beautiful chasuble brought here at the time of the Reformation from Old St. Paul's in London. I wondered, when I looked at it, whether Catherine of Aragon, Henry VIII.'s consort, had been instrumental in its removal from England.

The Cathedral of El Pilar is thus named as it possesses the identical pillar on which the Virgin descended from Heaven and appeared to St. James. At first a modest chapel, it has grown by the addition of cloisters and subsidiary chapels to the present stupendous building. The length is close on five hundred feet and the breadth two hundred. The possession of this miraculous pillar has brought untold wealth to the Cathedral. Votive offerings on the anniversary of the festival at the shrine often amount to many thousands of pounds. Jewelry, gems and costly objects of every description are given; these are now sold by auction, the large sum of £20,000 being realised a few years ago. To these sales we owe a fine rock crystal and gold medallion, given to the Virgin of El Pilar by Henry IV. of France, and now in South Kensington Museum. Many examples of old Spanish goldsmith's work have also been acquired for the same collection in this way.

The towers and pinnacles of El Pilar pile up

grandly, and are best seen from the fine bridge which spans the yellow flood of the river Ebro. Silhouetted against the evening sky, with the smooth running waters below, it seemed to me a worthy example in brick and stone of the church's magnificence.

The interior is an immense temple, the frescoes of which are from the brush of that extraordinary genius, Goya, who turned his talent to any job that was productive of the cash he spent so freely. The *retablo* of the High Altar is a fine piece of work from the alabaster quarries at Escatron. Composed of three good Gothic canopies with tapering finials, it has seven smaller divisions below. Damian Forment was the artist who designed and carried out this, one of the most beautiful *retablos* in the country. The *reja* which stands in front of *coro* is superb, and considered to be Juan Celma's masterpiece. Behind the High Altar is the celebrated chapel of the Virgin. The figure itself is of very old blackened wood, evidently a specimen of early Christian work. On October 12, the anniversary of her descent, thousands of pilgrims flock hither to kiss her foot through a hole in the wall at the back of the chapel. The city is then full of visitors and it is next to impossible to find quarters or a room of any sort.

I happened to be in Saragossa for *Semana Santa*,

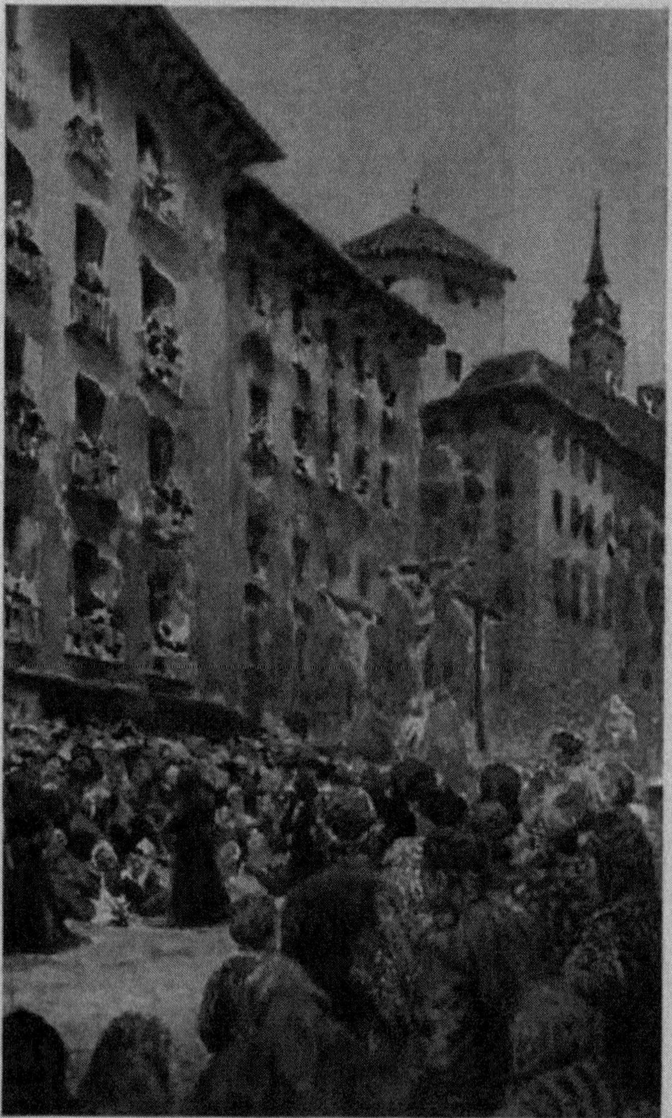

SARAGOSSA

and watched the processions of groups of heavy wooden figures, illustrative of our Lord's life-history, proceed through crowded streets. My sketch shows the last *paso* of the Crucifixion, with a figure of the Virgin bringing up the rear, as they passed the intensely devout throngs on Good Friday. Masked members of different religious brother and sisterhoods, walk along keeping the route clear. The whole procession was led by soldiery, and "Romans," men attired in the garb of ancient Rome, while an infantry band followed the Virgin. The *pasos* are deposited in the Church of Santiago built on the spot where St. James passed a night. In the belfry of this church is an old Gothic bell of which the inhabitants are justly proud.

San Pablo is a very interesting fabric, dating from the year 1259. The floor of the church is a dozen steps below the street. The *retablo* is another fine example of Damian Forment's art. The aisles are cut off from the nave by a flat wall with square pillars and ill-proportioned pointed arches. The *coro* is at the west end, from whence also issue the notes of a very beautifully toned organ. The extraordinary octagonal brick steeple might pass as of Russian or Tartar origin.

Of all the gateways to the city, there remains but one, the Puerta del Carmen. It has been left as it stood after the French bombardment, and retains many marks of shot and soft-nosed bullets. The site of the historic Puerta del Portillo, where the Maid of Saragossa won immortal fame, is in the square of the same name. Outside it stands the Castillo de la Aljaferia, the Palace of the Sheikhs of Saragossa, and the residence of the Kings of Aragon. Ferdinand gave it to the Holy Office, and from out its portals issued many terrible orders for the suppression of the wretched heretic. There still remains a small octagonal mosque, and many of the rooms have their original *artesonado* ceilings. In it also is the "Torreta," the dungeon in *Il Trovatore*; while from the tower can be seen the Castillo de Castlejar, mentioned in the drama by Garcia Gaturrio, from which the libretto of the opera was taken. This one-time fine palace is now a barrack, and I used to watch the recruits drilling and exercising outside. When the recruiting season commences, the numbers are drawn among those liable to serve — the lucky ones being those who are not compelled to take any part in the military service of their country. There exist societies in Spain to which a sum of 750 pesetas can be paid, that undertake to pay another 750 pesetas to the State, if the payee's name is drawn for service, 1500 pesetas being the sum which enables any one to forego his military career. If his number is not drawn, he loses his deposit, if it is, the society pays the full sum.

In the old days the nobles of Aragon safeguarded their privileges by the Fuéros de Sobrarbe, a code something like our Magna Charta, which reduced the King's authority to almost vanishing point. Pedro IV. got rid of the Fuéros by cutting to pieces the parchment incorporating the union or confederacy, whose members, if the King was thought to have exceeded his prerogative, were absolved from allegiance. They were a hardheaded race, these Aragonese, and are still like those of the other northern provinces, very independent and jealous of Castile's rule.

Among other things handed down from time immemorial is a national dance, and the Jota Aragonesa, the national air, known beyond the limits of Spain. Very few of these old airs still exist. As a fact, the old songs of Spain and their music are better known in the Jewish colony of Salonika than in the country of their origin. The upper classes of this colony still speak the pure Castilian of Cervantes' time, and being the descendants of Spanish refugees hounded out of the country by the Inquisition, still observe the customs, songs and language of their immigrant forefathers.

The Aragonese also have a national game, Tirando a la Barra, which consists in passing an iron bar from one hand to the other, thereby gaining impetus for the final swing which sends it hurtling through the air towards a mark on the ground, like a javelin. One or two good old houses still remain in Saragossa to testify to its former greatness, notably that of the great Luna family. Two gigantic uncouth figures with clubs stand on either side of the doorway which is the centre of a simple but good façade. The cornice above is very heavy and the eaves project far out, a feature that I noticed was very characteristic of the old quarters of the city. It was in this house that the besieged, during the French war, held their councils. The Casa Zaporta can boast of a very fine staircase and beautiful *patio* with elegant fluted columns and reliefs and medallions breaking the spandrils. A few other good houses still exist, but as they are in the old quarters of the city, and as these are rapidly disappearing, I fear that Saragossa will not contain for long anything beyond her Cathedrals that is of tangible interest.

SANTIAGO

THE evening train from Pontevedra deposited me sometime about midnight at Cernes, the hamlet outside Santiago where the line ends. The full moon during the latter portion of the journey had been a source of endless delight. My face was glued to the window watching the ever-changing hills and valleys through which the train crept, shrouded in that mystery which obliterates detail and suggests so much in great masses of subdued light and deep shade.

I reached the hotel, procured a room, threw open the window, and stood on the balcony listening to the intense stillness of a wonderful night. Suddenly a dull rumbling down some side street disturbed my reverie of the Santiago of days gone by. The only thing to be expected at this time of night was the station 'bus, but I heard no clattering hoofs and was lost in surmise, when out of the dark shadow of a narrow lane into the moonlight swung a yoke of oxen drawing a long cart with slow majestic pace. But what a cart! a low sort of wooden box balanced between two solid

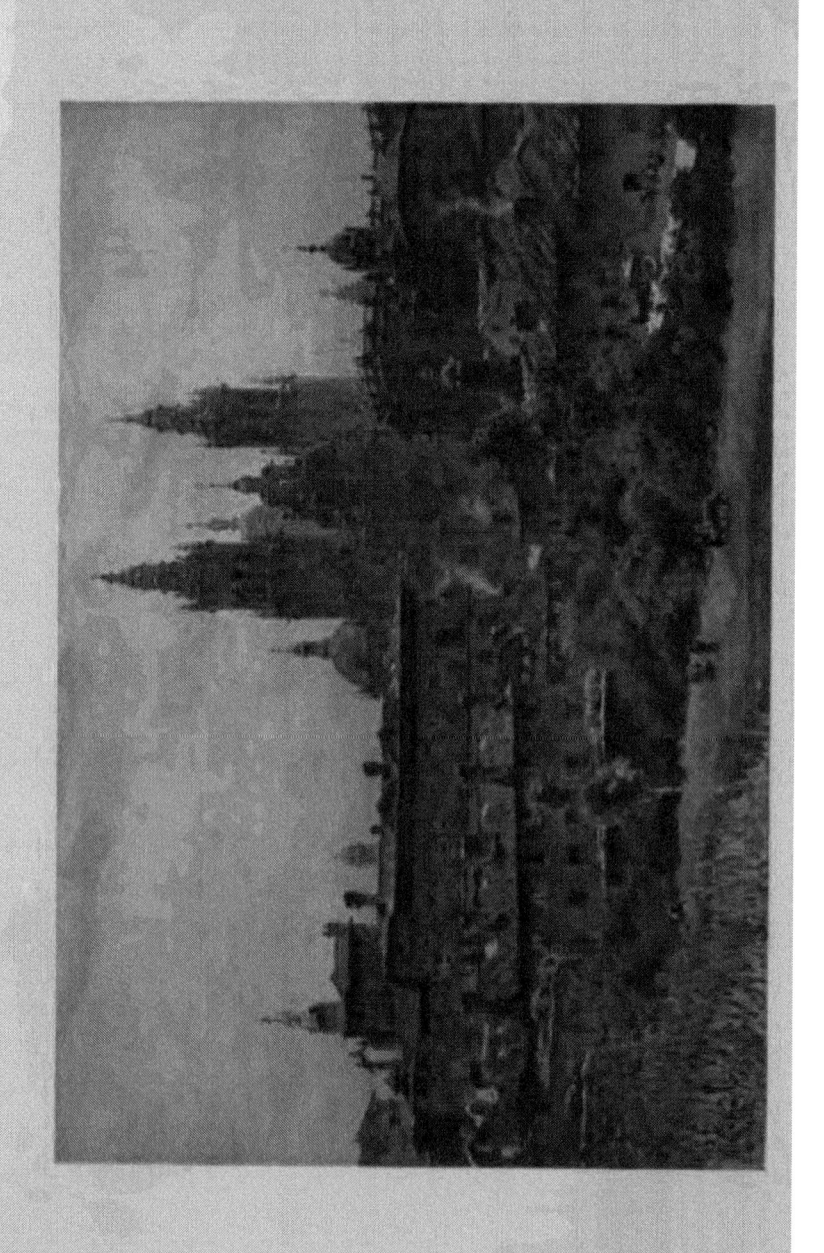

SANTIAGO

Cathedral. In the course of time their whereabouts was forgotten and it remained for Bishop Theodomir to rediscover the sacred spot in 829, guided thither by a star. Hence the Campus Stellæ—or Compostela.

The shrine of the saint is still visited by innumerable pilgrims, and perhaps more arrive in Santiago than any other city of Spain. In olden days so great was the number that "El Camino de Santiago"—"The road to Santiago," gave rise to the Spanish term for the "milky way." I have watched them in the Cathedral, peasants, men and women, come from afar, to judge by their dress. They each carried a staff decorated with tufts of herbs and little star-shaped pieces of bread tied on with gay ribbons. I have seen women making the round of the altars in the different chapels with great bundles of clothes, through which were thrust umbrellas, balanced on their heads. They never lost the poise of their burden as they knelt and rose again. But of all the pilgrims I saw, one who might have stepped out of Chaucer's pages carried me back to the days of long ago. She wore a short skirt of thick brown material, sandals protected her stockinged feet, from her girdle hung rosary, scallop shells and a stoneware pilgrim's bottle, a hooked staff lent support to her bent, travelled-stained figure. Her leather wallet was stuffed with bread, and covering her short cropped hair was a grey felt hat, mushroom shaped. A little black dog entered the Cathedral with her, and squatted silently by his mistress's side as she knelt praying in the dim light of a grey day. Chaucer's " Wyt of Bath " had made a pilgrimage to " Seynt Jame," and my pilgrim with her little lame companion might very well have been with him too.

The Cathedral, founded in 1078, was built on the site of one destroyed by Almanzor in 997. The legend of the destruction of the first church, which had been standing for just one hundred years, was thus—Almanzor, after sacking Leon and Astorga, swept all the country westwards with his Moorish hosts until he reached Santiago. So great was his fame and in such terror was his name held that no one had the courage to face him and fight for saint and city. Riding through its deserted streets he came to the church, and to his surprise at last espied a solitary Christian, a monk, praying alone at the shrine of the saint. "What dost thou here?" inquired the haughty Moor. "I am at my prayers," curtly answered the holy man, continuing his devotions. This reply and the courage of the single enemy so called forth the admiration of Almanzor, that his life was spared and an infidel guard set over the tomb.

SANTIAGO. SOUTH DOOR OF THE CATHEDRAL.

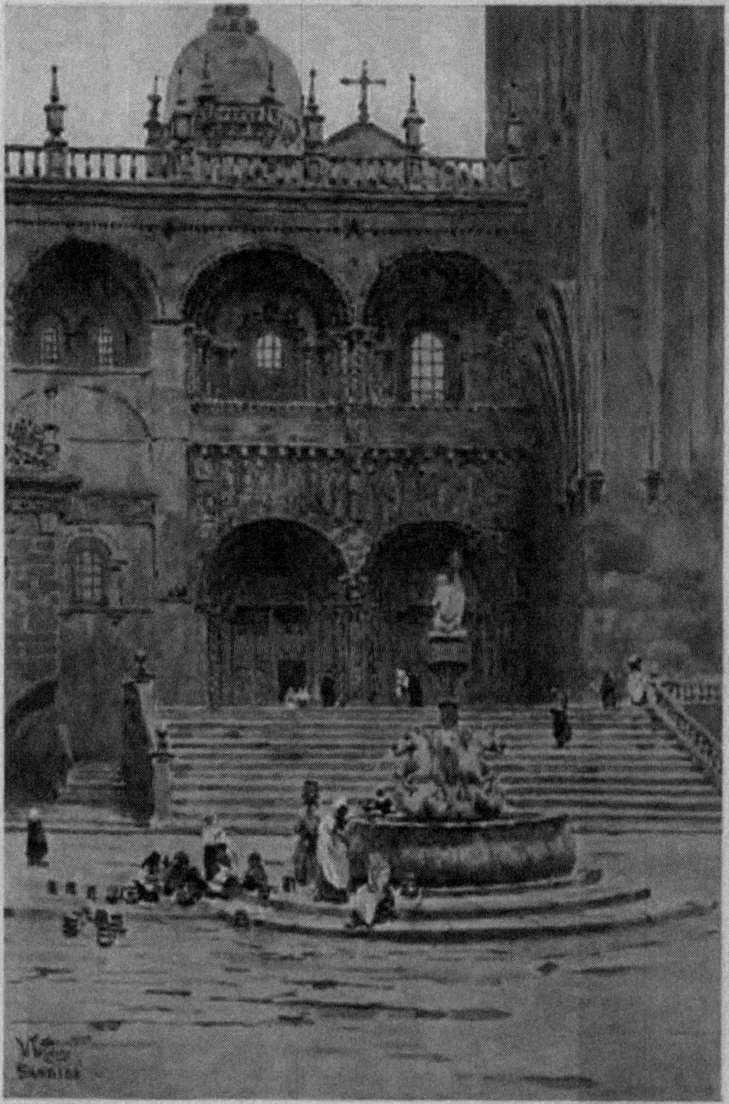

SANTIAGO

The west façade, a Renaissance outer covering, so to speak, of the older façade, would not look so imposing as it does if granite had not been used in its construction. The grey tones of the lichen-covered stone redeem the somewhat overdone florid design, and it stands well above a double flight of steps on the east side of the huge Plaza Mayor.

The south door, or Puerta de las Platerias, takes this name from the silversmiths whose workshops are still under the arcades around the Plaza on to which it opens. It is the oldest portion of the Cathedral and dates from the foundation. The shafts contain tiers of figures in carved niches, and the tympanum has rows of smaller ones.

The north door fronts on to the Plaza Fuente San Juan, and faces the convent of San Martin Pinario, which was founded in 912 by Ordoño II. In the days before this Plaza was officially given its present name, it was known as Azabacheria, *azabache* is jet, and it was here that vast quantities of rosaries made of this were sold to pilgrims.

In the south-east angle of the Cathedral is the Puerta Santa, bearing the inscription "Hace est domus Dei et porta cœli." It is only opened in the Jubilee year and then by the archbishop himself. The entrance to it is from the Plaza de los Literarios. It will be seen from this that the Cathedral is practically set in four great Plazas, el

Mayor, de las Platerias, la Fuente San Juan, and de los Literarios, and for this reason, although the roof towers high above, it is one of the few Cathedrals the size of which can be appreciated by an exterior view.

The early Romanesque interior is superb, and not unlike our own Ely Cathedral. The finest thing in it of archæological interest is the "Portico de la Gloria," which Street calls " one of the greatest glories of Christian Art." This Portico, situated at the west end of the nave, formed at one time the façade. The idea of the whole doorway is Christ at the Last Judgment. His figure, twice life-size, occupies the centre. Below Him is seated St. James, while around them are angels worshipping. Four and twenty elders are arranged in the circumference of the archivolt; each one holds a musical instrument, most of which are shaped like violas and guitars. A most beautifully sculptured marble column supports this in the centre, resting on a base of devils, with the portrait of Maestro Matio, who executed the whole from his own designs, facing the nave. An inscription under this doorway states that the work was finished in 1188. To the right and left are smaller arches, portraying in well-cut granite good souls on their way to Paradise and wicked ones in the clutches of devils on their way to Hell. Nothing can exceed the primitive religious feeling pervading this work. Mateo must have given his whole soul with fervour to his labours; and the almost obliterated traces of painting and gilding enhance their result by giving a touch of warmth to the cold colour of the stone.

West of the portico, above which are the remains of a fine wheel window, has been built the present Renaissance façade known as El Obradorio, the two being connected by quadripartite vaulting. The nave itself has a walled-in triforium, but no clerestory and the vaulting of the roof is barrel.

The saint's shrine is in the crypt beneath the Capilla Mayor. The extra extravagant *retablo* above the High Altar is chirrigueresque, and hardly redeemed by the lavish employment of jasper, alabaster and silver with which it is decorated. A jewelled figure of St. James is seated in a niche above the mass of precious metal in which the altar is encased.

It is all very gorgeous and must impress the pious pilgrim who has journeyed hither from afar, but I could not help wishing it were simpler. However, the one living vital thing in Spain is her religion, and her Church knows so well how to conduct its business that my feelings of regret are purely æsthetic.

The *cimborio* is a fine creation, under which swings on certain *fiestas* the huge silver *incensario*, a lamp wellnigh six feet high. The two bronze pulpits are real masterpieces of cinquecento art and are adorned by subjects from the Old Testament by Juan Bautista Celma.

In one of the side chapels, known as the Relicario, are recumbent figures on the tombs of Don Ramon, the husband of Urraca, Berenguela 1187, Fernando II. 1226, Alfonso XII. of Leon 1268, and that faithful, pitiable figure Juan de Castro, wife of Pedro the Cruel. Even now, after the spoliation by Soult, who carried away ten hundredweight of precious metal in sacred vessels, the Relicario is a perfect museum. All the other chapels contain good tombs, especially that of Espiritu Santo in the north transept; and among other beautiful objects with which the Cathedral is replete are two ancient *limosneras* or alms-boxes, two very ancient gilt pyxes, a carved wooden cross, similar to the much-revered cross of los Angeles at Oviedo, given by Don Alfonso and Doña Jimena in 874.

The large cloisters to the south-west of the Cathedral were built by Archbishop Fonseca in 1521. They are bad Gothic enriched with Renaissance details. The centre court is paved with granite and gives an impression of bareness which is not redeemed by the architecture.

It was in this Cathedral that John of Gaunt, Duke of Lancaster, was crowned King of Spain.

SANTIAGO. INTERIOR OF THE CATHEDRAL.

SANTIAGO

Santiago possesses a much frequented university, which is extremely well provided with books.

In the church of Santa Maria de la Sar may be seen relics of the Holy Office which held its sittings in the adjoining monastery. The president's chair, marked with a palm, a cross and a red sword is perhaps the most notable. This monastic church, at one time owned by Templars, is situated outside the city boundary on the Orense road. Like all the others, in fact like the whole of Santiago, it is built of granite. It possesses a triple apse; the nave is of five bays without a triforium or clerestory, and the interior, in consequence, is very dark, heavy and gloomy. In it is the tomb of Archbishop Bernardo, 1242. The cloister at one time must have been exceptionally fine, but alas! only nine arches now remain; and the whole edifice is of the fast-crumbling away type not uncommon in the country.

The fine Plaza Mayor, or Plaza Alfonso Doce, is bounded on the north by the huge Hospice erected by Enrique de Egas for Ferdinand and Isabella for the use of poor pilgrims. The royal coat-of-arms is in evidence over the entrance portal, enriched, in addition, with figures of saints and pilgrims. The massive cornice has a course of heavy chain work and the ball decoration so common in Toledo. This huge pile of buildings is now used as a hospital. It is divided into four courts with fountains and is admirably adapted for its present use. The small chapel is one of the gems of Santiago. The roof springs from four arches with Gothic statues and niches clustered round a central column.

On the west side of the Plaza stands the great Seminario founded in 1777 for the education of young priests. The ground floor is now occupied as the Ayuntamiento of Santiago.

To the south is the Collegio de San Gerónimo, with a remarkable early doorway. The college was known as *Pan y Sardina* from the poverty of its accommodation. Sardines, the staple industry of Vigo and other coast towns of the district, are the cheapest food obtainable, hence the appellation. Santiago is delightfully situated amidst heather-clad hills, the lower slopes of which are well wooded with oak, fir, and eucalyptus. Great boulders of granite stand out like the monoliths of pre-historic ages. Many a pleasant walk through the purple heather revealed to me a landscape such as one sees in parts of Cornwall and Scotland. The grey city with its red-tiled roofs, its huge deserted monastic buildings, the many spires and domes of the Cathedral and other churches, all set in patches of brilliant green meadows and maize fields look particularly beautiful from Monte Pedroso, a fine vantage point surmounted by a huge Calvary.

SANTIAGO

The climate is comparatively moist, ferns of all sorts grow in the shade of garden walls, and bracken is thick in the oak woods. The Galician is well favoured by Nature, and being a patient, hard-working man of not much mental capacity, very pious and an ardent advocate of small holdings, gets through life with a contented spirit. He is very close and knows the value of a peseta. Unfortunately he is looked down upon by the Castilian, and the term " Gallego " is rather one of abuse than respect. Driven to emigration by the subdivision of land which cannot support more than those who own and work it now, he goes south in great numbers and is the trusted *concierge* in many a large house and hotel in Madrid and elsewhere. The Panama Canal too attracts him from his native hills, in fact the Gallego is to be met with wherever Spanish is the spoken language.

TUY

THE train deposited me one morning at this little frontier town. It was very hot, and it was Sunday. The only porter in the station volunteered to carry my bag to the Fonda, so we joined a long file of peasants and tramped up the dusty road to the old Gothic capital which stands splendidly situated above the river Minho.

From a distance the Cathedral rises like a fort, capping the white houses and brown roofs which are terraced below. At one time in the far away past Tuy was a town of great importance. Greek remains have been dug up here, but history does not go further back than Ætolian Diomede, the son of Tydeus, who founded what became under King Witiza the Gothic capital. This was in the year 700. Ordoño I. rebuilt it two hundred years later, and I did not find it difficult to trace the massive granite walls which sheltered the inhabitants, and preserved it as the most important city of these parts.

Truly a crown to the fortress, the castellated walls of the Cathedral give it a martial air. The nave of five bays is early pointed, with a blind triforium and blocked up clerestory. So narrow and dark are the aisles and so massive the columns which support the fine vaulting of the roof, that I could never get rid of the feeling that I was in some great hall of an ancient castle. It only wanted a few halberdiers or men-at-arms, instead of the black-garbed peasant women kneeling at the different altars, to make the illusion perfect.

The transepts, which have aisles, are Romanesque with an early pointed triforium. After the great earthquake at Lisbon many strengthening additions were made to the interior, blocking out most of the light. In the case of the aisles arches were run up at different intervals with no sense of proportion, quite hap-hazard, and creating a very much askew appearance in this part of the building. Transoms were built across the nave to add to the disfigurement of one of the most perfect little Cathedrals in Spain.

The west doorway is very fine, with four detached columns on either side, thus forming a narrow porch. The upper half of these columns each consists of a good figure of a saint whose feet rest on a devil. In the tympanum are good reliefs and a well-cut Adoration of the Magi. The archivolt is seven-fold and is an excellent piece of rich carving. All is granite, and all is solemn, quite in keeping with this hard material.

TUY

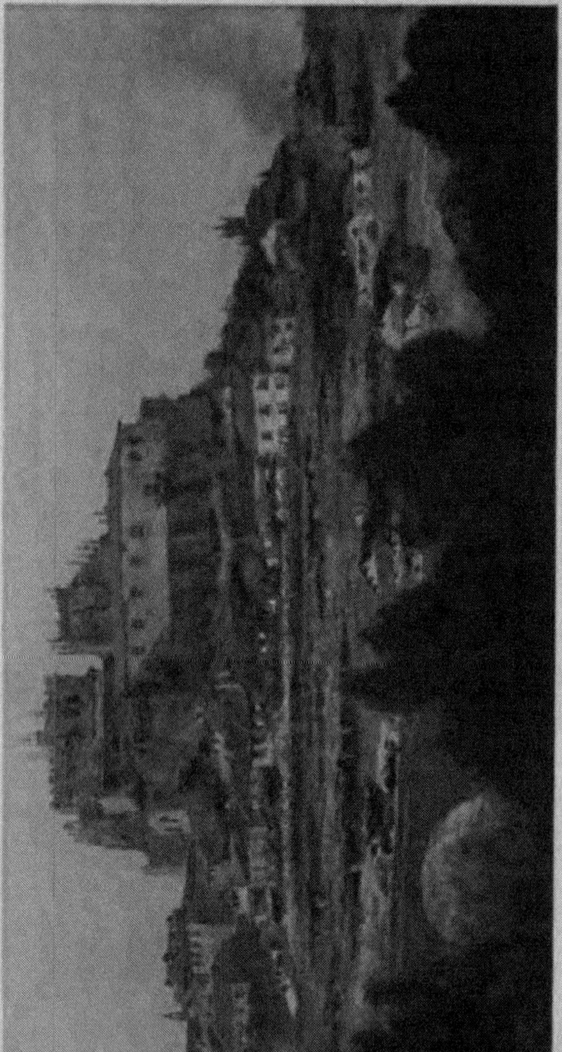

TUY

The Cloister Court, round which runs a most beautiful arcade of early pointed work with detached shafts, has unfortunately fallen into decay. But the charming little garden in the centre somewhat compensates for this. When I strolled in the silence was only broken by the cooing of doves and the hum of bees. The sun seemed to find his way into every nook and cranny, and here, thought I, is peace.

Away beyond the outer wall, a wall which is part of the old defence of Ordoño's day, is the road to Portugal. Passing through vineyards it reaches the river a mile distant and crosses the water by a very fine bridge. It was from this road that I made my sketch of the quaint old-world town. Down by the river at the end of the one broad street that Tuy possesses is the old Convent of Santo Domingo. Now a barrack, it still keeps its grand Transitional church. The chancel is extremely fine and among its many tombs a knight in armour with his lady at his side I thought the best. On the grassy platform in front of the church I spent one or two pleasant evenings. The river flows below and the mountains of Portugal rise sublimely from the opposite bank. I was decidedly pleased with my short sojourn in this typical Spanish town, the wonderful position of which, right on the frontier overlooking another land, makes it one of Spain's most unique Cathedral cities.

ORENSE

"IN the gold district," such is the meaning of Orense. In Roman days it was the headquarters for working the gold in which the district abounded.

Three warm springs, situated close to the road which leads out of the town to the south-west, also brought fame to Orense, though they possessed, apparently, no medicinal properties. Nowadays the poorer classes use the water for domestic purposes, thereby saving fires.

In Visigothic times Orense was the capital of the Suevi, and was the scene of the renunciation of Paganism by this tribe. Besides its warm springs the town boasts of two other wonders, its bridge and its Cathedral. The former is certainly a grand piece of work. The centre arch rises one hundred and thirty-five feet above the river Minho, with a magnificent span of one hundred and forty feet. Of the six remaining arches some are pointed and some are round.

The Cathedral is a most interesting structure, more's the pity it is so little known. Built on an

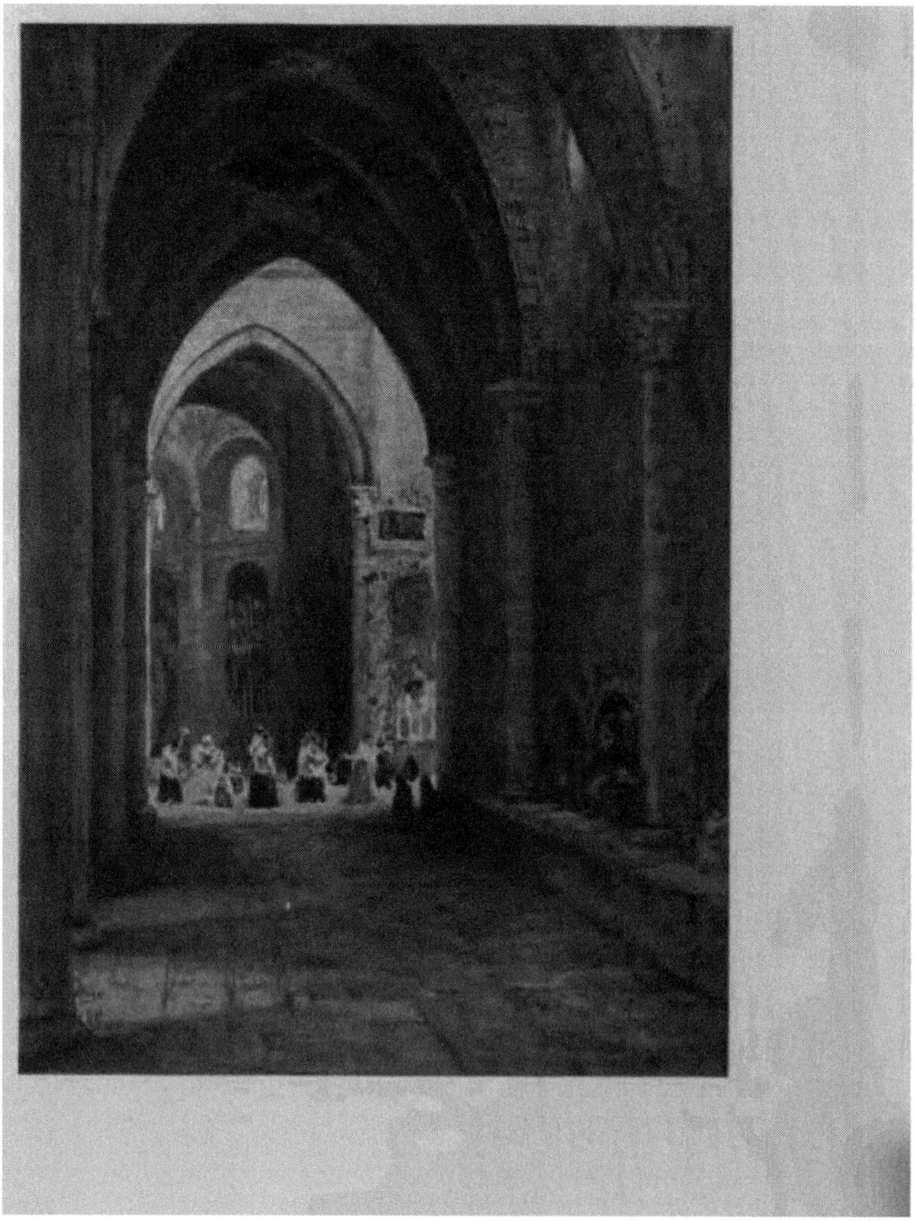

bosses. The spandrils between the arches are recessed with well-carved figures of angels and archangels playing on musical instruments. Of course this octagon bears no comparison with that at Burgos, it is much simpler and much smaller, but has a tentative beauty of its own.

The transepts are of earlier date, and have been altered, though not injudiciously. The *coro* is small, very dark and solemn, and in this respect bears favourable comparison with many another which may be far finer. Its *reja*, like that of the Capilla Mayor, is a very good example of wrought and hammered iron-work, and does credit to the skill of those who no doubt sat in the little shops below giving their life-work to the adornment of the church above.

The High Altar is a mass of silver with a background of glittering carving which forms the gilded *retablo*. The warm yellow of the Cathedral stone and the time-worn colour of the figures which decorate this *retablo* have a very pleasing effect to the eye. The ashes of Santa Eufemia, Orense's patroness, rest beneath her effigy which stands to the south of the High Altar, and those of SS. Facundo and Primivo under theirs on the north side. Santa Eufemia's body was found by a poor shepherdess lying out on the mountain slopes of the Portuguese border, and was brought here to rest.

CATHEDRAL CITIES OF SPAIN

The Cathedral is full of fine tombs, among which that of Cardinal Quintata in Carrara marble is the best. It is placed on the north side of the chancel, facing a much earlier Gothic tomb with a well-carved canopy which stands on the south side. The present edifice was founded in 1220 by Bishop Lorenzo, displacing the older church erected in 550 and dedicated to Saint Martin.

Wandering at random up the narrow streets which covered the hill I found myself outside the Convent of San Francisco. Like so many institutions of a kindred nature it is now a barrack, and difficult of access. However, I managed to get in and found the chief interest centred in the cloisters. They are beautiful relics of the thirteenth century. Sixty arches complete the arcade, with coupled shafts standing free. The capitals are well carved and the dog-tooth moulding above them has not suffered much from the ravages of time.

Here, as in other towns where money in late mediæval days was scarce, it is pleasant to find untouched remains of an earlier past. The streets are mostly arcaded and very tortuous and quaint. The market is held on the Plaza of the Cathedral, and fruit vendors sit in the sun on the steps which lead into the Holy Fane. The *Alamedas* are thronged at night with a crowd which, for Spain, seemed to take life seriously.

ORENSE

I had finished my usual after-dinner stroll one evening, and returned to my hotel. It was a balmy night and I pulled my chair out on to the balcony. The lights in the cottages on the hill opposite went out one by one, and away down below, amongst the dark foliage of a vineyard, I heard the sound of a guitar. A voice breathed out a love song, and once more I felt the romance of the South—that indescribable feeling which comes over one when nerves are attune to enchanting surroundings.

ASTORGA

"NO, you won't find much for your brush to do in Astorga, señor"—was the answer to a query addressed to a fellow passenger in the train. I fear he was not far wrong, though I knew with the Cathedral I should not be disappointed.

It was a wet evening, and I landed at the station in the dark; gave my traps to a porter, and found myself after a tramp through the mud at the only Fonda in the place. My baggage was deposited in a sort of glorified cupboard containing a bed. The small window had no glass, and I discovered the next day that it opened on to the stables. I objected to these quarters, and later on in the evening my belongings were moved into a room just vacated by some one who had gone on to Madrid in *el rapido*.

The next morning I made my way to the Cathedral. It stands well and quite isolated, except for the "New Art" Bishop's Palace which is in course of erection. The Cathedral is late Gothic, built in the fifteenth and sixteenth centuries on the site of a former church. The interior is lofty and very beautiful, though spoilt by a bad *trascoro* in execrable taste and quite out of keeping with the elegant columns of the nave. This consists of seven bays. The bases of the piers run up ten feet or more, and resemble the later additions to Leon Cathedral and those at Oviedo. The intersecting mouldings on them are the very last style of Gothic work and exemplify the beginning of a more florid taste. There is no triforium. The clerestory windows are of unusual height, as at Leon, and are filled with very fine glass.

The aisles are also very lofty. The chapels attached to that on the north have their vaulting carried up to the height of the aisle, a very unusual feature. All the windows on this side, with one exception, are blocked. In the south aisle the vaulting of the lateral chapels is low. The windows are glazed and contain good glass; and in the first chapel from the west is a very fine early German *retablo*.

The transepts are of one bay only. The south has perhaps the best glass in a Cathedral which is specially rich in this.

There is much good iron work in the different *rejas*, and the walnut *silleria* in the *coro* are exceptionally well carved. But the gem of the Cathedral is undoubtedly the magnificent *retablo*

ASTORGA

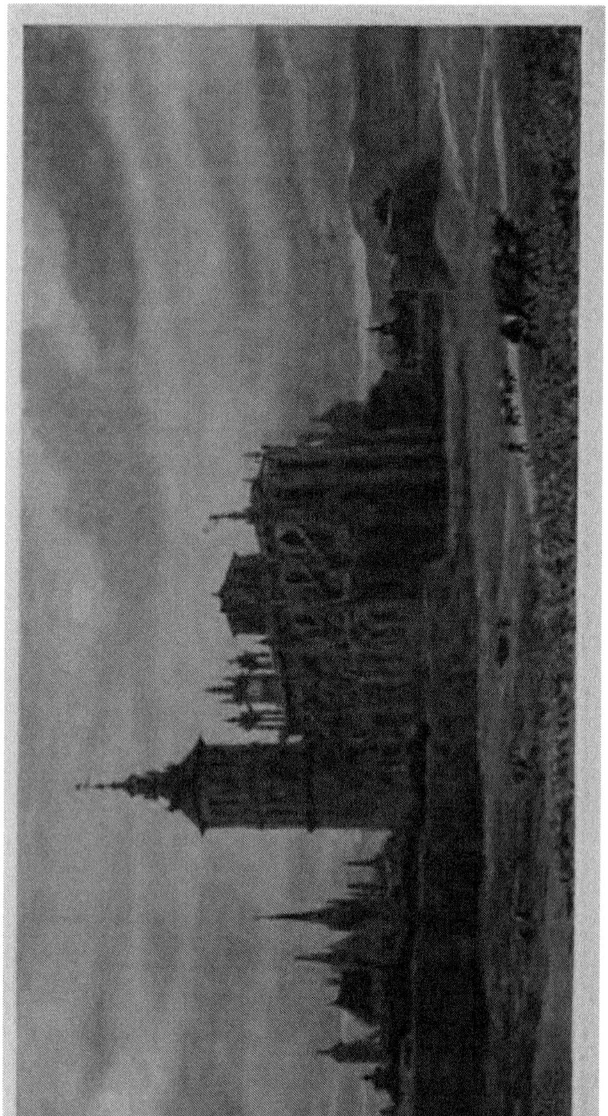

over the High Altar. Its author, Gaspar Becerra, was a native of Baeza, and studied in Italy under Michael Angelo. It is his masterpiece, and well merits this title. Of the fourteen panels, *The Disputation* and *Ascension* are the best. The exterior of this lofty church is much enhanced by its flying buttresses. The west façade is good Renaissance work, with flanking towers, only one of which is, however, finished. A flying buttress connects them with the centre of the façade as at Leon, in fact I could not help drawing comparison, when I knew them both, between these two Cathedrals.

The warm red stone of which this at Astorga is built has weathered most beautifully, and contrasts with the grey balustrade composed of figures holding hands—a very quaint device, by the way— which adorns the ridge above the clerestory. At the south-east corner, instead of the usual pinnacle, a huge weathercock stands. It is a wooden statue of Pedro Mato, a celebrated Maragato, in the dress of his tribe.

La Maragateria is a territory of small extent in the middle of which Astorga is situated. The inhabitants, the Maragatos, mix with no one. They live exclusively to themselves, preserve their costume and their customs, and never marry out of their own clan. The men hire themselves out as carriers, the women stay at home and work. It is supposed that as they have many Arabic words still in use, they are a remnant of the Moorish occupation left behind when Christian armies finally swept the Infidel back into the south. This may be so, for the Moors are past masters at caravan work, and the Maragatos are the great carriers of Spain. When on the road their strings of mules take precedence, and everything clears out of their way. The men dress in loose baggy knickers and the women attire themselves in short red or canary-coloured skirts with green or light blue lining, one pleat remains open and shows either of these colours. They wear white stockings, black shoes, and very gaily-coloured handkerchiefs cover their heads. On a Sunday they swarm into the town, going off in the evening at sundown to their different villages in picturesque chattering throngs. Twice a year the whole tribe assembles at the feasts of Corpus Christi and the Ascension, when they dance for an hour, el Cañizo, a dance which if an outsider dare join in is immediately stopped.

I had heard a great deal of the dignity of the Spaniard, before I went to Spain, and had failed to find that this reputation was at all justified, except in the case of the *Guardia Civil*, until I came across the Maragatos. I found them to be among

ASTORGA

the most self-respecting and courteous folk that one could meet anywhere; they certainly are amongst the most interesting of the many distinct tribes that people the Peninsula.

Astorga, the Asturia Augusta of the Romans, is described by Pliny as a "magnificent city." It was once the capital of southern Asturia and was always an important outpost fortress. As indicative of its strength I may mention that Astorga bears for arms a branch of oak.

Like Leon, the importance of its position as a base, both for those who lived in the mountains to the north and west, as well as for those who came from the plain, was always appreciated, and was for ever a bone of contention between the inhabitants of these districts. The Bishopric was founded in 747 by Alfonso el Catolico, but no man of note has ever been appointed to the See as far as I could discover. Indeed, Astorga is another of those old Spanish cities which are passed by in the train, with the remark—"How nice the old walls look, I do wish we had time to stop here."

A saunter round the walls I must own is very disappointing. It is so evident that but little veneration is felt, or respect shown, for any antiquities or historical associations. In many places they have been pulled about for the sake of the building materials they yielded. They are the

...the...
affords...
view is o...
Here, at any...
for the sake of...
women walk, in...

At the spot where...
deal of demolition has...
the huge new château-like...
now in process of erection,...
and detracts from the little...
in this corner of Astorga. ...
Spain. Besides its walls, Astorga...
its *mantecadas*, small square...
folded in pieces of greased paper,...
way all over this part of the...
farther off you find them the less...
the originals, and these are very good.

ZAMORA

TRAVELLING through the great plain of Leon by train is apt to become intensely monotonous, especially when, as in the case of reaching Zamora, fate decreed that I should sit baking for hours in the slowest of all, the undesirable *mercantilo*. Very few villages enlivened the yellow landscape, which bare of vegetation lay blistering under the midday sun; those that were visible were all *tapia* built with unglazed lights, and seemed to have grown outwards from the little brown-walled churches in their midst. On rising ground beyond the limits of these sad-looking hamlets, I could see the dwellings of the poorest of the poor. Dug out of the bank-sides, they resemble rabbit holes more than anything else. A door gives light, ventilation and access to the interior, a tiny chimney sticking out of the ground above carries off the extra fumes of smoke. Life inside must be nearer that of the beasts than that of any other race in Europe; and as the slow *mercantilo* crawled along I had plenty of time to note the stunted growth and wearied mien of those whose day of toil ends in these burrows

ZAMORA

one hour) became a proverb. It was at this siege that five Moorish sheiks brought the Cid tribute and saluted him as "Campeador."

There are more tangible remains of the quaint old city's importance to be found in its Cathedral and streets than its proverbs and anecdotes. Here is the house of Urraca, with an almost obliterated inscription over the gateway—"Afuera! Afuera! Rodrigo el soberbio Castellano"—culled from the ballad of the Cid, and referring to his exclusion from the place.

In the church of San Pedro y Ildefonso are a couple of fine bronze-gilt shrines containing the remains of SS. Ildefonso and Atilano. The Romanesque church of the Templars, La Magdalena, dates from the twelfth century. Its rose window is formed with small columns like the Temple Church in London; and within are some beautiful tombs.

The Hospital is a good building with an overhanging porch, very effectively coloured and having the appearance of glazed tiles. Many old houses of the nobility now slumber tranquilly in slow decay, and Zamora, like so many other Spanish towns of its class, seems left behind in the modern hurry of life; and this is one of its greatest charms, the charm that is so typical of old Spain.

CATHEDRAL CITIES OF SPAIN

The Cathedral abuts on to the city wall and is almost surrounded by a bare piece of ground where the remains of dismantled fortifications give a deserted and forlorn air to the very unecclesiastical aspect of the exterior. I made a sketch among these ruins and could not help feeling the result looked more like an Eastern farm enclosure than a really fine Cathedral. There was the huge unfinished square tower, baked a brilliant yellow, the *cimborio* and dome, with its eight curious little domes, all roofed in cement, and a copy of, if not contemporary with, the same in the old Cathedral of Salamanca; the low mud walls and almost flat roofs; a party of peasants in a sort of nomad encampment, innumerable fowls pecking at the dust—what more could you have to remind one of the East. The sun was broiling, and nothing disturbed this " bit " of the Spain of long ago.

The exterior of the Cathedral has been much marred by the poor Renaissance north façade, not visible in my drawing, and a tower with a slate roof. The south porch is, however, intact, and from it, for the building stands high above the Douro, the view must have been grand before the Bishop's Palace was built and obliterated the whole prospect. A dozen steps, narrowing as they approach the portal, lead up to the door which is surrounded by four good round arches with scroll mouldings

of simple design. Inside this I found myself in the south transept.

The interior, with the exception of that portion east of the crossing, which is poor Renaissance with perpendicular vaulting, is exceedingly massive. The nave is but twenty-five feet in width, the columns which support the bays are ten feet through; the aisles are very narrow, but so good are the proportions of all these that this miniature Cathedral is one of the finest Romanesque churches in the country.

The *cimborio* is round in plan with sixteen windows from which the ribs of the vaulting spring. Unfortunately the columns have been decorated with a spiral pattern of a chocolate colour, quite destroying the beauty and simple grandeur of a feature which for simplicity ranks next to that of the Catedral Vieja at Salamanca.

In the Capilla del Cardenal at the west end of the nave is a very fine *retablo* divided into six panels painted by Gallegos, whose signature is on the central one. I was examining this one morning when an old priest passed through into the adjoining sacristy. He stopped and explained the subjects to me, taking particular interest in this when he learnt I was a painter and what my mission to Zamora was. I cannot forget his courtesy and pride while showing me some of the treasures the Cathedral possesses, and shared his regret that the wonderful tapestries were only on view at certain festivals. In this chapel are some good tombs of the great Romero family, others too of interest are in the Capilla de San Miguel, and the finest of all that of Canon Juan de Grado has the genealogy of the Virgin sculptured above the effigy of the Canon. I was very grateful for the seats which here are available for a rest and quiet examination of the church. In Burgos is the only other Cathedral where it is possible to sit and gaze.

LEON

SITUATED on the edge of the great plain which stretches away south to the Sierra de Gredos and beyond to Toledo, Leon served as a sort of buffer town between the Highlanders of the north and the dwellers on the Castilian uplands.

The headquarters of the seventh Roman Legion, from which the name is derived, it may be described as a great fortress of bygone days. Astorga, some thirty miles westwards, being an outpost in that direction no doubt helped to preserve Leon from the ravages of the Galician Visigoths.

The Romans held their fortress for five hundred years until Leovigild in 586 captured it after a long and strenuous siege. So highly was the position and strength of these two towns appreciated, that when Witiza, the King of the Goths, issued a decree levelling all defensive works to the ground, they were exempted and their fortifications preserved.

The Moors held Leon for a very short spell, and then only as a defence against northern invasion. When Ordoño I. descended from his mountain fastnesses and drove them out, Leon changed front with its new occupants, and became a stronghold to be held at all costs against invaders from the south.

The great Almanzor, in his victorious march north with the soldiery of Cordova, swept away all opposition and this buffer town was sacked. However, after his defeat at Calatanavor and subsequent death, the banner of Christ was once more unfurled to the breeze from what little was left of its walls.

These were almost entirely rebuilt of *tapia* and cob-stones by Alfonso V., since whose time they have remained or slowly fallen away.

Leon stands in a verdant pasture valley intersected by many streams and shady roads lined with tall poplars. The fields on either side are divided from one another by hedges and willow trees, thick scrub follows the streams and grows down to the water edge, and walking in these pleasant places it was not difficult to imagine myself back in England. The city itself is really little better than a big village, and considering the important part it has played in the history Spain, seems sadly neglected and left out in the cold. This, too, despite the fact that it is an important junction and railway centre. There are no buildings of any present importance, and those that once could lay claim to this are in a state of decay. It is only on Sundays and market days, when the peasants in picturesque costume and gay colours come in, that Leon can boast of the smallest animation. I remember one Sabbath evening as I stood on my balcony, that vantage ground from which one sees all the life of the place pass by in the street below, watching the folk parade up and down. A military band discoursed " brassy " music, the crowd was packed as tight as sardines in a tin, when suddenly the " toot, toot " of a motor horn was heard above the clash of cymbals and boom of the drum. A large car came down a by-street opposite, turned sharply and charged the crowd. The Spaniard is of an excitable temperament, loud cries of disapproval, and screams from the gentler sex drowned all else. The chauffeur discovered his mistake none too soon and attempted to turn the car. At this the uproar grew louder and he brought it to a standstill. Youths climbed the steps, boys hung on behind, " Toot, toot " went the horn ; the bandmaster, with an eye to the situation, waved his *bâton* more energetically than ever, the big drum boomed, the trombones blurted out for all they were worth, but the hooting and whistling drowned everything.

At last the car began to back and became disengaged, the chauffeur adroitly turned, and started down the street followed by the noisier elements of the crowd eventually pulling up at a café, just out of the parade zone. In Leon as

CATHEDRAL CITIES OF SPAIN

elsewhere, fashion dictates a limit to the speed in either direction and the chauffeur had not gone beyond this. The two occupants of the car got out in a very unconcerned manner, sat down at a café and ordered a drink. For at least a quarter of an hour, while these two were taking their coffee, the crowd stood round booing, whistling and shouting. I do not think I have ever seen anything cooler than the way in which, their thirst satisfied, and the account settled, they got up and walked slowly after the car which long ago had disappeared out of danger.

By this time, despite the presence of a couple of the *Guardia Civil*, the crowd was excited. A cart full of peasant folk next essayed the perils of the thoroughfare, they however got through safely after much badinage and fun. No sooner had they gone, the band meantime had vanished, when out from a wine shop came some peasants with castanets a little light-headed for once. There were four of them, two men and two women. They immediately began a dance on the pavement. A ring was formed and a storm of hand-clapping encouraged them, for ten minutes they footed it admirably. More castanets appeared from somewhere and soon half Leon was dancing in the middle of the Calle. The feeble-looking policemen, who had been terribly worried over the motor-car incident, thrust

LEON. THE CATHEDRAL

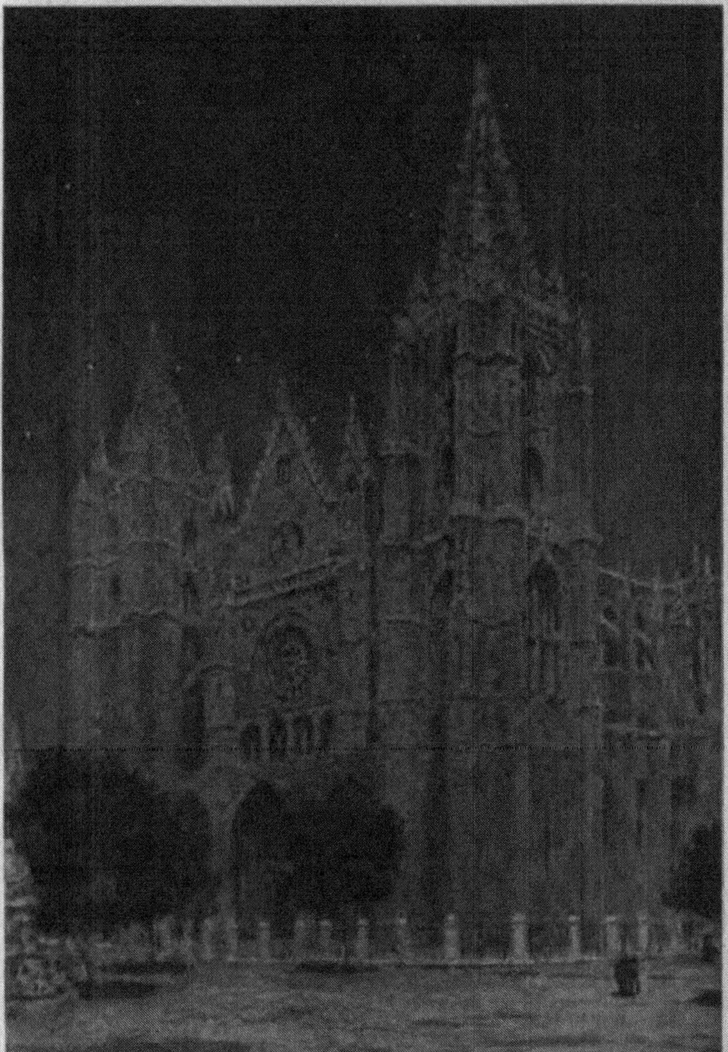

out their chests, or tried to, and beamed all over. The scene had changed from what had first looked very much like an ugly row, to one of pure enjoyment, they were safe, every one else was out of danger, and Leon too was saved.

The night I arrived in Leon, having finished dinner, I left the hotel and taking the first turn haphazard wandered up the street. The electric lights were soon behind me and I found myself in what seemed to be a huge deserted square. The dark night was lit by milliards of twinkling stars, and gazing upwards at them my eye followed the line of what appeared to be immensely tall poplar trees. I looked again, I had never seen trees that colour, then it slowly dawned on me that I was in front of the great Cathedral. Slowly, slowly as my eye became accustomed to the dark I made out tapering spires that met the very stars themselves embedded in the purple-blue sky, an infinitude of pinnacles, with a wonderful building beneath. The mystery of a beautiful night conjures up all that is best in this country. Squalor and dirt are hidden; one's thoughts take flight and wander back to the Spain of old, the glorious Spain of bygone days. At moments like this I certainly would never have been surprised to hear the clatter of hoofs and see a band of knights with pennons flying and armour glinting appear suddenly in the semi-darkness.

CATHEDRAL CITIES OF SPAIN

Well, the days of chivalry have gone but the romance of a starry night will never die.

The next morning I returned eager to discover what my impressions would unfold. Much to my delight I found the restoration of the Cathedral, which I knew was in progress, so far finished that not a single scaffold pole, nor any rubbish heaps of old stones were anywhere to be seen. Extremely well have the designs of Señor Don Juan Madrazo been carried out, and the Cathedral to-day stands a magnificent church and grand monument of Christianity.

Santa Maria de Regla is the third Cathedral which has existed in Leon. The site of the first is supposed to have been outside the city walls. The second was built where once stood the Palace of Ordoño II., and this had been raised on ground occupied by Roman baths.

The present edifice was founded in 1190 by Bishop Manrique de Lara, a scion of a great family which was always in revolt, but was not completed until the early part of the fourteenth century.

With Toledo and Burgos, Leon's Cathedral forms the group of three great churches that are distinctly French, and closely resemble Amiens and Rheims. It would be difficult to find another building the interior of which exceeded the colour elegance and grace of this airy structure.

LEON. THE WEST PORCH OF THE CATHEDRAL.

a figure of San Froilan, at one time Bishop of Leon.

A beautiful balustrade follows the sky-line of the whole Cathedral. This is broken by many pinnacles, some of which are spiral, with others on the façades and finishing the supports of the flying buttresses, give the exterior a resemblance to a forest of small spires.

The interior is a marvel of beauty and lightness. The nave and aisles consist of six bays, no lateral chapels disfigure the latter with chirrigueresque atrocities. The triforium runs round the whole Cathedral. So cleverly has the spacing here been arranged, that with the clerestory it makes one magnificent panel of gorgeous light. The windows of this, forty feet high, were at one time blocked up for safety. They now contain stained glass, and soar upwards to the vaulting of the roof. Every window in the Cathedral is coloured and the effect as the sun streams through can well be imagined.

No flamboyant *retablo* spoils the simplicity of the east end, the place of what might have been a jarring note amidst the Gothic work being taken by good paintings in flat gilded frames. It was Señor Madrazo's idea to remove the *coro* from the centre of the nave, and had this been done Santa Maria de Regla would have gained immensely.

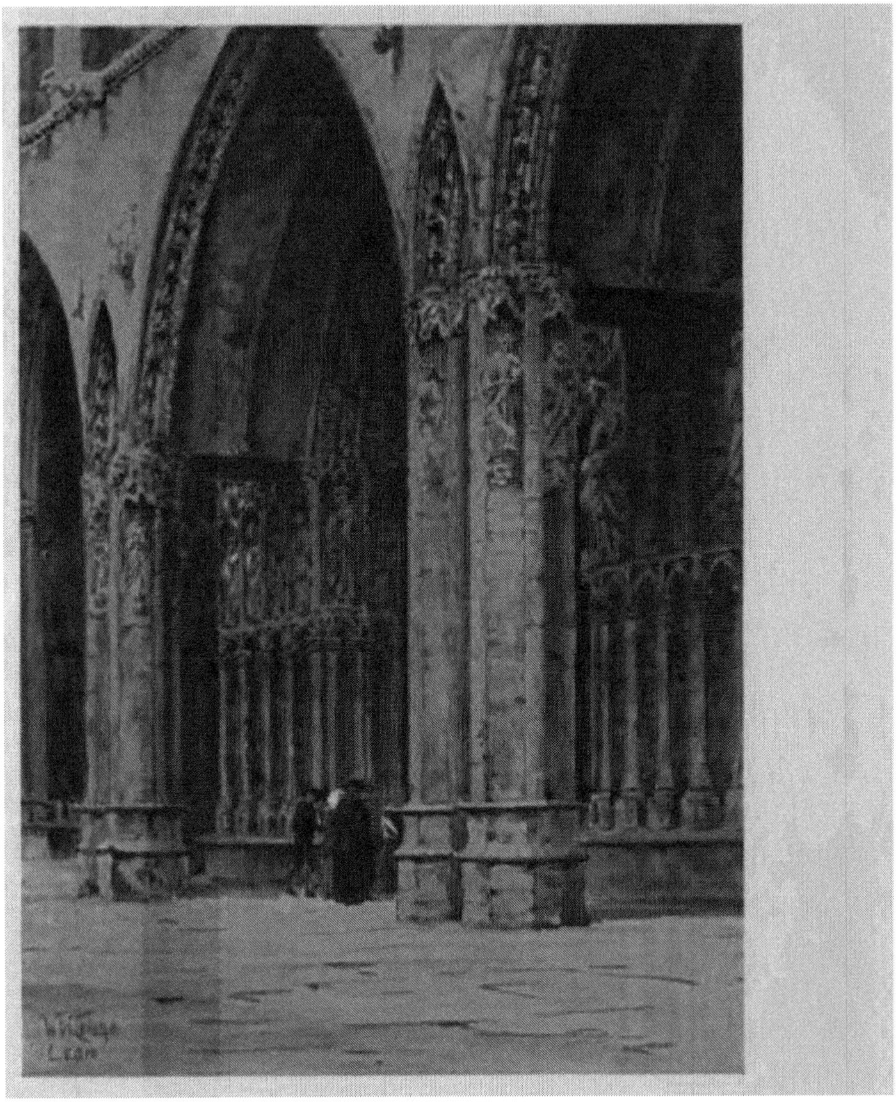

LEON

The west porch is the finest Gothic specimen of its kind which exists in Spain and recalls those of Notre Dame de Paris and the Cathedral at Chartres. Three archways are supported by cloistered columns to which are attached figures under beautiful canopies. The archivolts and tympanum are covered with sculpture representing the Reward of the Just and Unjust, the Nativity, Adoration, Flight in Egypt, and Massacre of the Innocents. All are extremely interesting, many of the figures being in contemporary costume. Two grand towers flank the west façade, of which the north is the older and some thirty feet less in height than its neighbour. Both are surmounted by spires, that of the south being an excellent example of open filigree work, rivalling those at Burgos and very much better than that of Oviedo.

Between these towers and above the porch is a pediment with spires and a glorious wheel window, underneath which is a row of windows that corresponds to the triforium. This portion is part of the late restoration.

The south porch also has three arches, which have been well renovated. The centre one alone has a door to admit into the interior, it is double and surrounded by figures in the archivolt with reliefs in the tympanum. On the centre column is

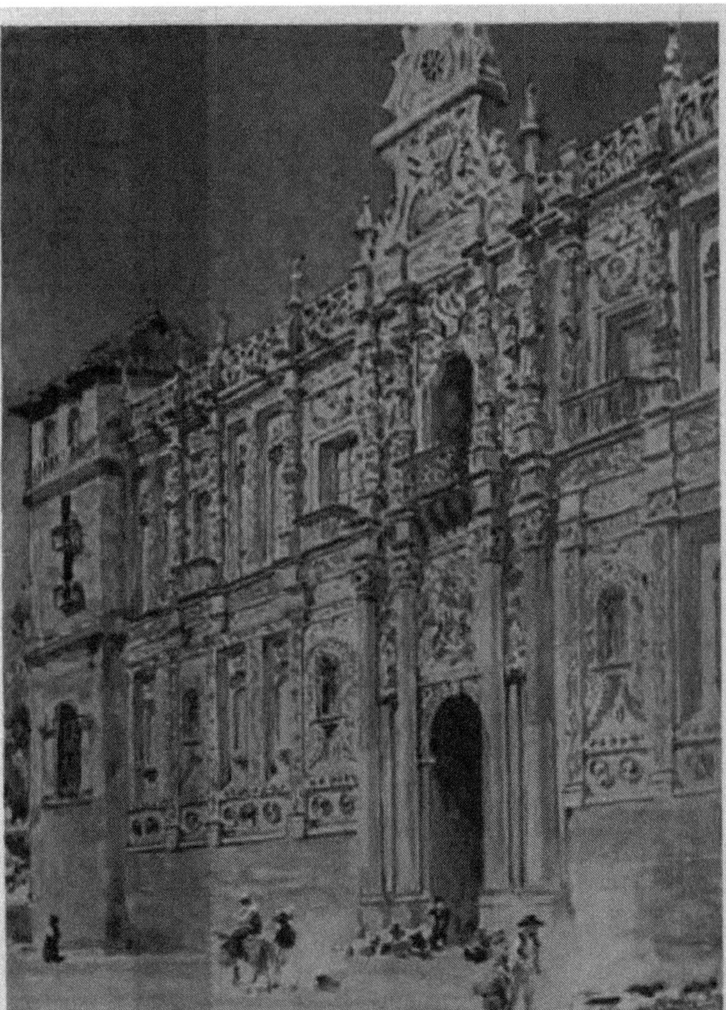

LEON

In the Panteon, a small low chapel at the west end, lie buried the Kings and Queens and other royalties of Leon. The columns are very massive with heavy capitals; the ceiling is adorned with early frescoes which happily escaped the depredations of the French, they are crude, but the colour adds to the impressiveness of this gloomy abode of the Dead. Representing scenes from the Lives of our Lord and His Apostles, with signs of the Zodiac and months of the year, they date from 1180. The whole convent is replete with mural paintings, and before Soult sacked it contained many extremely interesting and rare missals of the seventh and eighth centuries.

Unique is another convent, that of San Marcos, which stands on the river bank outside the city on the road to Astorga. Founded as a chapel in 1168 for the knights of Santiago, it was rebuilt in 1514-49 by Juan de Badajos, and is certainly his masterpiece. It would be difficult to find a façade of greater beauty than this marvel of plateresque work. The remarkable pink and golden colour of the stone, intensified against the background of a deep blue sky, the delicacy of the carving in which angels and cherubs, griffons and monsters intermingle with floral wreaths and branches of fruit in orderly confusion, the elegant pillars and pilasters, all so truly Spanish under the blazing sun,

CATHEDRAL CITIES OF SPAIN

fascinated me immensely as time after time I turned to wonder and admire.

Here again I could conjure up the past, the romance of Spain's greatest Order; well housed were those knights of old in their glorious Hospice, and now—the river still runs under the walls of what afterwards became a convent, its banks are lined with tall poplars, far away rise the mountains of the north in rugged outline just as they did of yore—and San Marcos? Alas! half is a museum and the rest a barrack. A forlorn air pervades the place, the old garden wants tending, and despite the life of the military, I could not help sighing once again, as I have so often sighed in Spain —" How are the mighty fallen!"

OVIEDO

OVIEDO, seldom visited by the foreigner, lies well situated on rising ground in a fine open valley. Grand mountains surround and hem it in on the east, south and west, to the north the country undulates until it reaches the Biscay coast twenty odd miles away. These natural barriers gather the clouds and the climate is humid; on an average there are but sixty cloudless days in the year. While I was in Oviedo it rained almost incessantly, and the " clang of the wooden shoon" kept the streets lively with a clattering "click-clack." All the poorer classes wear sabots in wet weather, sabots that are pegged on the soles, difficult to walk in, but kept well out of the mud and puddles by these pegs. This particular make is common to Asturias, just as the ordinary French shape is to Galicia.

Oviedo is one of Spain's university cities, and I happened to strike the week when the festivities in celebration of its tercentenary were in progress. Wet weather and pouring rain never damp the ardour of the Spaniard during a *fiesta*, and despite

CATHEDRAL CITIES OF

the rain, powder was kept dry somehow, and enthusiasm vented itself regularly up to o'clock every night by terrific explosions. tions of some sort seemed to be going on long. Societies from the country paraded streets, led by music, in most cases bagpipes drum, and Oviedo was evidently "doing proud."

I happened on a ceremony in the Cathedral one morning. The bishop was preaching to immense crowd when I entered. Seated in the nave were the Professors of the University, Doctors of Law and Medicine, the Military Governor and his Staff, the Alcalde and Town Councillors, besides representatives from the universities of every European country, except, strangely enough, Germany, and one from Harvard, the first to attend a function of this sort since the war. It was a really wonderful sight, for the Cathedral is not marred by a *coro* in the nave. The hues of the many-coloured robes, from canary yellow and scarlet to cerulean blue and black, the vast throng literally filling every available bit of space, even on to the pulpit steps, gave me a subject for my brush, and I surreptitiously made a hasty sketch, to be finished afterwards in my room.

The Cathedral was founded by Fruela in 781, and enlarged in 802 by Alfonso the Chaste, who

OVIEDO. IN THE CATHEDRAL

[illegible]

[illegible]

[illegible] the [illegible]

[illegible]

[illegible]

[illegible] Community, [illegible]

[illegible]

[illegible] hers, [illegible]

[illegible]

[illegible]

[illegible] fro[illegible]

[illegible]

[illegible] cathedra[illegible]

[illegible]

[illegible]

[illegible] through [illegible]

[illegible]

[illegible]

[illegible] in [illegible]

[illegible]

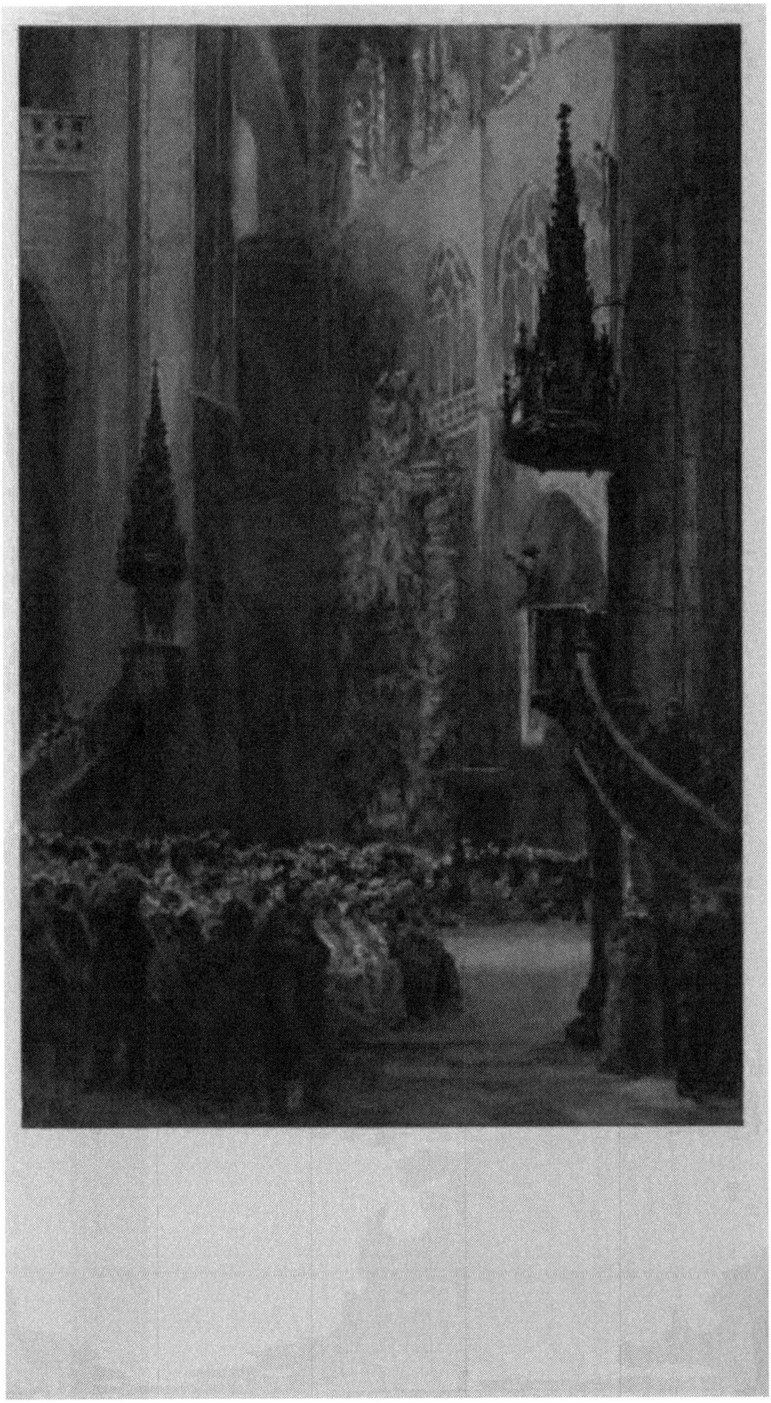

OVIEDO

made Oviedo the capital of Asturias, and with his Court resided here. He created the See in 810. The present edifice was begun by Bishop Gutierrez of Toledo in 1388, and the tower added by Cardinal Mendoza in 1528.

Hedged in, although fronting on to a little *plaza*, the grand west façade with its beautiful porch can hardly be said to be visible. This lofty portico of richly ornamented Gothic, under the shelter of which the gossips parade to and fro, leads into the Cathedral and stands thrust out and between the two towers. Only one of these towers is completed, and it is surmounted by a good openwork spire the top of which rises two hundred and seventy feet from the ground.

I wandered about hopelessly trying to gain some idea of the exterior of the Cathedral and found that it was only by walking outside the city that anything at all can be seen of it, and then the towers and roof of the nave, with the flying buttresses attached, were the only features that came into view.

The entrance by the south door leads through a dark passage, in which many votive offerings hang over a tiny shrine where burnt a little flickering lamp; going in I found myself at the spot from which I had made my sketch the previous day. What a relief it was to find no *coro* blocking up the nave! The eye could wander over the whole of this lofty interior—could follow the beautiful open work of the triforium and rest on the stained glass of the clerestory windows. The aisles are very shadowy, all the light being concentrated in the nave and the crossing, and the vision, with a great sense of good effect, is led up to the white tabernacle on the High Altar and the immense *retablo* beyond. A little theatrical if you like, but it is business, and the Church understands this so well.

Among the chapels, good, bad and indifferent, is one containing a gorgeous silver-gilt shrine wherein rests the body of Santa Eulalia, Oviedo's patroness. In another, tucked away behind the north transept, the Capilla del Rey Casto, lies buried Alfonso the Chaste who did so much for the city. Six niches in the walls contain stone coffins, which are supposed to hold the remains of Fruela I., Urraca, wife of Ramiro I., Alfonso el Católico, Ramiro, and Ordoño I. The bodies of these royalties at one time lay here, and a modern inscription on a mural tablet relates how they were removed, but not how their tombs were destroyed. Many other kings and princes we are told by this tablet also lie here, and as there are but half a dozen coffins their bones must be *bien mélangé*.

There are the usual overdone chirriguerésque altars which do their best to mar this imposing church, though I am glad to say they hardly succeed. From them, however, it was a relief to be taken by a very intelligent verger up the winding stairs which led to the Cámara Santa.

This is by far the most interesting portion of the Cathedral. Built by Alfonso in 802 to hold the sacred relics brought hither from Toledo at the time of the Moorish invasion, it stands above a vaulted basement; the reason for this arrangement evidently being the damp climate, and the wish to keep so holy a charge free from moisture. The chapel is divided into two parts. The inner, of very small dimensions, has a low barrel vaulting borne by arches with primitive twelfth-century figures. The *sanctum sanctorum* is slightly raised, and from this inmost Holy of Holies the relics are shown to the devout who kneel in front of a low railing every day at 8.30 A.M. and 3.30 P.M. The cedar wood *arca* in which they are kept is of Byzantine workmanship. The relics include some of Mary Magdalene's hair, and crumbs left over from the feeding of the five thousand.

The outer chamber of the chapel has a finely-groined roof, attached to the columns supporting which are statues of the twelve apostles. The richly-tesselated pavement resembles the Norman-Byzantine work of Sicily, and was not uncommon in Spain prior to the thirteenth century.

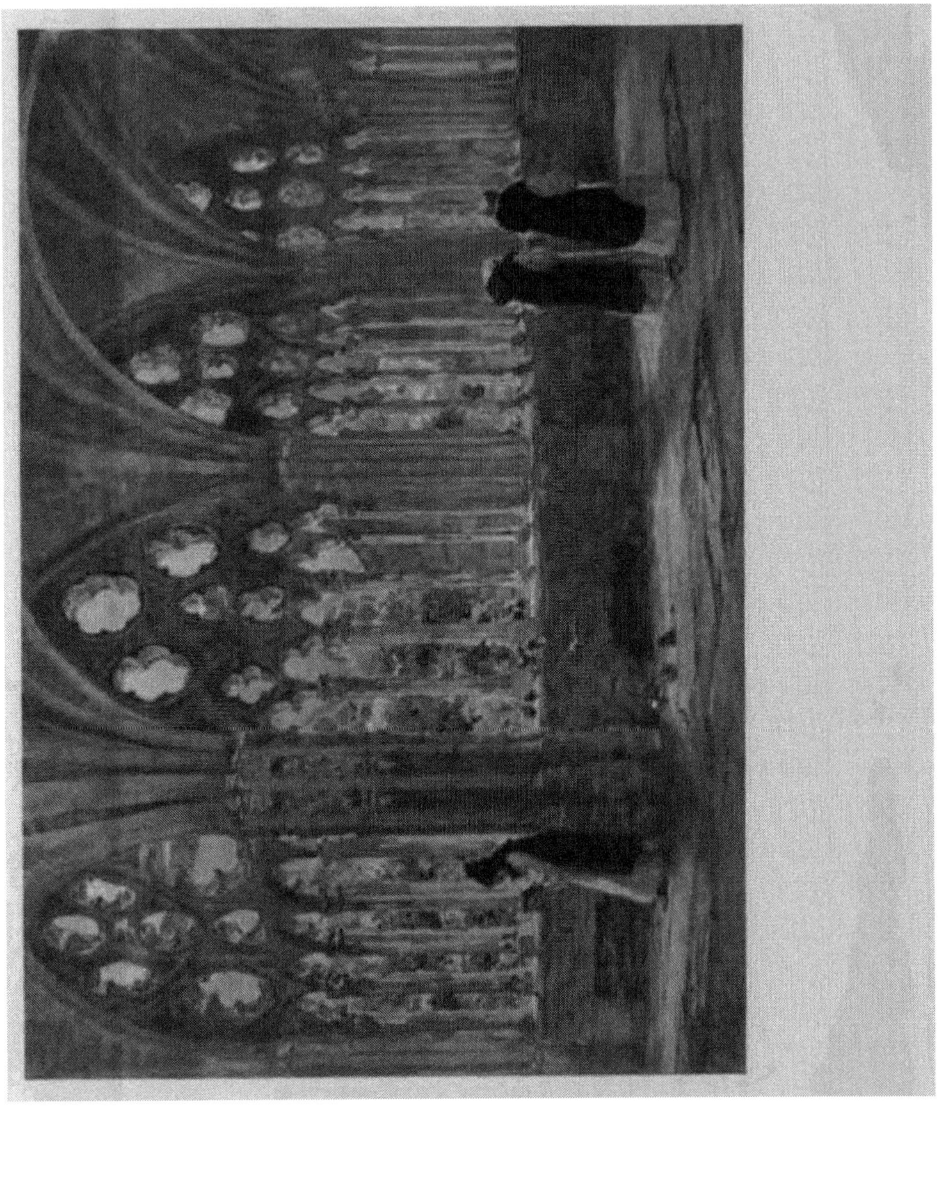

some of those I know. The capitals of the columns are well carved with prophets and saints under canopies, angels and angels' heads, grotesques and good floral cutting; while into the walls beneath them and round the arcades are let many tombs and gravestones brought here from different ruined or desecrated churches.

I went off one morning to see the earliest Christian church in the country. Braving the rain I tramped through mud ankle-deep for an hour up the hill slopes westward. It was a case of two steps forward and one back, but the spirit of the tourist was on me. I could not leave Oviedo and acknowledge I had not been to Naranco. I was desperate and I got there. What a charming out-of-the-way spot it is! Hidden behind a grove of ancient chestnut trees, under the brow of the mountain, stands Santa Maria.

A triple arched porch at the top of a dozen steps gives entrance on the north side to this minute and primitive place of worship. I entered and found myself in a barrel-vaulted parallelogram, with a curious arcade running round the walls. The west end is raised three steps above the nave, from which it is cut off by three arches ten feet high at the centre. The east end also has this feature, but the floor is level with the nave. All the columns in the church are of twisted cable design

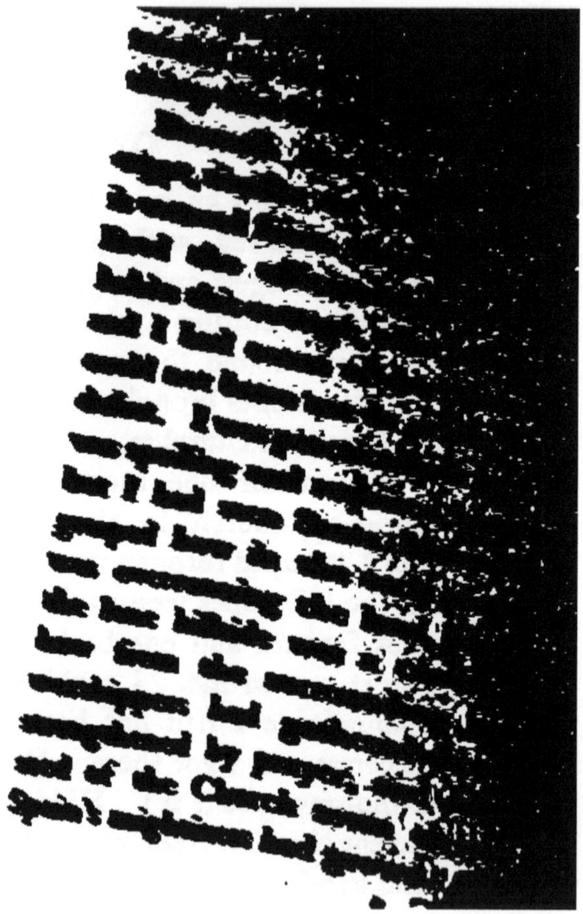
and of the Church
Spain's neighbours had

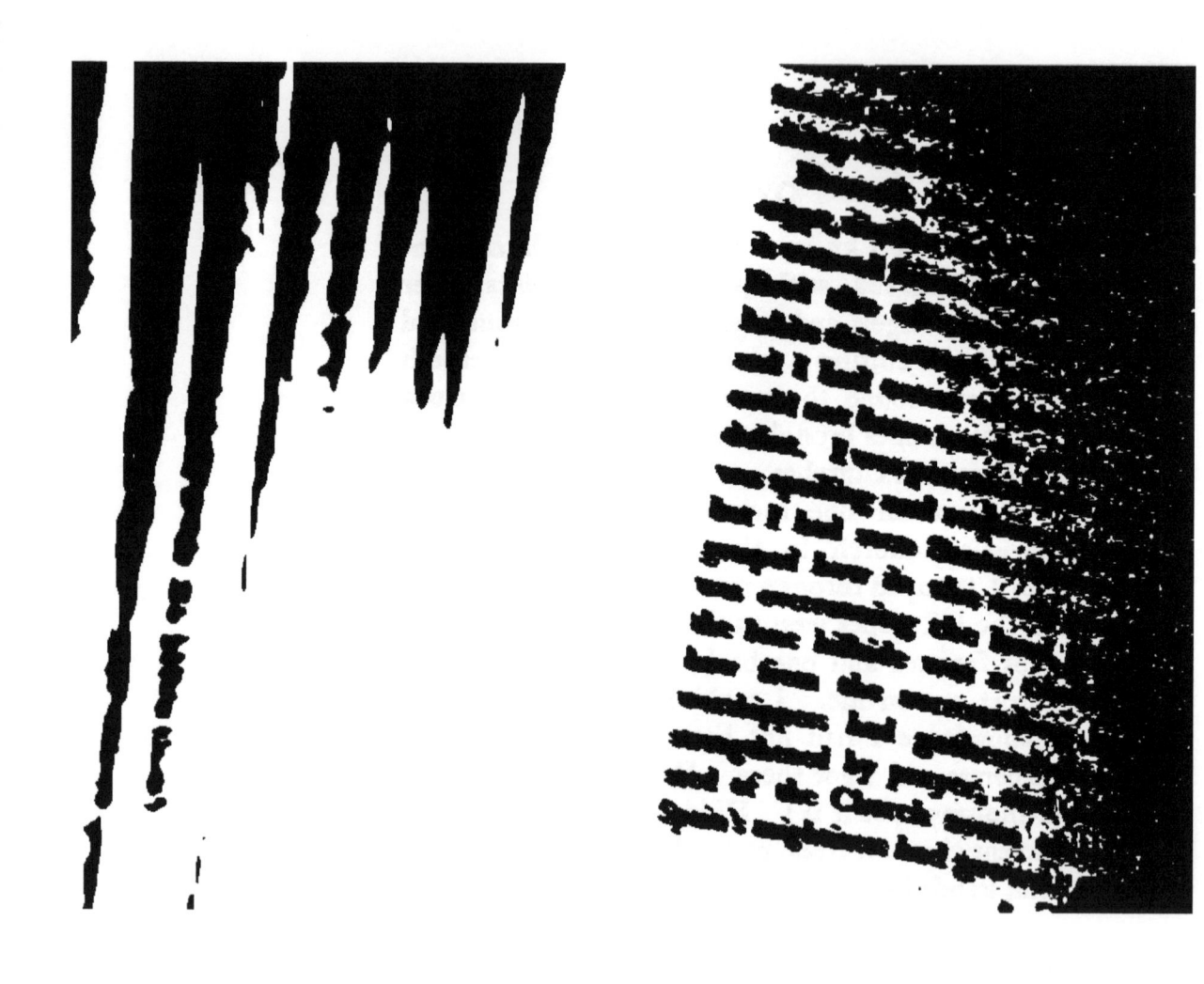

VALLADOLID

FOR nearly one hundred and fifty years, from the reign of Juan II., 1454, to Philip II., 1598, Valladolid was a royal city and the capital of Castile. It lies on the plain through which the river Pisuerga meanders, just touching the outskirts of the city on the western side. In the Moorish days Valladolid was known as Belad al Wali, "The Town of the Governor," and flourished as a great agricultural centre. It is still the focus of the corn trade of Old Castile. It was here that Prince Ferdinand, despite attempts on the part of his father Juan II. to frustrate it, was introduced to Isabella the reigning Queen of Castile and Leon. Many suitors had proposed themselves and paid their addresses to this paragon among women, but possessing a will of her own she made her choice and selected the Prince whom she married on October 19, 1469.

Valladolid suffered more severely at the hands of the French than any other city of Spain. They demolished most of the good houses and despoiled the churches; among those that are left, however,

I found plenty to interest me and to make a stay, after I had discovered them, well worth the while.

I made a sketch of Santa Maria la Antigua, which is the most interesting edifice in the place. The fine Romanesque tower is surmounted by a tiled steeple which recalls Lombardy, and although many additions have been made to the original fabric the whole building piles up very well, the early Gothic east end being particularly beautiful. This church dates from the twelfth century, but the greater part of it is pure Gothic. The roof is richly groined; there are three parallel apses, and the *coro* is at the west end—an always welcome place to find it. The *retablo* by Juan de Juni, whose work is scattered throughout the churches of Valladolid, is fine though over-elaborate.

Another good church is San Pablo, partly rebuilt by the great Cardinal Torquemada, whose name will for ever be associated with the terrors of the Inquisition. I found another subject for my brush in its very intricate late Gothic west façade. The upper part of this contains the arms of the Catholic Kings, below which on either side are those of the Duque de Lerma. The niches are luckily all filled with their original figures, and the wonderful tracery of the round window is also in good preservation. The grey finials are weather-worn and contrast well with the rich yellow and

VALLADOLID. SANTA MARIA LA ANTIGUA

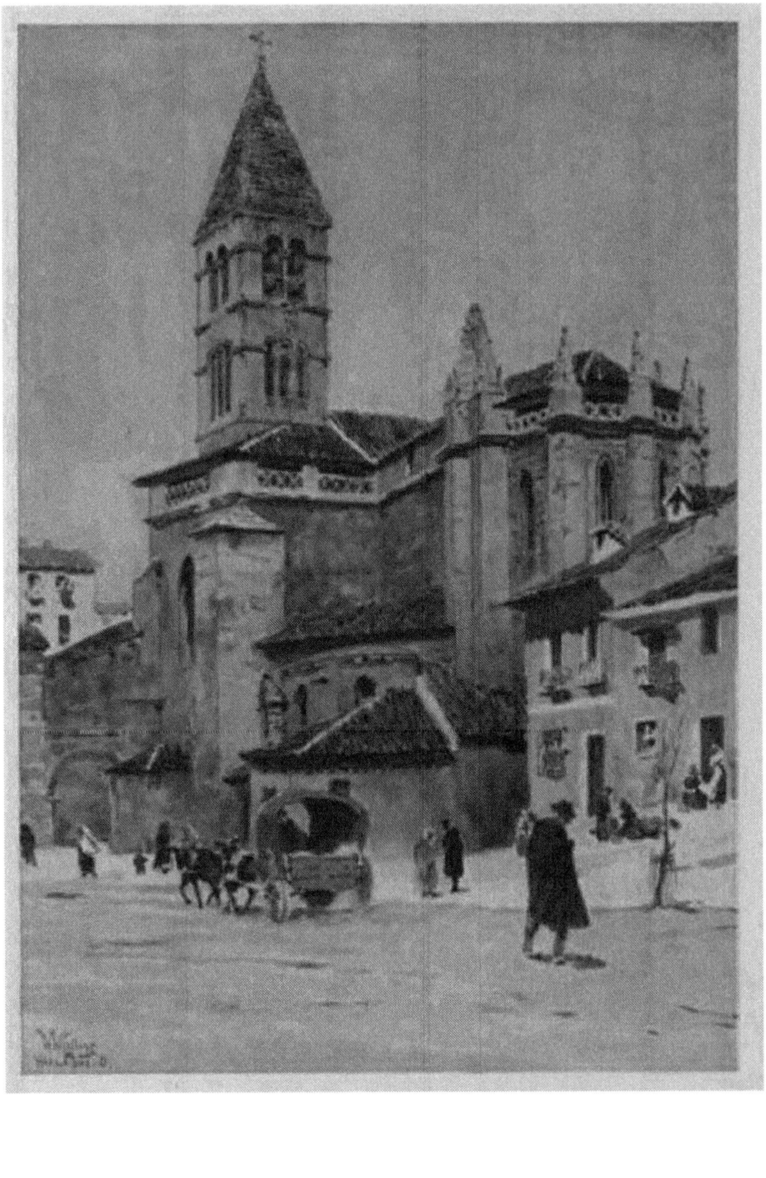

VALLADOLID

pink of the rest of the front, a façade which is absolutely crammed with intricate design. Two hideous towers of later date and of the same stone as that with which the Cathedral is built, flank this and detract unfortunately from one of the best examples of late Gothic work in the country.

Hard by, up the street pictured in my sketch, stands the Colegiata de San Gregorio, with an equally fine façade, though being an earlier Gothic it is more severe in type. The doorway of this is surmounted by a genealogical tree and the arms of Ferdinand and Isabella. Some of the figures of rough hairy men with cudgels are very primitive. San Gregorio was a foundation of Cardinal Ximenes, it is now used as municipal offices. Passing through the doorway I entered a beautiful little court, rather dark, but with sufficient light to enable me to appreciate the good artesonade ceiling of its cloisters. The second court is a blaze of light. Spiral fluted columns form the cloister, the ceiling of which is picked out in a cerulean blue and white; they support a recently restored gallery, a mixture of Moorish, Romanesque and plateresque work, into which the sheaves and yoke of the Catholic Kings is introduced as at Granada and Santiago, making a very effective whole. A fine old stone stairway leads from this court up to what in the old collegiate days was a library.

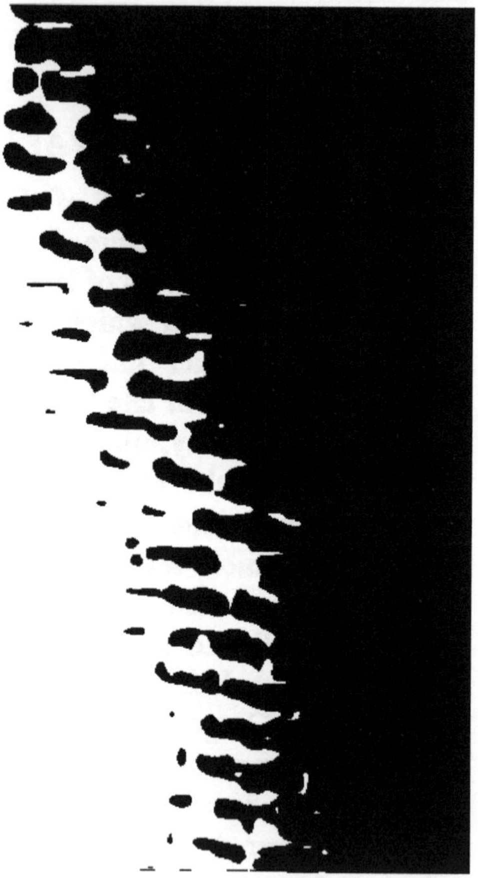

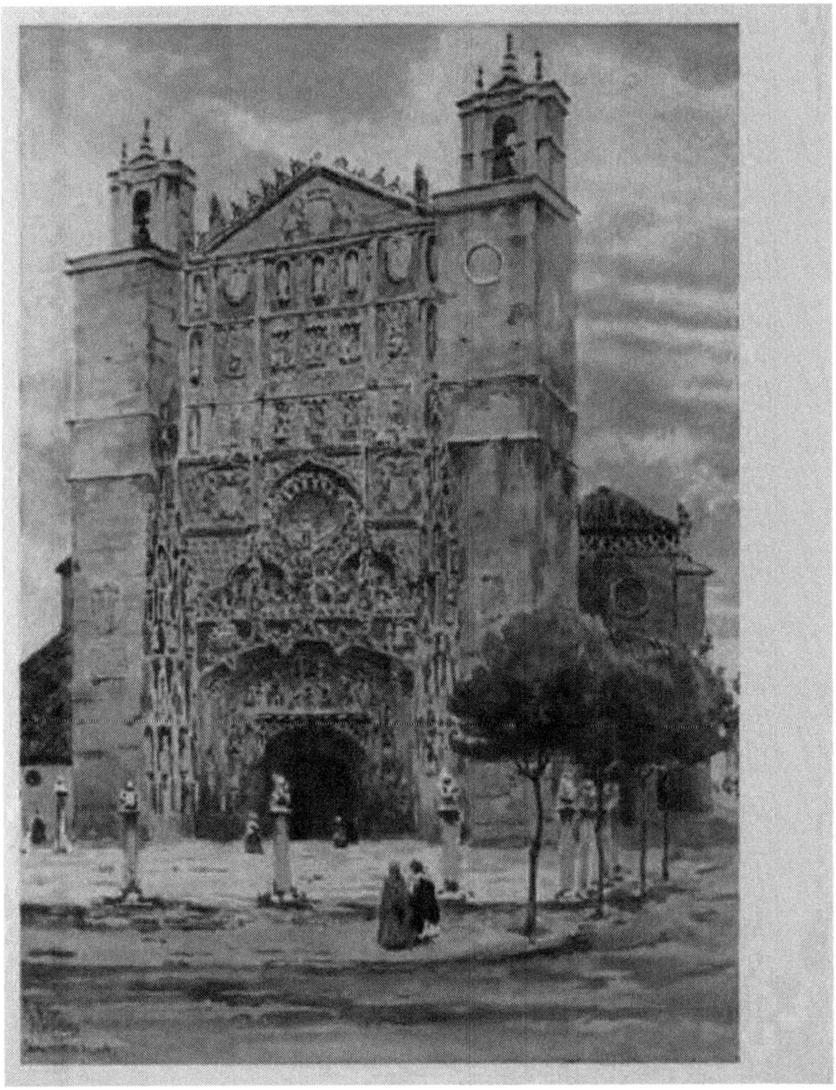

Hernandez and Juan de Juni can be examined here at leisure. Some of the life-size carved wooden figures of the last named, formerly used on the processional cars which parade the streets at certain festivals, are remarkable more from the extravagant attitudes of the figures than from their artistic merit. The custodian who accompanied me was a pleasant fellow, and evinced surprise that a *pintor* could not see the beauties he pointed out. I fear he thought little of my artistic discrimination; especially when in the Sala de Juntas he invited me to ascend a pulpit over which hung a large crucifix, and with fervour solicited my admiration of the face of Christ, on which was a most agonised look, "cheap" and quite according to academic rules. "No, no, it is bad." "But, señor, He suffers." I could not make him understand that acute suffering need not be so painfully apparent.

In this Sala are placed the whole of the *silleria de coro* from the church of San Benito. Arranged on either side of the room they give it a superb effect. At the far end are the red velvet-covered chairs of Spanish Chippendale used by the Council of the Academy of Arts at their meetings. Beyond them, on a raised platform, are the two bronze-gilt kneeling figures of the Duke and Duchess de Lerma. A few pictures hang on the walls and other treasures and relics [...] this fine Sala an ideal council cham[ber ...] academicians.

Of the hundreds of carved figures in [...] those by Berruguete, very Greek in type, fla[t] and straight nose, are artistically by far [the ...] though the "Death of our Lord," a [...] composition by Hernandez, follows not far beh[ind]. Just as Madrid contains the finest armoury in [the] world, I doubt if any other museum can comp[are] with Valladolid's for figures and composition[s in] carved wood.

The University holds at present a high ran[k], most of its professors being progressive. Th[e] building itself is a chirrigueresque concern of th[e] seventeenth century with a very extravagan[t] façade. It possesses a good library which is get-at-able, and not like others belonging to th[e] church which are very difficult of access. A propos of this one of the professors here told me the following hardly credible experience of a friend of his, whom I will call A.

There is a movement at present in Spain to catalogue some at least of the many thousands of priceless historical Arabic documents and MSS. which, hidden away in Cathedral and other libraries, would throw invaluable light on the history of early times if they could be examined. A. is

VALLADOLID

engaged in trying to compile this catalogue, and, hearing that in a certain Cathedral city—not Valladolid— the Cathedral library contained some treasures of Arabic lore, procured an introduction to the bishop, and requested permission to search the archives of the diocese.

Explaining that he was unable to help in the matter, the bishop sent A. to the chapter authorities. The basis of their refusal was that any MS. if taken down from its shelf might be injured, and if once taken down might not be replaced in the same position! "Yes, they certainly possessed many supposed Arabic documents, but as none had been disturbed in living memory, why take the trouble to make a catalogue? Surely this would be superfluous, the books were there no doubt, A. could see them in their shelves, the librarian would be happy to show them, but no, they could not be taken down."

In the library of the Escorial the books are all placed with their titles against the wall and their edges turned towards the spectator, so that no vulgar touch could defame them by reading. Small wonder that the Progressists of Spain shrug their shoulders sometimes at the many petty obstacles encountered in their attempts to better their country, and regard it as an almost hopeless task.

Two foreign colleges are situated in Valladolid,

the Scotch and the English. The [first]
was founded by Colonel Semple [who]
removed hither in 1771, the second by [Sir Francis]
Englefield, who came to Spain after the [death]
of Mary Queen of Scots. They are both [used]
for the education of young priests and [the]
Irish College in Salamanca complete the [trio].

The focus of the city's life is in the Plaza [Mayor,]
a fine square where the first *auto de fé*, [which]
Philip II. and his court witnessed, took place [in]
October 1559. It was here also that Alvaro [de]
Luna was executed, after faithfully serving [his]
King, Juan II., for thirty years. Spain thereby [lost]
the strong will and the arm which enforced [it,]
and which out of chaos had brought the country
into a semblance of order by quelling the turbulent
nobles. Such has been in the past the fickleness
of Spain's rulers that not one of the great men
who have served their country, with perhaps the exception of General Prim, and he died a disappointed
man, has ever ended his life in peace and quiet.
They have nearly all died at the stake, on the
scaffold, or been foully murdered.

The much dilapidated house in a narrow street
where Columbus died is fast falling into ruin, but
that in the Calle de Rastro, where Cervantes lived
and wrote the first part of Don Quixote, is in better
condition.

BURGOS

UNLIKE most folk who enter the country from the north, I left Burgos for the end of my last visit to Spain, and found it in a way not unlike Cadiz, the first place I arrived at. They are both clean cities—for Spain; the streets in both are narrow, and the houses tall with double-glazed balconies. There is but little traffic in either, the squares in both are numerous, but the resemblance stops at this. The streets of Burgos run east and west in lines more or less parallel with the river Arlanzón. They are draughty and cold. The city stands 2785 feet above sea level and the winds sweep down from the distant sierra in bitter blasts. The life of Burgos is eminently ecclesiastical with a large sprinkling of the military element, for here all three branches of the service are quartered. It is a quiet place and I worked in peace unmolested.

What a pity the builders of the great Cathedral could not find another site whereon to erect their wonderful church. How much better it would have looked if placed on the flat ground near the

river than on the spot where a [...]
Gonzalez once stood. However, [...]
mountains and I was perforce obliged [...]
easel on the slope of the hill and paint [...]
view from in front of the west façade.

In 1075 Alfonso VI. moved the Arch[...]
See from Oca to Burgos and gave the [...]
royal palace for its erection. The present [...]
was founded in 1221 by Ferdinand el Santo [...]
occasion of his marriage with Beatrice of [...]
who in her train brought the Englishman, [...]
Maurice. Employing a French architect, M[...]
was more or less responsible for the [...]
building, though another foreigner, John [...]
Cologne, added the beautiful open work spires [...]
their parapets to the towers of the west end. [...]
is curious that this, the most richly [...]
Cathedral in the country, should be the outcome [...]
patronage of the foreigner, though at the same
time it is the most Spanish of the three "foreign"
Cathedrals. So rich is this magnificent Church
in every style of architectural decoration that it
would take a lifetime to know it thoroughly.

John of Cologne's beautiful spires are better than
those at Leon and Oviedo, and rise with the towers
that support them to a height close on 300 ft.
The gorgeous central lantern, with its twelve
traceried pinnacles, the grace of those that sur-

mount the Constable's Chapel, the many, many others that break the skyline and adorn this glorious fabric, all go to make it a building that, despite the different styles employed, will be a wonder and a joy as long as man's handiwork lasts.

The lower portion of the west front was renewed in 1790. The Puerta Principal in the centre is flanked by two small doors, with reliefs of the Conception and Crowning of the Virgin, while the chief door has four statues of Ferdinand el Santo, Alfonso VI., and Bishops Oca and Maurice. Large Gothic windows occupy the third stage of the front, their bases being filled with statues. The central stage, which has a single arch, contains a splendid rose window. The upper portion of the two towers is occupied by very beautiful perforated double windows in which crochet decoration is profusely used. It is altogether a wonderful façade which I greatly wished could be seen from the level.

The chief entrance on the north is closed. It is on the street, and through it the descent into the north transept is by the well-known Escalada Dorada. The early Gothic portal—Puerta alta—is adorned by statues and with the whole of this façade is one of the earliest portions of the Cathedral. The door, which on this side leads into the Cathedral, is the Puerta de la Pellejeria and opens on to the north-east angle of the transept [...] Staircase.

On the south the Puerta del [Sarmental is] approached from the street by three [flights of steps;] it is also part of the original Gothic [and is de]corated with statues and coats-of-arms. [Above] rises a similar façade to that of the north [transept.] The arcading in both these façades is most beau[tiful,] and from some points, where the roof-line can [be] seen cutting the sky, they look like two [towers] surmounted by an elegant balustrade. [Very] probably the pitch of the roofs was intended [to] be higher, and the building of the central lant[ern] has interfered with the original design.

The nave of pure early Gothic is lofty but sadly spoilt by the height of the *coro*. The aisles are low, but very beautiful. The *cimborio* runs up in double stages with windows in each and balustrades; it is a perfect maze of intricate design and fine carving. The walls are covered with the royal arms of Charles V, and the City of Burgos; there are figures of patriarchs and prophets standing in the niches, seraphim and angels occupy the recesses of the spandrils, and the beautiful groining of this superb octagon is quite unmatched anywhere in Spain. It all looks as if just finished, the stone is white and in perfect preservation. How my neck used to ache when looking aloft, un-

BURGOS   THE CAPILLA MAYOR

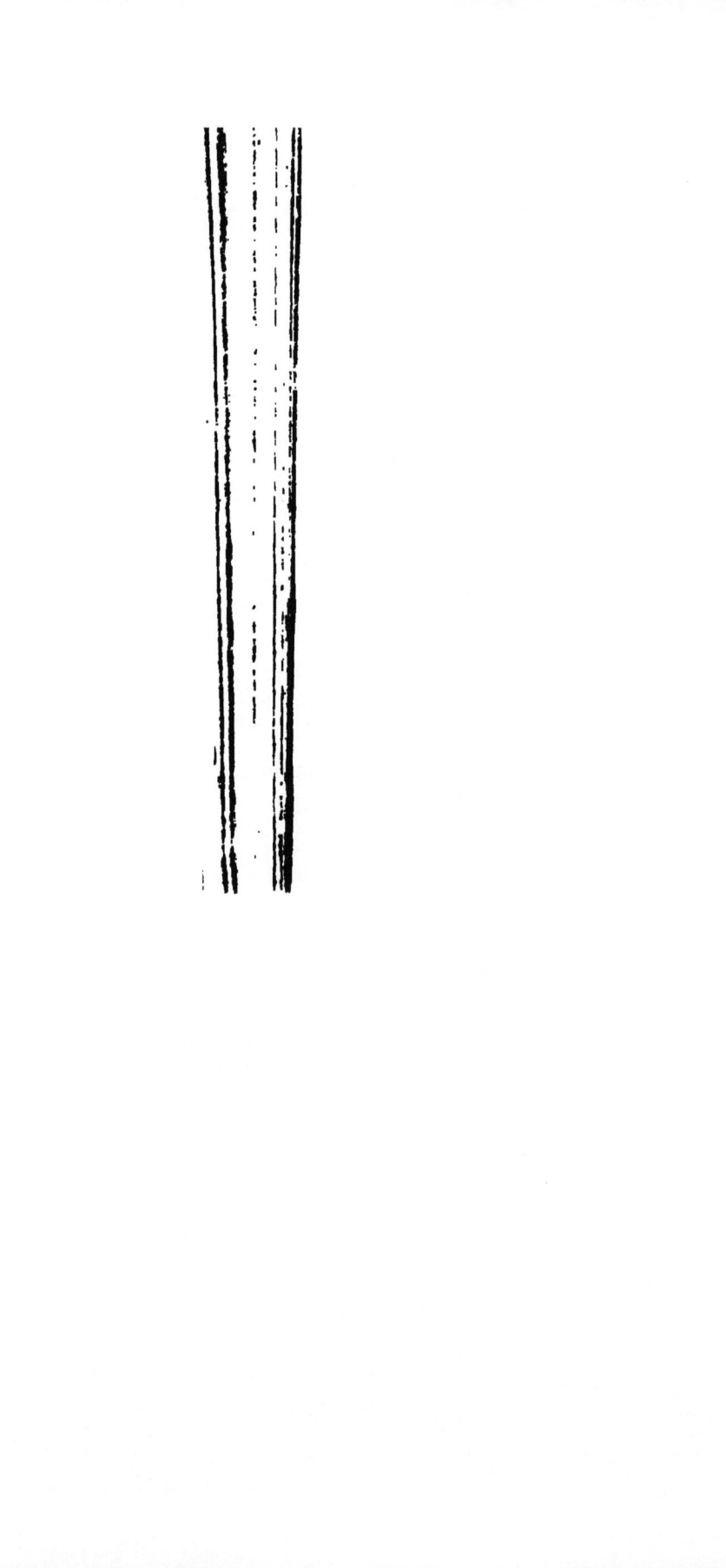

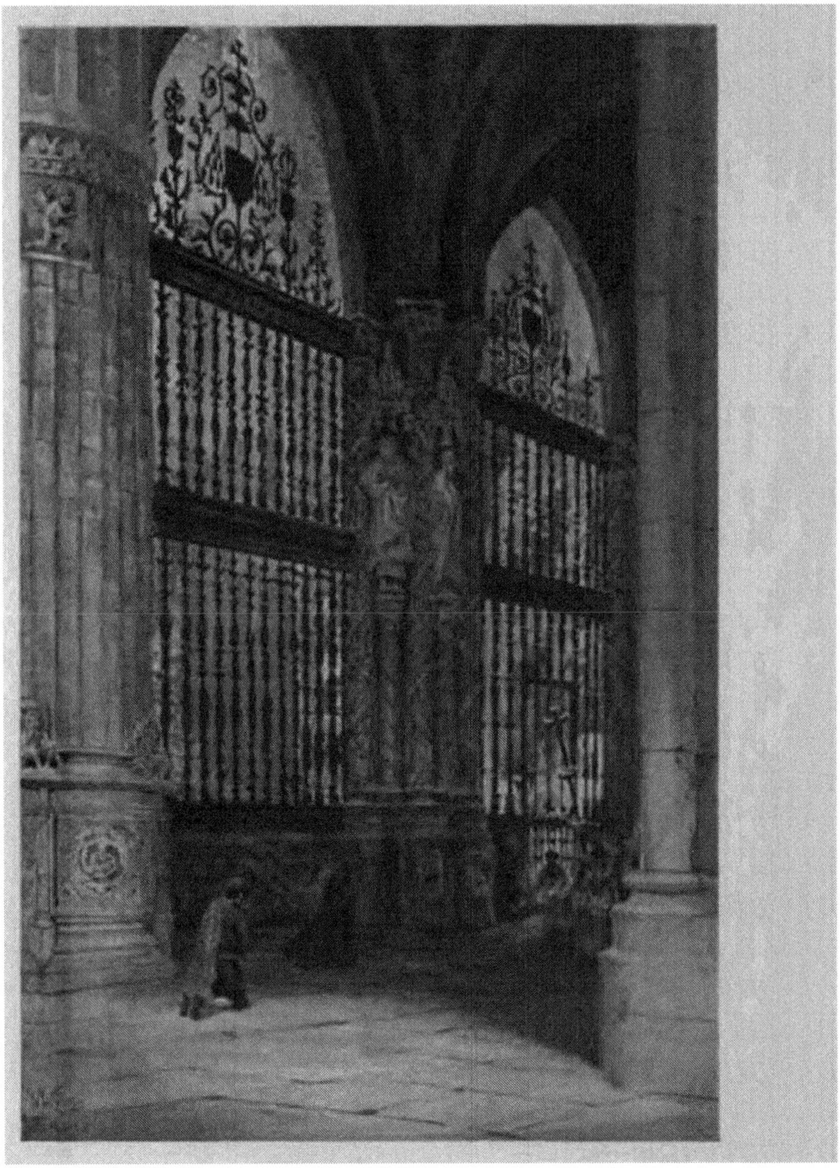

weaving the intricacies of that splendid interior! To strengthen the Cathedral and support the weight of this addition, the original piers were altered at the crossing, and the huge cylindrical columns, which are richly chased with Renaissance decoration, substituted. One can hardly say that Juan de Vallejo has spoilt the church by this octagon, for his work here would grace any building, but all the same I think the Gothic of the interior has suffered by the introduction of his designs, and I would sooner have seen the crossing in its original state.

The triforium is composed of wide bays with an uneven number of closed lights in each. A single arch, the mouldings of which are surmounted by carved heads, spans each group.

The clerestory contains a little modern glass, most of the old having been destroyed by a powder explosion in the fort on the hill above.

In the *coro* the *sillería* are exquisitely carved; the main panels represent subjects from the New Testament, the lower, which are divided by pilasters with arabesques, represent scenes of martyrdom. Philip Vigarni, who was responsible for this fine *coro*, surpassed himself in some of its decoration, which adds one more item to all that ought to be thoroughly studied in the great Cathedral.

On the north side of the High Altar, in front

CATHEDRAL CITIES OF

or which hangs a magnificent silver
tombs of three of the Infantes of Ca
this, the *trascoro* is covered with
reliefs in white stone, some of this is
has crumbled away a good deal. E
a deposit of dust is swept up and it
necessary to thoroughly restore these
the designs will be lost for ever. They
the Agony in the Garden, our Lord bear
Cross, the Crucifixion, the Descent, the Re
tion and the Ascension. The three centre
Vigarni, and the others by Alfonso de los Rí

Nearly all the chapels are replete with in
be it architecture, tombs, pictures or relics,
them all the Capilla del Condestable is
grandest. Built in 1487 by John of Cologne
the Hereditary Constable of Castile, Don P
Fernandez de Velasco, it is the private property
the Duque de Frias. The *reja*, the masterpiece
Cristobal Andino, bears date MDXXIII. and is
certainly the finest in the Cathedral. It is
worthy entrance to this magnificent octagon, which
viewed from outside, rises detached from the main
building with eight elaborate pinnacles pointing
heavenwards. The tracery of the pierced ceiling
of the Lantern with its gilded bosses, vies in
intricacy with that of the Cathedral itself. There
is a double clerestory with sculptured knights at

the bases of the columns holding coloured metal banners. The undercutting of the mouldings in the arches is very marvellous, the lowest course is formed of detached figures hanging downwards and from a little distance off looks like a piece of lacework. In front of the *retablo* and High Altar are the superbly sculptured tombs of the Constable and his wife. He is in full armour, she lies by his side on a richly embroidered cushion with her little lap-dog nestling comfortably in the folds of her robe near her feet. The chapel teems with interest; the wealth of red marble from the quarries of Atapuerca and the very effective chequer arrangement of black and white steps leading to the High Altar give it just the note of colour its whiteness otherwise would lack.

Attached to the chapel is a small vestry entered through a diminutive plateresque doorway of exquisite design. Amongst other priceless relics the vestry contains a fine gold chalice studded with precious stones and a good Madonna by Luini.

Another fine picture, a *Virgin and Child* by Sebastian del Piombo, hangs over the altar in the Capilla de La Presentacion. In the Capilla del Santissimo Cristo is a very ancient crucifix of life-sized proportions. Tradition and the vergers say that it came from the East and was carved by Nicodemus. The figure is flexible and very attenuated, it is covered with a thin leather to represent dried flesh and is very fine. In San Juan de Sahagun are six panels of the fifteenth century; good specimens of the early Spanish school, they represent the Nativity, Presentation and four scenes from the Passion.

The great Bishop Alfonso de Cartagena is interred in the Capilla de San Enrique, and his tomb is remarkably fine. Others in this chapel and in the cloisters are cut in slate and have been worked with great cleverness considering the way in which a blow splinters this material so easily.

The Chapel of Santa Ana, unfortunately restored recently, belongs to the Duque de Abrantes and contains the best *retablo* in the Cathedral. On it are displayed incidents in the Life of Christ which spring from and are enclosed by the branches of a genealogical tree. It is a quaint idea very well carried out.

It is a difficult task to try and give an idea of the contents and admirable style of all these chapels in the space of a short chapter, suffice it to say that they are, one and all, worthy pendants to the rest of the great church, and exemplify in their contents the glorious age of the ruling bishops and nobility of Old Castile.

In the south transept is a wonderful low doorway in front of which I had often stood examining the well-carved wooden panels on the doors themselves. It leads into the cloisters, but it was not until I had become thoroughly acquainted with the groups representing the Entry into Jerusalem and the Descent into Hades which grace this portal, that I passed through. The door dates from the early fifteenth century and considering the many thousands of times it has swung open and shut is in most excellent preservation.

The cloisters are fourteenth-century work and form an upper storey to a basement cloister of low arches surrounding a courtyard which at the time of my visit was undergoing extensive repair. In the centre is a huge cross; the flagstones of the court were all up, and the bones from many disturbed graves were being thrown into a pit. The beautiful cloisters proper are filled with modern opaque glass—" Muy frio" answered the verger to my question, " Por que ?"—and no doubt it is in the winter months. But the charm about a cloister is the vista through the arches; this Burgos has lost for the sake of the well-being of her priests; the pity is that funds would not allow of better glass when the utilitarian aspect demanded the shutting out of the cold winds.

The sacristy on the east side of the cloisters is a very beautiful early fifteenth-century room with a fine groined roof, the peculiarity of which is that

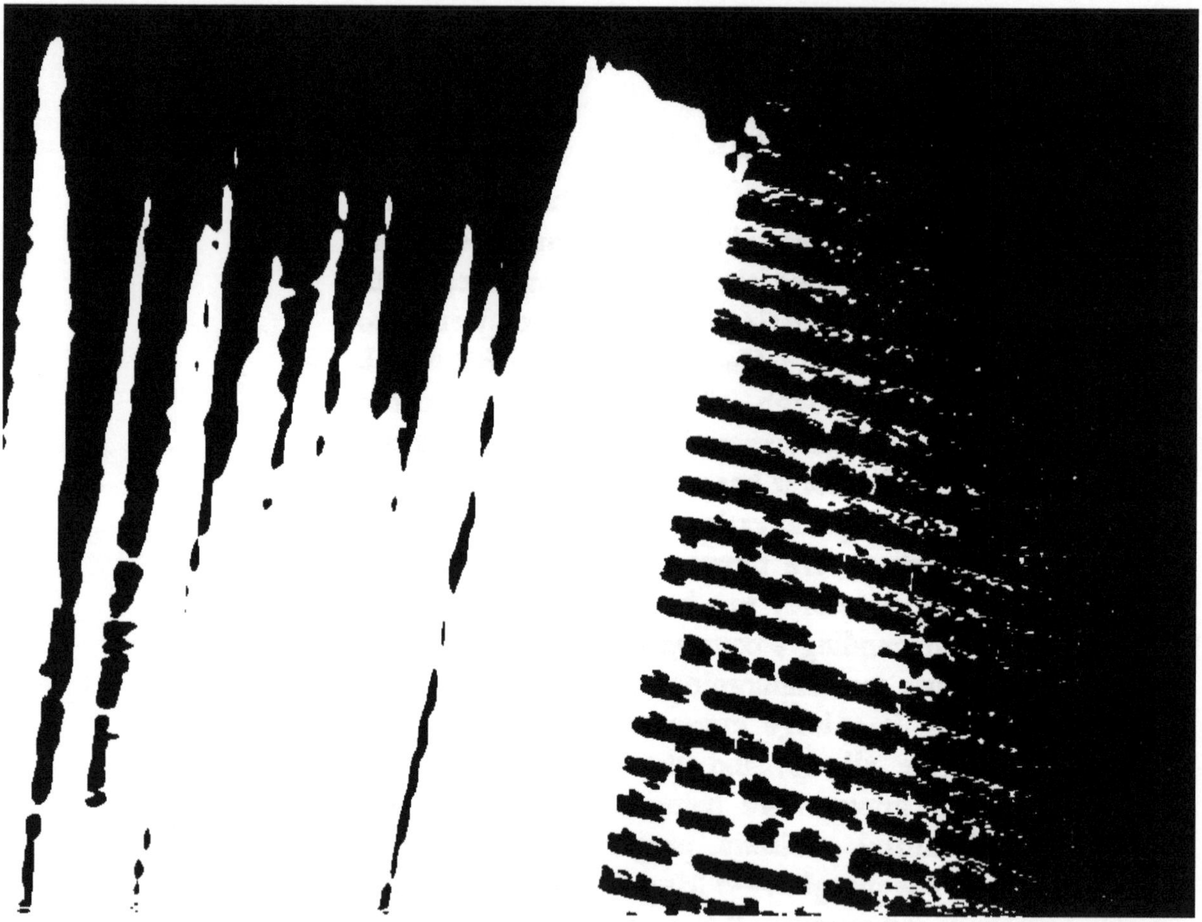

BURGOS. ARCH OF SANTA MARIA

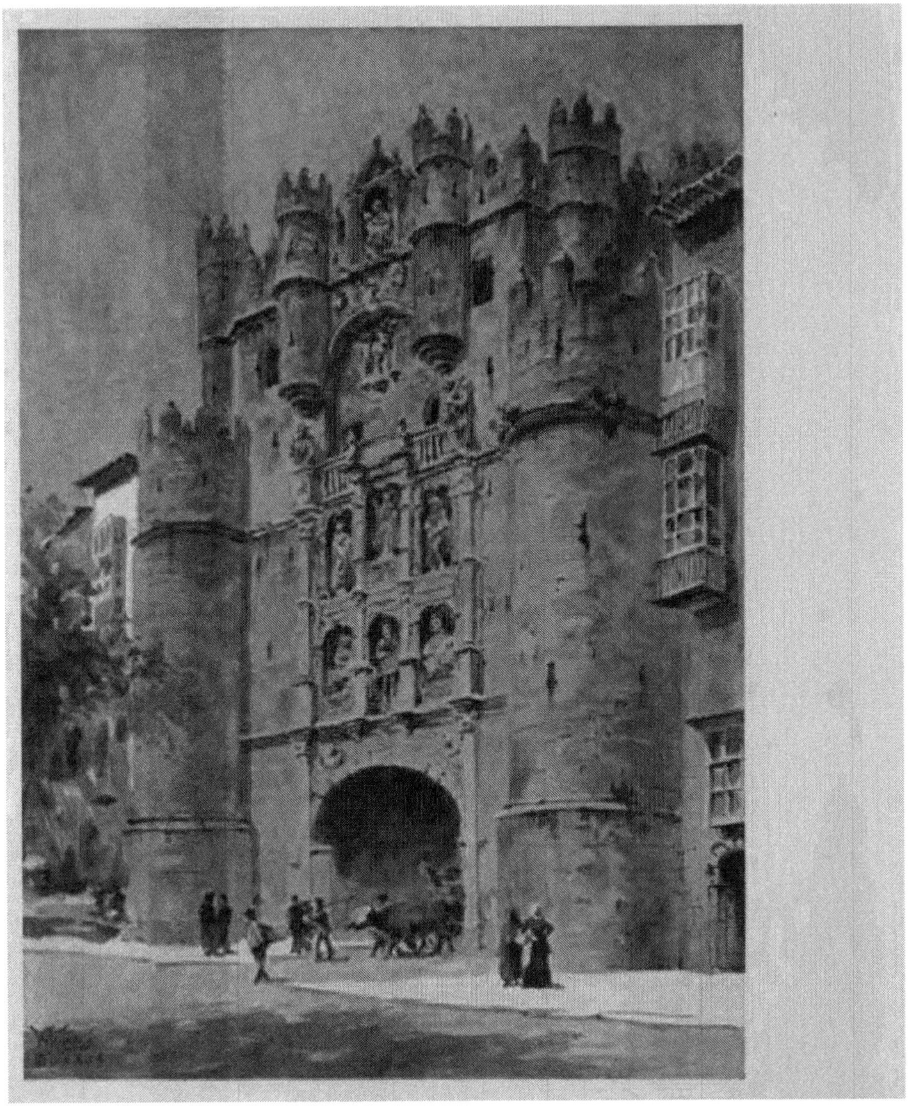

the capital of Castile. At the marriage of Ferdinand I. in 1067 Castile and Leon became one and ten years later the seat of Government was removed by Alfonso VI. to Toledo. Serious troubles ensued between the inhabitants of the two cities. Old Castile could not brook the interference of the great archbishops of New Castile and the loss of prestige attached to royalty and its court.

In Charles V.'s reign Burgos joined the Comuneros, the opponents of centralised government, but was wisely pardoned with other towns by the King, who held a court in state for this purpose in the Plaza Mayor at Valladolid. As a result of this forgiveness the inhabitants erected the fine entrance gateway of Santa Maria of which I made a sketch. Since that day, except for Wellington's futile sieges, Burgos has slept the sleep of the just and being an eminently ecclesiastical city will continue in this happy state.

Much of interest lies tucked away in the narrow streets. There is the Casa del Cordon, at one time the palace of the Velasco family, and a royal residence. Within its walls the Catholic Kings received Columbus on his return from the New World, and here was signed the incorporation of Navarre with Castile. This fine example of a town house is flanked by two square towers, with a rope from which it takes its name carved over the

CATHEDRAL CITIES OF

portal. The Casa de Miranda, with its yard and well-proportioned fluted columns, which is the Casa de Angulo a strong building. The façade of the old College of Nicolas is replete with fine workmanship, church of this name with tombs. The carved stone *retablo*, illustrating events of the life, is also a work of real art. Under the the cemetery stood the house wherein the Cid was born, and in the Castle on the hill, now a ruin, was married. The nuptials of Edward of England with Eleanor of Castile were celebrated in this fortress, which can also claim the birth of Peter the Cruel.

For a provincial town Burgos possesses a most interesting museum. Among the many curios I saw was a bronze altar font with coloured enamels of saints and a Moorish ivory casket, both from the monastery of San Domingo de Silos. The fine kneeling figure in alabaster of Juan de Padilla, who lost his life at an early age during one of the sieges of Granada, is almost as beautiful as that of the Infante Alfonso in the Cartuja. Roman and mediæval remains, found at different times and taken from disestablished convents, added to the interest of a short visit. There is so much to see in Burgos and its surroundings, and the seeing of it all is so pleasant, so undisturbed, and so different to the south, where for ever I was annoyed by touting loafers and irrepressible boys, that when I left it was with feelings of great regret.

Across the river, about an hour's walk one morning brought me to the Convent of Las Huelgas, which is still inhabited by shy nuns. Founded in 1187 by Alfonso VIII. it has always loomed large in the history of Castile. Many of her kings have kept vigil before the High Altar, when receiving knighthood, our own Edward I. among them. Many royal pairs have been wedded within the church, and many sleep their long sleep within its quiet precincts. The Abbess was mitred, she possessed powers of life and death, she ranked as a Princess-palatine next to the Queen, and she was styled "Por la gracia de Dios." Her nuns were, and still are, daughters of noble houses, and some even of royal birth. In the chapel of Santiago hangs a copy of the embroidered banner captured at the great fight of Las Navas de Tolosa, a victory which crippled and drove out the Infidel from the north. The original hangs in the nun's choir, a fitting pendant to the splendid tapestries which cover the walls. I was told of other treasures invisible to the eye of man and once again wished I could have changed my sex for a short time. Being mere man, I heard the gate shut as I left the convent with a rather crestfallen

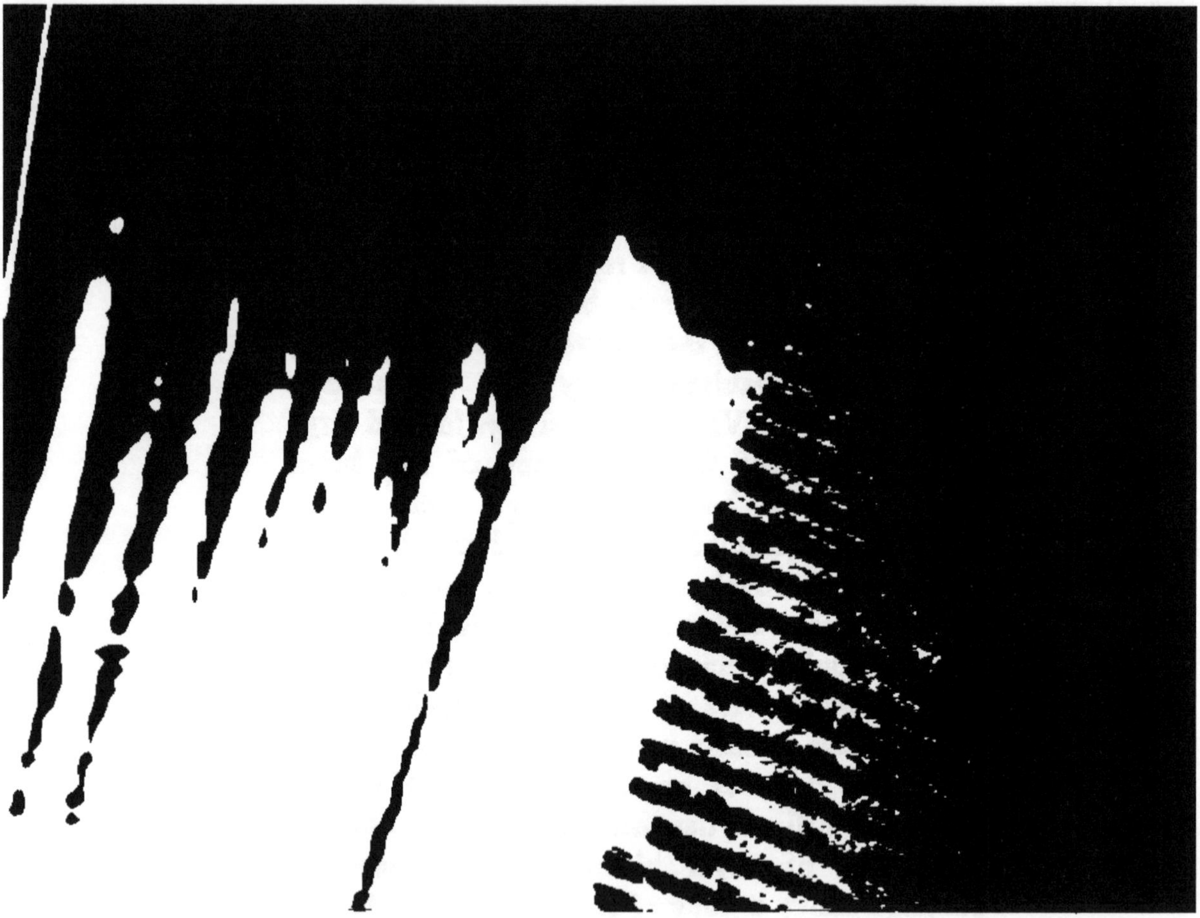

BURGOS

Gothic arch. A monk in the stalls was at prayer, he also kept an observant eye on the two visitors. Our footsteps seemed to sound intensely loud on the stone pavement, and we spoke in very low whispers. The cold white-washed walls and this solitary figure droning out his prayers were depressing.

We furtively admired the finely-carved stalls, the grand *retablo* over the High Altar with its terribly life-like crucifix, all the time with a feeling on my part of that vigilant eye boring a hole in my back like a gimlet. We next examined the alabaster tomb the masterpiece of Gil de Siloe, executed to the order of Isabella the Catholic, which stands in front of the altar. Juan II. and his wife Isabella of Portugal lie side by side clothed in their robes of state. At his feet are two Lions, at hers a Lion and a Dog. I forgot the solitary monk and the gimlet stopped its work as I became lost in admiration while following the intricacies of Gil de Siloe's greatest production.

At the eight corners of this magnificent tomb, most undoubtedly the finest I have ever seen, and by some considered unsurpassed in Europe, sixteen lions support the royal arms, above them along the cornice beautiful little statuettes stand under canopies which are a marvel of delicate tracery. The embroidery on the robes of the royal pair is exquisite and the imitation of the lace work unsurpassed.

CATHEDRAL CHURCH

For a long time we [stood]
admiring the marvellous cleverness
of a monument which is worthy of the
pious woman who erected it to the [memory of her]
parents.

Hard by in the west wall of the [church is the]
tomb of the Infante Alfonso, whose death at the
early age of sixteen left the accession to
Isabella and so changed the history of [Castile,]
is likewise a wonderful piece of work by the
skilful hand. The young Prince kneels in an
attitude of prayer which gains dignity from the
half-shadow thrown by the recess in which the
monument is placed. The arch above is decorated
with a twining vine, while men-at-arms guard
the tomb.

We turned from the contemplation of these
memorials and the monotone of the old monk's
prayer filled the church. I think we both felt
a feeling of relief when we found ourselves once
more outside under the grey sky, though I shall
ever remember the impression of that ancient
church with its magnificent tombs, that white-
robed monk with his droning voice, the chill of the
autumn air and those long lines of stately poplars
under which I passed in my last pilgrimage in
Spain.

INDEX

Abderrhaman, mosque of, 80
Adrian IV., Pope, 81
Albornoz, Cardinal, tomb of, 121
Alfonso VI., 234, 235
Alfonso VIII., 245
Alfonso de Cartagena, Bishop, 240
Alfonso el Catolico, 197; coffin of, 220
Alfonso the Chaste, 218, 220
Alfonso the Learned, sarcophagus of, 10
Alfonso de los Rios, 238
Alhambra, 31, 46, sqq.
    Court of Lions, 50
Almakkari, historian, 23
Almansor, 200
Alva Garcia, 138
Alvaro de Luna, 232
Antequerra, 48
Arabic documents, 230
Aragon, union of, with Castile, 67
Arfe, silver monstrance by, 142
Arfe, Juan de, 228
Arlanzón, river, 233
Astorga, 193–198
    Cathedral, 193 sqq.
    Historical sketch, 197
Augustus, Emperor, 84
Averroes, 30
Avila, 137–144
    Cathedral, 81, 138

Avila, Historical sketch, 137
Avila, tomb of, 143

Badajos, Juan de, 215
Baeza, 195
Barcelona, 83, 91–99
    Cathedral, 92, sqq.
    Church of San Pablo del Campo, 94
    Church of Santa Maria del Mar, 95
    Church of Santa Maria del Pi, 95
    Historical sketch, 91 sq.
    Rambla, 97
Barceloneta, suburb of Barcelona, 96
Bartolomé, and the Capilla Real, Granada, 39
Beatrice of Swabia, sarcophagus of, 10
Becerra, Gaspar, 195
Beggars, at Cordova, 29, 30; at Seville, 30, 35; at Madrid, 30
Bernardo de Aragon, tomb of, 164
Berruguete, carvings by, 113, 141, 228
Boabdil, figure of, at Granada, 41
Brutus, Junius, founds colony on the Turia, 66

INDEX

El Calvario, 150
El Campanario, tower at Cordova, 27
El Cristo de la Luz, Toledo, 125
El Grao, port of Valencia, 67
El Parral, Segovia, 154
El Transito, Toledo, 124
Englefield, Sir Francis, 232
Escovedo, Juan, 150
Essex, siege of Cadiz by Lord, 4

FERDINAND I., 200, marriage of, 243
Ferdinand and Isabella, monument at Granada, 40; portraits, 41, 44, 225; arms of, 227
Ferdinand el Santos, 234, 235
Francisco de Lara, ceiling by, 112
Francisco de Palenzuela, tomb of, 126
Fruela I., coffin of, 220

GALLEGOS, panels by, 203
Gayá, 84
Genil, river at Granada, 34
Geronimo, tomb of, 126
Geronimo, 200
Gerona, 101–10
    Cathedral, 103 sqq.
    Church of San Pedro de los Gallegans, 105
    Historical sketch, 101 sqq.
Gibraltar, 58
Gil de Siloe, 247
Giralda Tower, Sevilla, 13, 14
Gomar, Francisco, work at Tarragona
Gonzalo de Cordoba, 45
Grado, Canon Juan de, tomb of, 204

Granada, 31–35
    Albaicin, 31
    Alhambra, 31, 239
    Antequeruela, 31
    Capilla de la Antigua, 39
    Capilla de Pulgar, 44
    Capilla Real, 41
    Capilla de Trinidad, 38
    Cathedral, 38, 44
    Church of San Juan de los Reyes, 44
    Church of San Nicolas, 44
    Church of Santa Anna, 44
    Convent of Cartuja, 45
    Convent of San Geronimo, 45
Greek remains, Tuy, 185
Guadalete, river at Cadiz, 53; battle on banks of, 58
Guadalquiver, position of Cordova on, 23
Guadalmedina, the, 61
Guillermo Boffy, 104
Gutierrez, Bishop, 219

HERNANDEZ, 229, 230
Hontañon, rebuilt dome of Seville Cathedral, 12; Salamanca Cathedral, 135, Segovia, 150
Hospital de Santa Cruz, Toledo, 116

INFANTE Alfonso, tomb of, 248
Inigo de Mendez, tomb of, 112

JAMES I., of Aragon, armour of at Valencia, 70; tomb of, 86
Jews at Sevilla, 15
John of Cologne, 234, 238
John of Gaunt, 178

251

INDEX

Juan Granadino, builds western façade of Cathedral, Granada, 98
Juan II., 24
Juan Bautista Celma, 178
Juan Frenca, tomb of, 242
Juan de Borgoña, frescoes by, 232, 242
Juan de Castro, 178
Juan de Juni, 228
Juan de Mena, 30
Juan de Padilla, figure of, 244
Juan de Vallejo, 237
Juanes, Last Supper by, 71

La Mantera, Zamora, 201
Lambeán, Bishop, 80
La Peña Cajoro, 254
La Petarah, 158
Las Nieves de Triana, 245
Leon, 205–216
  Cathedral, 209
  Chapel of La Nuestra Señora del Dado, 213
  Convent of San Isidoro el Real, 214
  Convent of San Marcos, 215
  Historical sketch, 205 sqq.
Leovigild, 205
Life, 48
Lopez, relic of, 95
Lucas, 30

Manara, designs by, 110
Maestro Mateo, portrait of, 176
Malaga, 57–63
  Alcazaba, 61
  Cathedral, 59
  Historical sketch, 57 sqq.
  Mercado, 61
Malaguera, river, 61

Manriq...
Maraga...
Marcellu...
Maria Pa...
  the Cru...
Maurice, ...
Mena, Pedr...
  60
Mendoza, C...
Meshwir, 53
Miguelete T...
Minho, river, ...
Monte Mauro,...
Morales, 30
Mulhacen, 48
Murillo, pictur...
  San Antonio ...
  Seville, 11; in ...
  20
Museum, Seville, ...

NAPOLEONIC Wars, ...
Naranco, 223
  Church of S...
    223, 224
Nicodemus, 239
Nicolas Florentino, ...
  128
Nicolas de Vergara, ...
  113
Notre Dame de Paris, ...

Oca, Bishop, 235
Oñar, river, 102
Ordoño I., coffin of, 220
Ordoño II., 213
Orense, 187–191
  Cathedral, 187, sqq.
  Convent of San Franc...
    190
  Historical sketch, 187

252

INDEX

Oviedo, 217–224
    Capilla del Rey Casto, 220
    Cathedral, 218
    Historical sketch, 218, sq.

PANTEON, Leon, 115
Parapanda, Mount, 48
Pedro the Cruel, coffin of, 10; trees planted by, 14
Pedro Mato, statue of, 195
Pelayo, 222
Petrucci Orto, chalice by, 242
Philip II. destroys mosques at Cordova, 24
Philip Vigarni, 137, 138
Philip and Juana la Loca, tomb of, at Granada, 40; coffins of, 42
Pisuerga, river, 225
Pliny quoted, 197
Pradas, work of, at Granada, 43

QUINTATA, Cardinal, tomb of, 190

RAMIRO II., 200
Ramiro, coffin of, 220
Ramon Berenguer I., Count, 91
Ramon Berenguer II., and Encesendia, tombs of, 104
Reus, 83
Ribalta, painting by, at Valencia, 71
Ribera, *Adoration* by, 71
Roman remains, at Tarragona, 84; at Segovia, 149
Roman Sculpture at Tarragona, 89

SALAMANCA, 122–135
    Capilla del Carmen, 126
    Capilla Mayor, 128

Salamanca, Capilla de San Bartolomé, 128
    Capilla de Talavera, 128
    Cathedrals, 123, 124, sqq.; 127
    Church of San Pedro, 143
    Collegio Mayor de Santiago Apostol, 132
    Convent of las Agustinas Recoletas, 136
    Grammar School, 131
    Historical sketch, 123, sqq.
    University, 131
San Pedro, river at Cadiz, 5
Santa Eulalia, body of, 9d, 221
Santiago, 171–181
    Cathedral, 173 sqq.
    Collegio de San Geronimo, 180
    Historical sketch, 172
Santos Cruz, pictures by, 142
Saragossa, 191, 159–170
    Church of San Pablo, 167
    Cathedrals, 162 sqq.
    El Pilar, 165
    Historical sketch, 149 sqq.
    La Seo, 162 sqq.
Sebastian del Piombo, 239
Segovia, 145–158
    Capilla del Cristo del Consuelo, 152
    Cathedral, 150 sqq.
    Chapel of Santa Catalina, 152
    Church of San Martin, 153
    Church of San Millan, 153
    Church of la Vera Cruz, 153
    Convent of Santa Cruz, 155
    Historical sketch, 149 sqq.
Semple, Colonel, 132

Simancas, 50
Seville, 7-21
    Capilla de San Pedro, 13
    Capilla de Santiago, 12
    Cathedral, 8 sqq.
    Historical sketch, 7
    Jewish quarter, 15
Sierra de Elvira, 48
Sierra Nevada, 48, 55
Souchet, sacks Valencia, 67

TARRAGONA, 83-90
    Cathedral, 84 sqq.
    Historical sketch, 83 sqq.
Toledo, 107-119
    Bridges, 116, 117
    Cathedral, 109
    Capilla de la Descension de Nuestra Señora, 112
    Capilla de Reyes Nuevo, 111
    Capilla de San Ildefonso, 111
    Capilla de Santiago, 112
    Church of San Juan de los Reyes, 114
    Church of Santa Maria la Blanca, 114
    Convent of San Domingo el Real, 115
    Historical sketch, 107 sqq.
    Jews' quarter, 114
Torquemada, Cardinal, 226
Tortosa, 77-82
    Carving at, by Cristobal, 81
    Cathedral, 80 sqq.
    Historical sketch, 78 sqq.
Triana, 19
Tribunal de Aguas, 69
Tuy, 183-185
    Cathedral, 183 sqq.

Tuy, Cathedral
    Historical sketch

Urraca,

VALENCIA, 65-76
    Cathedral, 69
    Church of San
    Church of Santa
        71
    Convent del Carmen
    Convent Espinosa
    Convent Jesus
    Convent Ribalta, 75
    Historical sketch
    Mercado, 72, 74
Valladolid, 225-232
    Church of Santa Maria Antigua, 226
    Colegiata de San Gregorio, 227
    Collegio de Santa Cruz, 228
    Historical sketch, 225
    Scotch and English Colleges, 232
    University, 230
Vargas, Louis de, La Gamba de Seville, 11, 12
Vega, the, 62
Velasquez, tomb of, 146
Vigarney, carvings by, 115
Viladomát, pictures by, at Barcelona, 95

"WAMBA," great bell, Oviedo, 222
Wellington, Duke of, 48

254

INDEX

XIMENES, 112, 227

YAHYA, Moorish King, 65

ZAMORA, 199–204
    Capilla del Cardinal, 203
    Capilla de San Miguel, 204

Zamora, Cathedral, 201, *sqq.*
    Church of la Magdalena, 201
    Church of San Pedro of Ildefonso, 201
    Historical sketch, 200
    Hospital, 201
Zurbaran, pictures at Cadiz, 4; at Seville, 11, 12

Milton Keynes UK
Ingram Content Group UK Ltd.
UKHW021237240324
439834UK00007BA/279